Family Structure and Effective Health Behavior

The Energized Family

P9-CRP-242

Family Structure and Effective Health Behavior

The Energized Family

Lois Pratt

Jersey City State College

Houghton Mifflin Company • Boston

Atlanta   Dallas   Geneva, Illinois
Hopewell, New Jersey   Palo Alto   London

Library of Congress Catalogue Card Number: 75-29817

ISBN: 0-395-18702-8

To

Sam and Pamela Pratt

CONTENTS

/

PREFACE

We can deepen our understanding of both the family and health by examining each in relation to the other. This book explores the type of structure the family needs in order to function effectively in contemporary society. It assesses the effectiveness of alternative forms of family structure in the family's performance of one of its major functions—personal health care. After examining the scope of the contemporary family's health care responsibilities, the family's effectiveness in performing these tasks, and the nature of the family's relationships with the professional medical system, the book concludes that the "energized" family is best equipped to handle the health care task in contemporary society. The term *energized family* derives from the stimulation and exchange that occur between family members who interact a great deal, both within the family and with outside groups, and who generate ideas and learn to cope with the pressures and demands of contemporary society. The energized concept refers to the unleashing of people's potential so that they may develop themselves to their fullest capacities.

This book can be a useful supplement for courses in sociology of the family, medical sociology, and courses offered in departments of health education, health administration, maternal and child health, and within schools of public health.

Interest in the family as a unit of health behavior is growing, and concern is now focusing on questions such as these: What is the role of the family in mobilizing health behavior? How much health care is practiced at home and how good are family health practices? How does the structure of the professional medical system affect families' efforts to care for their members' health? Is health best served by the autonomy of the individual within the family or by control of the individual? Which approach is likely to generate greater improvement in health behavior—training patients to comply with doctors' instructions or incorporating the family in the therapeutic team?

The book focuses on the family as a unit of action. My research investigated family units of father-mother-child: each of the members was interviewed, and the structure of relationships among family members was examined. This study approaches health care from a family perspective: the family is viewed as a major unit through which health care is organized and carried out, and the professional medical system is shown as the consumer-family encounters it rather than as the professionals view it. My research shows the impact that family life has on health and health behavior.

My study also illuminates the difficulties families experience in negotiating with the medical care system and the influence that the family's ties to other institutions have on its own ability to function.

The first of the book's three parts describes and evaluates the health care activities of the contemporary family, and analyzes the kinds of problems that families face in dealing with the professional medical system. Part Two offers a test of the energized family form. It presents the results of a study of the type of structure that enables families to serve their members' health needs most effectively. Here the reader has the option of examining my interpretations of the evidence in detail or of skimming over the evidence in favor of the conclusions. Part Three applies the evidence presented in the first two parts. It sets forth some propositions for increasing the family's effectiveness in health care. It then presents some theoretical propositions about what type of structure the family needs and how the family must function if it is to remain viable in contemporary society.

In the course of the book, then, readers are drawn into the range of activities that make sociology a productive adventure—research design, analysis of evidence, theory-building, and proposals for social action. The facts and theory that are presented on these two intimate and vital aspects of human existence—family life and personal health—also provide readers with a background against which to examine their own situations, assumptions, and goals.

ACKNOWLEDGMENTS

The field study was supported by a grant from the National Center for Health Services Research and Development (Public Health Service Grant Number HS 00065). I am deeply grateful for this support and for the sensitive concern which the members of this federal agency showed for my research. I appreciate the grant of time provided by the Jersey City State College Research Council during the writing of this book.

I am indebted to Agnes Meinhard and Barbara Rubinstein for their extraordinary dedication and talented assistance in the research. My colleague, John Dykstra, provided helpful consultation on many aspects of family sociology. Other colleagues whose generous efforts I especially wish to acknowledge are Philip Wallack, director of the computer center, and Ruth Arnold, Pauline Maggio, and Nicholas Senopoulos of the library. I am very grateful to several scholars who read early versions of the manuscript and made helpful criticisms and suggestions. They are Alex Boros, Kent State University; Robert N. Wilson, University of North Carolina; Klaus J. Roghmann, University of Rochester; Betty E. Cogswell, University of North Carolina; Alfred C. Clarke, The Ohio State University; and Mary Heltsley, Iowa State University.

My thanks are due to Victoria Berutti for faultless typing. I appreciate the cooperation of the families who participated in the research investigation. Finally, I acknowledge my debt to all the other researchers whose work I have drawn upon in writing this book.

Family Structure and Effective Health Behavior

The Energized Family

An Overview

An essential purpose of this book is to develop a distinctive viewpoint concerning the family and health. Briefly, the principal function of the contemporary family is to acknowledge the unique worth of individual members and to sponsor their personal development and well-being. A major dimension of this basic family function is to protect the health and to develop the unique physical capacities of individual members. Physical health is a resource that permits individuals to attain their goals and to achieve personal fulfillment. The family is a personal care system within which health is molded and health care is mobilized, organized, and carried out.

American families must carry on their health care tasks within a societal context of conflicting interests and coercion. The professional care system, on which families depend for service, is organized predominantly around the interests and objectives of its professional personnel and minimally around those of its clients.

Using this perspective, what type of family structure is most effective? We propose that the *energized family* is a structural form that may have the required capabilities. We will test the model to determine whether it works —whether this type of family can get better health services, practice better personal health care, and have healthier members than other types of families.

This overview introduces the three major parts of the book and indicates how we will use research evidence to develop social action strategies and to formulate social theory.

1

ORGANIZATION OF HEALTH CARE:
THE FAMILY AND PROFESSIONAL MEDICINE

The first objective of this book is to determine how important health care is as a family function and how effective families generally are in performing their various health care tasks. To understand the family, it is essential to know the characteristic tasks and activities that the family performs.

An additional incentive for looking at family health activity is simply that it has been hidden from view, especially by sociologists' own constructs. There has been a pervasive assumption in sociology that as society has become increasingly industrial, technical, urbanized, and complex, many functions formerly performed by families have been absorbed by specialized agencies. This interpretation has been applied with almost unflinching determination to the health care functions of the family. Some characteristic examples are:

> "In recent decades, much of this protective activity has been assumed by public organizations and by the state. In the matter of health care, for example, the increased use of physicians, the expansion of hospital facilities, and the rapid spread of accident insurance, hospitalization insurance, and workmen's compensation have tended to replace family nursing care" (Leslie 1967, p. 233); and "The medical function has been transferred to the doctor's office and hospital" (Adams 1971, p. 84).[1]

The general acceptance of this notion has inhibited serious examination of the family's former functions, including education, religion, production of goods, and recreation, as well as health care. In fact, many family sociology textbooks omit discussion of the family's health care functions.[2] Medical sociology has also neglected the family as a unit of health action, regarding the professional medical system as the locus of all health care activity.

This examination of the health functions of the contemporary American family also lays the groundwork for carrying out other objectives. A central focus of this book is how family structure affects the family's capabilities for meeting its health care responsibilities. Family structural requirements hinge on the functions it has to perform and what these tasks demand of the family. What type of structural capabilities do families require in order to meet such needs as these: to provide physical care and a sense of worth to a dying member; induce a school to provide education for their handicapped child or athletic programs for girls; get blood donations for a surgical emergency; bend the procedures of a hospital so that the family may participate in caring for a hospitalized member; get everyone in the family involved in some form of regular exercise; come to grips with faulty eating practices; track down self-help devices that will enable a wife and

---

[1] *See also* Bell 1971; Burgess et al. 1963; Eshleman 1970; Nimkoff 1965; Ogburn and Tibbitts 1934; Williamson 1966; Womble 1966.
[2] Bowman 1970; Cavan 1960; Kirkpatrick 1963; Landis 1970; Lantz and Snyder 1962; Merrill 1959; Queen and Habenstein 1967; Stroup 1966; Winch 1971.

mother with arthritis to continue to do housework; locate the best physician and hospital for cardiac surgery; or obtain compensation for an injury caused by medical negligence?

The second objective is to delineate the features of the contemporary American medical care system that hinder families in caring for health on their own as well as jointly with the professionals. Since families are highly dependent on the medical care system for services, family failures in health care may be due in part to defects in the organization and services of the medical care system—for example, the bureaucratic organization of hospitals, political power of the health care industry, unfettered self-rule within the medical profession, and conflict between financial and service goals in private medical practice.

FAMILY STRUCTURE: THE ENERGIZED FAMILY

The family's ability to function effectively depends on its own structure, and failures to care for health may be partly due to inappropriate family structure. We need to know what type of family structure does enable a family unit to serve its members' health needs effectively.

Our basic hypothesis is that a certain structural pattern—the energized family—enables families to function effectively in support of their members' health. Part Two reports on a study of urban families that tested whether members of energized families practice better personal health care, use professional medical services more effectively, and have better health than members of nonenergized families.

THE ENERGIZED FAMILY MODEL

The energized family develops persons through freedom and change. It is not bent on obtaining conformity to prescribed social patterns through control and stability.

Some families are highly energized in the sense that all members interact with each other regularly in a variety of contexts—tasks and leisure, conversation and activity, both inside and outside the home. Energized families maintain varied and active contacts with other groups and organizations—the whole range of medical, educational, political, recreational, and business resources of the community that can be utilized to advance family members' interests. These families actively attempt to cope and master their lives, for example, by grasping the opportunity to join a sports team, seeking out information on how to improve their diet, and weighing the advantages and disadvantages of various schools or hospitals.

The energized family tends to be fluid in internal organization. Role relationships are flexible; for example, house cleaning may be shared and everyone may take a turn at sick care. Power is shared, each person participating in decisions that affect him or her. Relationships among members tend to support personal growth and to be responsive and tolerant. Members have a high degree of autonomy within the family.

Energized refers to the sheer energy or exchange that occurs between family members who interact a great deal, the stimulation that comes from interacting with outside groups, the generation of ideas and problem-solving effort that results from family interaction, and the freeing of people to develop themselves. Energized families promote their members' capacities to function fully as persons and develop their capability for taking care of themselves, including their ability to deal with formal organizations. This type of family is an effective social group, both in the sense that it develops its individual members' capabilities, and in the sense that it provides backing and resources to take care of its members.

These individual and group capabilities foster sound personal health practices and appropriate use of professional medical services. The energized family contributes to members' health because it does not block, but rather encourages and supports all persons to develop their capacities for full functioning and provides them scope to act independently. Freedom is favorable to health.

DEVELOPMENT OF THE ENERGIZED MODEL

In 1969, we conducted a field study to discover what influence family structure has on health and health behavior. In the process of analyzing the data from this study we formulated the energized family model. We did not design the model in advance of testing.

The author had previously investigated the influence of socioeconomic status (SES) on health and health behavior. In the process of that analysis, it became clear that while SES was influential, it accounted for only a small proportion of the variance in health level and health practices of the population. Many low SES persons had excellent health practices and good health, and many high SES people had abominable practices and poor health. As other authors have also concluded, the SES variable is so broad that it is impossible to identify which particular features of life-style or heritage cause people in one SES category to behave differently from those in another. The author suspected that differences in the family structure of the various socioeconomic groups might be an underlying factor that caused low SES persons to have generally poorer health and health practices than high SES persons. Family structure might even explain some of the differences in health and health behavior that SES failed to account for. The author had made a documentary film, called *Family Legacy,* based on an in-depth study of the ways poor families react to and handle matters of health and illness. The crucial idea that emerged from the film-making experience was that the ways members of a family dealt with each other were inextricably bound up with their health.

The new study was hemmed in by this SES conception, and was focused on testing hypotheses consistent with assumptions about how SES affects behavior. Thus, our initial plan was to test the hypothesis that since high SES families comply most fully with societal norms and derive the greatest rewards from this compliance, the family form which will be most successful in fostering health and promoting sound health practices among its members is one that generates rewarding compliance with the mainstream of societal norms. Sound health practices would thus represent compliance with societal health codes. Hence, warm and loving families would be able to gain their members' willing compliance with normatively approved health practices, and close-knit families that exercise tight supervision over members' behavior could successfully constrain their members to conform to approved health codes. These same family patterns would also contribute to health. By encouraging adaptive conformity to societal standards, the family would help its members to minimize their exposure to stress in all types of social settings.

Rather than restrict the study by these arbitrary assumptions, the author constructed a number of alternative hypotheses concerning how family organization might possibly affect health and health behavior, and incorporated a variety of family structure variables that would permit testing of some of these alternative suppositions. The energized family emerged as a reformulation resulting from efforts to make sense out of these data. This model has very little to do with social class. It is not consistent with our earlier assumptions that high SES families are more successful because they reward conformity, for the energized family is not dedicated to conforming assiduously to societal standards. While the energized family form is found in slightly larger proportions among the more highly educated than among the poorly educated, it cuts across all socioeconomic strata.

The energized family model is, therefore, a conception of an effectively functioning family system that we developed in the process of designing and analyzing the results of an empirical study. It is not presented as the typical pattern of American family life. Even if this particular pattern turns out to be the most effective for protecting family members' health, it does not necessarily follow that it will be the prevalent form. Other social forces may have a more decisive influence in determining what family structure will prevail than effectiveness in protecting health. The frequency with which the energized form is found in the population is an important but separate matter, which will be discussed in a separate chapter.

The energized model is not presented as the normatively approved pattern. In certain respects the energized family is nontraditional, and its emphasis on individual freedom, personal fulfillment, and flexible role relationships between men and women and parents and children, might be faulted by some as disruptive of the social order. It is not presented as an idealized view of the *good* family. Even if it turns out to be good for health, some people will not regard it as an appealing style of family life or worth the hazards entailed. Some people may prefer a type of family life that is based on respect for convention and upholding of the traditional social order. The energized family might seem to be an anarchical life-style based on excessive freedom of the individual. Such freedom increases the risk of divorce and of children leaving home, and promotes stress in the continuous drive toward personal development, constant turmoil in innovating solutions to problems, and perils in confrontations with bureaucracies and other sources of authority.

IMPLICATIONS FOR SOCIAL THEORY AND ACTION

Our investigation raises some broad questions concerning social theory and social action, which we will consider explicitly in Part Three. We introduce these rather complex issues at the outset in order to indicate where we are heading. The critical task of readers is to examine the evidence presented and to analyze for themselves whether the conceptual viewpoint developed in the course of the book is a reasonable and useful point of view for interpreting the research evidence and, more generally, for looking at the family, health, and medical care system.

The theoretical issues revolve around the nature of social systems. As defined here, a social system is a group of interacting persons whose interaction is structured and oriented around common concerns or purposes. The two systems examined here are the family and the medical care system, but the findings have implications for other social systems as well. Various theoretical models offer different explanations of how social systems function. Consequently, one's theoretical viewpoint makes a difference in how one will interpret the evidence about the family and medical care.

A theoretical issue raised by the research concerns the nature of the relationship between different social systems, such as that between the family and the medical care system. One theoretical model—structural-functionalism—holds that societies tend to be cohesive and to be integrated by a consensus on values and norms. Since the various social systems within the society are bound together by these common values and norms, relations between social systems are based on cooperation and reciprocity and are generally harmonious. This theoretical formulation would be supported by research evidence which showed, first, that the medical care system accommodates the needs of families—for example, by setting up hospital visiting rules and doctors' appointments to suit the patients' needs rather than the professionals' own convenience. Second, the evidence would show that families which elicit the best service from the medical care system socialize and constrain their members to conform obligingly to the expectations and procedures established by the medical care system—for example, complaisantly relying on the physician to tell them what they should know about their condition, and having the parent present the child's complaint to save the doctor's time.

Another viewpoint—variously called conflict, power, or interest theory

—holds that in a highly differentiated society, deep differences in the goals and interests of various groups generate conflict and coercive tactics. Each of the various groups protects the distinctive interests of its members, and relations between various groups include disagreement, strain, conflict, and force, as well as consensus and cooperation. This view would be in accord with research evidence which showed, first, that the medical care system not only serves but also attempts to dominate and control the family—for example, by restricting contact with a family member in the hospital and by resisting review of professional mistakes by consumer groups. Second, the evidence would show that families must assert their own interests forcefully in medical care transactions to obtain good care—for example, by pressing physicians to explain their diagnoses and to disclose alternative types of therapy they are considering.

Another theoretical question that the research evidence illuminates concerns the type of structure needed by a social system in order to function and persist. The functionalist views society and its constituent systems as generally cohesive, in equilibrium, and tending to persist with minor amounts of adaptive change. The whole is integrated by common acceptance of role definitions, authority, and values. In the functionalist view of society, a social system requires a structure that enables it to socialize members to traditional role patterns and to transmit the societal values intact—to preserve the established order. The family is one of the units in the overall societal structure that contributes to the maintenance of the society by transmitting social values to the young, constraining its members to conform to social norms, and keeping its members healthy so they can perform their tasks to the prescribed standard. Health is viewed as a societal resource that enables the society to get its essential work done. Personal health is seen as the ability to perform one's expected social roles as prescribed. Since illness represents the inability to perform societal roles, it constitutes a form of deviancy that must be controlled in the interests of societal stability. The family and medical care systems both have responsibilities to keep people healthy and cure or control illnesses promptly. Research evidence which would sustain the usefulness of this viewpoint would show that the type of family which functions best in maintaining health and generating sound health practices has clearcut authority, firm control, conventional role distinctions between males and females, and parents and children, and binds members to the family circle—a traditional disciplinarian family.

If dissent and conflict are part of the normal social process, then any social system must also protect and assert its members' interests in relations with other systems, even by challenging the established order. No system can survive if it fails to maintain a favorable balance between its members' personal needs and the demands of the broader society. Thus, the family must function to protect the health and develop the physical capacities of its members so that they may achieve their goals and assert their interests within a societal context of conflict. Therefore, health is a resource that enables individuals to achieve their own goals, develop themselves, and assert their interests in taxing encounters with other assertive groups. This conceptual framework would be consistent with evidence that showed that the type of family structure which gets the best results is assertive rather than complaisant in dealing with outside groups—for example, insisting on redress when medical service is faulty; and individuating rather than controlling within the family—for example, accommodating the special needs of the person who wants to pursue a demanding type of sport.

The present work weaves back and forth between data and theory, attempting at the outset to set our hypothesis within a larger conceptual framework, then determining whether the conceptual formulation is consistent with the research results, and finally reformulating the conceptual framework to accommodate the data. The data did not spring neatly into place within the functionalist conceptual scheme with which we began. The last chapter is a reformulation brought about by the results of the research, and is a blending of functionalist, conflict, and systems theory. The result is not a grand sociological theory. It is a modest set of propositions for which some relevant evidence was available in an investigation of family and health, and which can now be subjected to further testing with different samples, measurement tools, and types of behavior.

The investigation also raises questions about what type of action strategies will prove most effective in getting families to care adequately for their members' health. The social action proposals presented did not emerge directly from our empirical research. The choice of action strategies was directed by the resolution of the basic conceptual issues raised by the research evidence: whether the relationships between the family and the medical care system can more usefully be viewed as based on harmonious reciprocity or conflict and coercion; whether a family requires a structure based more on control and stability or more on freedom and change; and whether the family and medical care systems function largely to preserve the societal order or to serve the interests of their own members.

These conceptual choices translate into the practical choices that must be made in forming social policy and selecting social action programs. Adoption of the first conceptual formulation leads to recommendations of programs for training patients and families to comply with physicians' medical instructions and to appear faithfully for medical appointments. Acceptance of the other formulation leads to recommendations that consumer-families get representatives on the governing boards of the health services and that home care services be expanded. While these two theories are not as incompatible as they appear here, the sharp contrast drawn between them is designed to emphasize that one's basic assumptions about the social world direct one's choice of practical programs to promote health and aid the family as a whole and its members as individuals.

PART ONE

Organization of Health Care:
The Family and
Professional Medicine

To understand the organization of contemporary health care, we must examine the activities carried on both by the family and by professional medicine. But our present concern focuses much more pointedly on the family's role in health care than on the professional component. Chapter One surveys the volume and range of health-supportive tasks performed by contemporary families, and Chapter Two evaluates how competently and effectively families generally perform these health care responsibilities.

The next two chapters examine the professional medical system from the vantage point of the family. Since families are highly dependent on professional medicine for service and for access to drugs, information, and other benefits controlled by the profession, the structure and functioning of the professional sector affects the family's own health care performance. Chapter Three examines problems in the structure of the medical care system, and Chapter Four discusses some aspects of professional medicine's performance that may limit families' capacity to carry out their health care responsibilities.

ONE

Health Functions
of the Family

WE WILL USE TWO GENERAL criteria to determine the extent of the family's health maintenance functions. The first criterion is whether or not the family's health care responsibilities constitute a significant share of the *family's* total responsibilities—whether they are central to family life. This criterion requires that we determine whether health matters are reflected significantly in the family's concerns, communication and interaction among the members, the time and energy spent in the household, and the amount of family resources dedicated to health (money, physical plant, and equipment); and whether the family's health responsibilities are given the force of law. The second criterion is whether or not the family's health maintenance activities constitute a significant share of *society's* total health care endeavors—whether the family is an important unit through which societal health action is organized. This criterion requires that we look at the evidence in terms of whether or not the commitment of resources by families (money, time, energy, and services) looms large in comparison with the total contribution made by all social agencies involved in health care.

The present chapter concentrates on describing the extent of health care action by families. It does not evaluate the quality of the action; that will be done in Chapter Two. Nor does it assess the impact of the family on its members' health; that will be discussed in Chapter Seven.

Since sociology has provided few systematic accounts of this area of family functioning, we had to seek evidence from a variety of other fields, including law, economics, medicine, architecture, engineering, health education, nutrition, and industrial sources. The resulting picture is sketchy in some areas.

LEGAL RESPONSIBILITIES AND RIGHTS

The family's involvement in the care of the human body in health, sickness, and death is assured by laws that hold families responsible for performing certain health-related tasks for their members and which provide penalties that may be invoked if those tasks are not performed. The family's involvement in health activities is buttressed by laws that vest in the family certain rights concerning the health of its members, rights which supersede those of other interested parties.

SUPPORT

Members of a family are legally responsible for providing for the needs of all the members, including food, clothing, shelter, and health care. A man has the obligation to support his wife and minor children. Some states, however, specify that the support of minors is a joint responsibility of the husband and wife (Kuchler 1957). Desertion and nonsupport laws have made it a criminal offense for a husband to refuse to provide support and maintenance for his wife, and for a parent to neglect or refuse to provide support and maintenance for his or her children (Breckinridge 1972). Increasingly, the courts hold working women responsible for the support of dependent husbands as well as children.

MEDICAL AND HEALTH CARE

Health care and medical treatment are specifically included in the family's obligations. The law of support requires a husband to provide medical care for his wife and children. A man is liable for support of his child from the moment of conception, including all prenatal care and expenses of the birth (Ludwig 1955). This holds true whether the man is married to the mother or not. If the father cannot be found, then the mother is held responsible. Statutes specify that failure of a parent to provide medical or surgical treatment, or to provide proper and sufficient food, clothing, and a clean home, or to do any act necessary for the child's physical well-being, constitutes the offense of child neglect. Failure to care for a child so that the child is exposed to physical risk without proper protection constitutes abandonment. Exposing the child to unnecessary physical strains or hardship that may injure the child's health is considered cruelty (N. J. Statutes).

In twenty-six states and the District of Columbia families are required by law to get necessary vaccinations and immunizations for their children (Jackson 1969). A law may specifically impose the duty of obtaining the immunization on the parents, as in New York's poliomyelitis requirement. Or the law may impose the duty indirectly by requiring schools to exclude children who do not have the necessary immunizations. Parents who fail to comply are then found in violation of the compulsory school attendance laws (Hershey 1969). The authority to enforce laws and regulations requiring personal health procedures is based on the state's police power.

DEATH

Recognition of the family's legal role in death goes back to English common law. Family members have the duty to dispose of the dead, and they also hold the right to control the disposal of their dead (Jackson 1950; American Hospital Association 1970). While kin do not hold property right in the body, they do have a right of possession or quasi-property right because of their duty to bury their dead. This includes the right to custody of the body for proper burial, and the right to determine the place and manner of disposition (Meyers 1970; Bernard 1966).

The family's rights also include possession of the body in the same condition in which it was at the time of death; from this stem their rights concerning whether or not an autopsy or organ donation will be made. The rights of relatives must yield to the coroner's authority to determine the cause of death in violent or suspicious circumstances. Apart from these limitations, the hospital must obtain the family's permission to perform an autopsy, and the kin may sue for damages for unlawful injury or mutilation of the corpse (National Research Council 1968; Meyers 1970).

Thus, from the moment of conception until disposal of the dead body the family has fundamental responsibilities and rights regarding its members' bodily care.

COSTS OF HEALTH CARE

In keeping with the two criteria for assessing the significance of the family's health functions, two questions are posed. How much does health care cost a family? How much of the nation's health bill is paid by families?

DIRECT COSTS OF HEALTH CARE

In 1970, families paid an average of $636 for nonfree health services. This represented 4.4 percent of family income (Andersen et al. 1973). However, health cost burdens vary enormously among families. For example, health costs represented 3.3 percent of the income of the wealthiest families, but 14.5 percent of the income of the poorest families. Families differ in their access to free medical services; almost three-fourths of American families received no medical care paid by such free sources as Medicaid, welfare, and tax-supported institutions (Andersen et al. 1973).

Families also vary in the total amount of illness experienced per year and in the costliness of their particular health conditions. For example, the cost of giving birth has been estimated to be $1,534 (Commission on Population Growth 1972). This particular cost falls on only a small proportion of families during a given year. There are health conditions that are far more costly than this, so costly that their impact is catastrophic for the family. One formula defines medical costs as catastrophic if they exceed 10 percent of the first $10,000 in gross income, 15 percent of the next $25,000 in gross income, and 25 percent above $35,000. Thus, a family with a $10,000 income would have catastrophic medical costs above $1,000, and a family with a $40,000 income would have catastrophic medical expenses beyond $6,000 (HEW 1971). There is no satisfactory estimate of how many families experience catastrophic medical costs. However, over one in five families, at all income levels, had health expenditures of $1,000 or more in 1970 (Andersen et al. 1973).

There are a number of health conditions that require a high level of expenditure year after year. A child with cystic fibrosis costs the family about $1,355 per year for the care of that disease alone (McCollum 1971). The cost of treating a hemophiliac child can run as high as $10,000 per year (Lazerson 1971). Charges for heart transplants average $18,694 (National Heart Institute 1969). The cost for a kidney transplantation is estimated at

$45,000, and the average cost over the succeeding years is between $2,000 and $15,000 (HEW 1971).

Cancer Care (1973) studied the total costs borne by 115 families as a result of a fatal cancer in one of their members. The median cost of the illness was $19,054 during an average of twenty-four months of illness, which, for most families, exceeded annual family income. Even though almost all the families had medical insurance, after the patient died more than a third had unpaid bills from the illness, ranging from under $1,000 to over $3,000. This level of solvency had been achieved by some through ruinous measures, as these examples show: a brother in his late seventies used his own life savings to pay the bills for his widowed sister's illness; daughters and sons left jobs in order to be closer; a mother took into her home the children of the patient; the medical care of other family members was neglected, and so on.

Indirect Costs of Illness

Earnings lost due to disability, illness, and premature death were estimated to total $23.8 billion in 1967 (Rice 1969). The average time lost from work owing to illness or injury was over five days per employed person per year, and more than half of the pay for days lost was not reimbursed (HEW 1972). Wages may also be lost by other members of a family who must care for and take on some of the workload of the ill person. The care of a terminal cancer patient frequently causes other family members to lose jobs, fail to get promotions, reject overtime work, or quit some jobs for lower-paying ones nearer to the patient (Cancer Care 1973).

Other indirect costs of illness include transportation costs for patients and their visitors, special diets and utensils for food preparation, comfort aids, bed clothing and specially constructed clothing for various forms of disability, dwelling modifications, special furnishings, and equipment to enable patients to get around and to carry on their activities. It may be necessary to hire special housekeeping and personal services, such as laundry, home visits of a barber or hairdresser, or home delivery of purchases. If the housewife is ill, it may be necessary to hire commercially the equivalent of her usual services, including restaurant meals and household cleaning help.

The funeral is another cost ensuing from some illnesses, and involves expenditures for a funeral director, casket, cemetery or cremation, monument, flowers, burial clothing, and transportation of the body. This is one of the largest expenses incurred by many families; the average funeral costs in excess of $1,500 (Harmer 1963; Moneysworth 1971).

The Share Paid by Families

How much of the nation's health bill is paid by consumer families? In the United States in 1971, the total direct costs of professional health care, including hospital care, medical services, supplies, research, and facilities construction, amounted to $75 billion. This was 7.4 percent of the gross national product (Rice and Cooper 1972). Consumers' direct share of this national health bill was 37 percent (HEW 1971). Another 25 percent of the total health bill was paid by private insurance, which was actually paid by consumers in the form of premiums and subscription fees totaling over $18 billion. While about half of these insurance premium charges were paid by employer contributions, the employers' share was part of the wage package earned by employees for work performed. Thirty-six percent of medical care costs were paid out of public funds, which were covered largely out of personal income tax revenues. Notably, only 2 percent of the health bill was covered by philanthropy. Thus, consumers covered 37 percent of the total health bill by direct out-of-pocket expenditures, plus the 25 percent covered by their private insurance, and a substantial share of the 36 percent paid for out of taxes.

GIVING

Individuals and families support the organized medical care system through voluntary giving. They contribute money to health organizations. They work as volunteers in hospitals and health causes. They even make contributions from their bodies, such as blood, organs, and cadavers.

CONTRIBUTIONS OF MONEY

In 1970 all philanthropic gifts totaled $18.3 billion. Of this total, 16 percent, amounting to $3.02 billion, was donated for health purposes. Individuals and families contributed 78 percent of the total ($14.3 billion in 1970), while foundations, corporations, and bequests accounted for the remainder (Am. Assn. of Fund-Raising Counsel 1971). It is particularly characteristic of health philanthropy that small personal contributions provide the sustaining financial support.

VOLUNTARY SERVICE

More than half of all American families contribute work to a voluntary agency (Morgan et al. 1966). In 1970 almost eighteen million persons volunteered time to the twelve major national health organizations. Over three million did voluntary work for the National Red Cross, and more than two million volunteered for the American Cancer Society, American Health Association, and the National Foundation (Am. Assn. of Fund-Raising Counsel 1971).

Some voluntary health organizations are based on family units in the sense that they are organized and sustained by the families of afflicted persons. In 1950, forty-two parents with mentally retarded children founded the National Association of Parents and Friends of Mentally Retarded Children.

This organization has expanded to more than a thousand local and state associations with over two hundred thousand members, and 30 percent of its total membership consists of family units. The Dysautonomia Foundation is another organization started and maintained by parents of afflicted children. The disease is found almost exclusively among Jewish families; its suspected genetic basis helps to account for the fact that families with afflicted members have banded together to draw attention to and foster research on the disease (Riley 1956).

More than half of all hospitals have auxiliaries, with an average membership of 343 per hospital. They are organized to provide voluntary work such as manning the information desk and performing escort, library, messenger, and recreation services. Auxiliaries also raise money for hospitals by running gift shops, coffee shops, and card carts. About half a million adult volunteers and one hundred thousand teenagers give voluntary service through hospital auxiliaries (Binkley et al. 1968).

BLOOD

In 1967 Americans received about 4,384,003 units of blood for transfusions, and these transfusions came from about 6,610,166 units of blood donated in that year (Titmuss 1971). Over half of these donations were obtained through some type of repayment contract requiring the recipient to pay blood debts. Generally, the recipient's family and friends furnished the repayment. The patient is charged for blood used and, in addition, is assessed a replacement fee by the hospital. Many hospitals also require the patient to replace each unit of blood used with two or even three units, thus obligating the patient not only for blood actually used but also for blood needed to replace outdated units and to maintain emergency reserves.

In the family credit system the family is the formal unit of blood obligation. The donor makes a predeposit donation of one pint of blood each year to insure coverage for the family's blood needs for one year. This plan is promoted on the theme of family unity and family welfare (Titmuss 1971).

BODIES FOR AUTOPSY

The public provides an essential form of support for medical education and research by contributing cadavers for autopsy. According to the American Hospital Association (1970, p. 12), "The autopsy requires no defense; it represents the instrument mainly responsible for the development of modern medicine." Many important medical discoveries are attributed to autopsy studies. Autopsy is also an essential method for training students for clinical medicine. So important is autopsy to medicine that the percentage of autopsies performed on persons who died in hospital is regarded as the best index for rating the quality of medical care in the hospital.

No fees are paid for cadavers; they are either donated by surviving family members or retrieved as unclaimed bodies. About four thousand to five thousand cadavers are required yearly for dissection by schools of medicine, dentistry, osteopathy, mortuary science, and chiropody, and by residents in surgical specialties. These needs are largely met nowadays, for in spite of the increased need, there has been an increased readiness to donate bodies.

DONATION OF ORGANS

There is a rapidly expanding demand for live organs for transplantation, but such operations can be performed only when people are willing to donate organs. Seventeen body organs and tissues are being used, including skin, heart, lung, kidney, liver, pancreas, and eye. Donation of an organ involves a rather different type of giving than is involved in donating a dead body for autopsy. Some organs, such as hearts, must be taken immediately after death; others, such as kidneys, may be removed from living donors. In the latter case, the recruitment of organs focuses within families, because the risk that the recipient's body will reject the organ is reduced when the donor is a close blood relative. Thus, of the 5,127 kidney grafts performed in the United States up to 1972, about half used kidneys donated by living relatives of the recipients, and half used cadaver kidneys (HEW 1972).

PHYSICAL PLANT AND EQUIPMENT

A basic characteristic of almost all American families is that they establish a home base which they outfit with a vast amount of equipment; perform the unremitting physical work of cleaning, maintaining, and developing it; encumber themselves with long-term financial indebtedness; and curtail their flexibility through these obligations. The fact that families must and do perform a wide variety of health maintenance and sick-care activities is a principal factor accounting for this pattern—probably a more influential factor than the desire for affectionate companionship and sexual intercourse. Not only are families able to perform health-care functions because they make heavy investments in facilities for this purpose, but from a societal point of view families provide a national network of home health-care facilities, more extensive by far than those provided by the professional health care system.

In 1970 the United States census reported 63.4 million occupied homes, of which about 40 million were occupied by their owners, and the others were rented. In that year the median value of owner-occupied homes was about $17,100 on a nationwide basis, and in metropolitan areas it was even higher—$23,500 in New Jersey, for example (U.S. Dept. of Commerce 1972). These homes provide basic accommodations for shelter, climate control, rest, feeding, bathing, clothes storage, laundry, and general sanitation, facilities that are essential for routine maintenance of health, as well as facilities for care of illness and disability. This is reflected in the fact that 20 percent of the energy consumed in the country is used in the home (Bird 1973), and some one hundred thousand gallons of water are used each year by a family of four (U.S. Water Resources Council 1968).

While the whole house structure provides shelter, certain spaces within the house have become functionally specialized in health care, particularly the bathroom, kitchen, laundry area, and bedroom.

THE BATHROOM

In the 1880s, five out of six American city dwellers had no facilities for bathing other than pail and sponge (Giedion 1948). The home bathroom became possible only when piped water and sewers were provided throughout cities. The particular form that the home bathroom took emerged decisively during the 1920s, when the sanitary fixtures industry became fully mechanized and geared to produce a standardized product. This turned out to be a five-foot-long enameled bathtub, and it was the size of this fixture that largely determined the size and character of the bathroom (Giedion 1948). The bathroom is generally a five-foot by seven-foot cell adjacent to a bedroom, and outfitted with door and window closings that assure complete privacy.

The standardized bathroom in the United States has had a significant influence on health maintenance practices. First, body hygiene is relegated almost entirely to the home; unlike some other countries, we have never developed public bathing facilities. Thus, in 1970 all but 7 percent of the occupied homes had full bathrooms (U.S. Dept. of Commerce 1972).

Second, the resources that have gone into the home bath are considerable. Although portable and hideaway bath fixtures were in use before 1920, this style lost out completely to the costly, permanently installed type of fixtures that required a whole separate room to house them (Kira 1966). The three basic fixtures and their associated plumbing constitute one of the most expensive clusters of equipment in the entire house.

Our bathrooms have developed a high degree of specialization; body hygiene and excretion are the focal activities. This means that other functions are excluded. Some societies have regarded bathing as part of a broader human purpose—rejuvenation of the whole person—and hence joined with leisure, sports, contemplation, reading, relaxation, and social intercourse. In marked contrast, our bathrooms have no easy chairs, the decor is cold and hard, and the room is cut off from the flow of life even within the household.

While excluding other pursuits, home bathrooms serve as shrines for carrying out elaborate health and hygiene rituals. The major ritual functions are: elimination, including measures taken to induce it; oral hygiene, including cleaning teeth and dentures, medicating the mouth, and using dental floss and water piks; sexual hygiene, such as douching and applying contraceptives and menstrual supplies; general bodily cleansing, using soap and water or lotions and creams; grooming activities, such as combing and brushing the hair, shaving body hair, applying deodorant, manicuring, pedicuring, removing calluses, and applying make-up. Certain sicknesses such as vomiting and diarrhea are apt to take place in the bathroom. Most forms of home medical care take place there also: taking medicines; cleansing and applying medication and bandages to wounds; treating rashes, sunburn, and skin blemishes; using hot- and cold-water soaks; and removing foreign particles from various parts of the body. Finally, evaluations of the state of health are made in the bathroom: weighing the body, taking the temperature, and inspecting the skin, teeth, and other body areas. These hygiene rituals tend to be carried on with a high degree of ceremony, and involve a vast collection of potions and paraphernalia that is kept in readiness in the bathroom.

FEEDING FACILITIES

Spatial arrangements and facilities for feeding assumed a quite different pattern from that established for body hygiene. By about 1910, scientific-management principles had been borrowed from industry and applied in kitchen planning to an extent that never occurred in bathroom planning. Efforts to increase the efficiency of housework coincided with feminist efforts to improve woman's lot, for feminists regarded household drudgery as one of the most degrading features of a woman's role (Giedion 1948).

A major work-saving method was to plan arrangements within the kitchen for most efficient use. One method was to store all equipment and supplies at work centers. Time and motion studies of specific work processes, such as dishwashing and canning, showed how time, footsteps, and motions could be reduced by better selection of equipment and rearrangement of the work area (Nickell et al. 1942). Another method of achieving efficiency was to design and arrange the equipment so that all the pieces fitted together into one coordinated whole. Still another aspect of mechanization of the kitchen was the use of electric power tools designed to perform a specialized function, thereby improving the quality of performance and reducing effort.

While factory design for the kitchen could have led to thorough isolation of the unit from the rest of household activity, as occurred with the bathroom, this did not turn out to be the pattern for household feeding. Recent American trends tend to make the kitchen a center of activity and to decentralize feeding activity throughout the home. The floor plans of houses are open so that neither the kitchen nor the dining room is isolated. Kitchens are now made large enough to serve as dining area as well as food preparation center, thus drawing all members of the family into the kitchen.

A trend toward combining eating and leisure activities has also encouraged spatial decentralization. Many meals are eaten in front of television sets, barbecues take place on a patio or in a backyard, snacks may be grabbed on the run, and a whole meal may be picked up from a drive-in restaurant.

As feeding has merged with leisure, sociability, and broad personal fulfillment activities in the home, it has gained renewed significance as a family activity. The vast technology of the kitchen has been directed toward simplifying work and enhancing leisure by providing convenient storage, easy preparation of processed foods, attractive service, and enjoyable consumption.

SICK CARE FACILITIES

The wealthy have always equipped themselves with sophisticated and commodious health care facilities in their own homes, and some have even maintained a physician and nurses in constant attendance. American homes, however, are not generally provided with permanent sickroom space. Bedrooms are converted to sickrooms when the need arises, and bathroom and kitchen serve as nursing stations.

When a family member becomes seriously ill or experiences long-term disability, special equipment must be obtained, and existing physical facilities must sometimes be remodeled for the patient's safety, convenience, and independence. It may be necessary to widen doorways to accommodate a wheelchair, to remodel existing bathtubs with low sides for easy access, and to provide handrails, nonskid surfaces, and long-handled levers on water taps (Elliott 1971). To enable a handicapped person to use the toilet independently, it may be necessary to change the height of the existing toilet to correspond to that of the wheelchair or to provide a separate lavatory wheelchair. A special bed may be needed; an electrically powered bed that turns the patient over costs about $1,000 (Preston 1972). A physically disabled woman may continue to work in the kitchen if adjustments are made in the facilities, such as providing storage space at wheelchair height or special utensils with thickened or curved handles.

A small amount of physician service continues to be performed in the home. Approximately 5 percent of all physician visits in the northeast take place at home, while in the nation as a whole little more than 2 percent are house calls (HEW 1972). Efforts are currently being made to reinstate some home medical service. A few agencies have been established to provide twenty-four-hour house call service by their participating physicians, and a number of home care agencies have been set up to provide nursing and other health services at home.

HEALTH MAINTENANCE

The family is the primary agency for protecting physical health, and the performance of health maintenance activities constitutes a major share of all the time and energy expended in households.

TIME AND EFFORT

Motion and time studies of household activity document the heavy focus of family time and effort on health-supportive tasks. A conservative estimate of the total amount of time spent in homemaking tasks by all family members is at least sixty hours a week. Food tasks account for the largest proportion, over one-third of the total homemaking time. House care and care of clothes each take about one-fifth of the total time, more than eleven hours per week for each. The other major homemaking task area is physical care of family members; this takes about eight hours per week (Walker and Gauger 1973; Baily 1962; Anderson and Fitzsimmons 1960).

BELIEFS ABOUT HEALTH MAINTENANCE

Families hold well-developed values and beliefs about the importance of their own actions within the family for maintaining health. When a group of homemakers with preschool children were asked to list their activities of the preceding day and then to give their reasons for doing them, the top-ranking reason given was health (Dyer 1962). Almost all the mothers and fathers in another study held instrumental beliefs about how to develop and maintain their children's health, and stressed food and nutrition as the most important method of maintaining health. In fact, about four in ten mothers and two in ten fathers believed that eating together as a family had a positive effect on the nutritional benefits to be achieved from food (Stolz 1967).

Three-fourths of the people in a study sample felt that a major reason for bad health was improper diet (FDA 1972). Other studies that asked how to keep a family in good health found that an overwhelming majority believed that personal health maintenance practices were most effective, and references to good food and nutrition were the most common. Notably, very few cited professional medical care as a means of maintaining health (Hassinger and McNamara 1960; Cornely and Bigman 1961; Litman 1971).

HEALTH EDUCATION

The family actively processes health information. It obtains, stores, exchanges, communicates to the young, and evaluates information concerning health problems and health care. Some professional health education organizations formally direct their efforts toward families; for example, school health programs use the child as the conduit to the family.

Families also actively seek out information on health directly from the media. About half of a group of respondents reported that they had read books dealing with health and medical topics, and almost a third had read consumer reports on these matters (Roney and Nall 1966). A national survey found that well over half the respondents read health articles in newspapers, over a third read them in magazines, and over half listened to health programs on television or radio. The most common pattern was to obtain information from all three media—newspapers, magazines, and radio. Only a fifth did not at least occasionally read or listen to health information from the media (Feldman 1966).

The distribution figures for books, pamphlets, and magazines on health topics attest to the widespread interest in the subject. Adelle Davis's four books on nutrition and health have sold around seven million copies (*Time* 1972). The record best seller of the United States Government Printing Office is *Infant Care,* followed not far behind by *Prenatal Care,* and a recent best seller is *Sanitation and Home Laundering* (Shenker 1972). Some widely circulated health magazines include *Prevention* (850,000), *Today's Health* (710,000), and *Family Health* (915,000) (Ulrich 1971–1972).

A considerable amount of health information is also exchanged within family units. Twenty-five percent of a National Opinion Research Center sample reported that their source of information on cancer symptoms was relatives, friends, and their own experiences with cancer (Feldman 1966). In our study sample, a large majority of fathers and mothers reported that they purposefully explained to their children (aged nine to thirteen) about proper health care procedures. While the figures shown below do not reveal the correctness of the information imparted, they do indicate that parents attempt broad-scale health education activity with their children. The only health area that a majority of the parents did not cover was how reproduction takes place.

These data indicate the higher concentration of health education responsibilities among women than among men. In all areas except reproduction,

	Percent of Parents Who Explained Various Health Procedures to Their Children		Percent of Children Reporting Their Parents Explained to Them
	Mothers	*Fathers*	
Proper way to use a toothbrush	95	68	90
Proper kinds of food to eat	96	77	92
Effects of smoking on health	78	75	77
When and how much to exercise	69	66	61
How to clean oneself in order to maintain a healthy body	97	78	94
Importance of moving bowels regularly	93	68	86
Effect of irregular or lack of sleep on health	92	78	86
How reproduction takes place between the sexes	47	32	36

however, at least two-thirds of the fathers also reported participating in the health education of their children. Women also absorb more and show greater interest in health and medical information than men. This reflects family structure, for the wife-mother has traditionally been assigned the major responsibility for maintaining the health of family members.

FAMILY AS THE UNIT OF HEALTH CONCERN

An indication that families assume responsibility for members' health is that health worries and concerns tend to focus within family units. In a 1950s study of what kinds of things Americans worried about most, 80 percent answered solely in terms of family and personal problems, and less than 1 percent were most concerned about societal issues, such as communism or civil liberties (Stouffer 1955). Health of self or family members turned out to be the second most frequently cited principal concern—reported by 24 percent of the cross section. In a more recent study, 18 percent of a group of Maryland families reported that a health-related matter was their largest problem (Wang et al. 1972).

Our study distinguished between the informants' worry about their own health and their worry about family members' health. The results showed that both men and women were more likely to worry about the health of other family members than about their own health. Over half of the women and about four in ten of the men worried about family members' health during the past week. More women listed family members' health as a source of worry than any of the other eight topics, except bringing up children. For men, on the other hand, bringing up children, getting ahead, and money ranked ahead of health of family members as a source of worry.

When asked what they had worried about most, 23 percent of the women and 16 percent of the men listed health of family members. This placed family members' health at the top of the list of problems most worried about by women, while bringing up children and money ranked ahead of family members' health as the problem most worried about by men. These findings agree with the evidence on the health education activities of men and women, which indicate the persistence of the traditional pattern of assigning responsibility for family health maintenance to women.

Not only do family members worry about each other's health, but a family member who becomes ill worries about the impact of his or her illness on the other members. Among a group of hospitalized terminally ill patients, those who were parents of school-age children were much more likely to be anxious and depressed than those without dependent children (Hinton 1963). A study of 323 incidents in which a person had had a close call with death by physical illness or accident found that the most frequent first reaction to finding oneself imperiled was concern about one's family and other survivors (Kalish 1969).

FAMILY DECISION MAKING

The definition of a state of illness, preliminary evaluation of symptoms, and decisions about what action should be taken are, in many important respects, family transactions. Initial discussion of symptoms with family members plays an important part in providing a person with provisional validation that she or he is sick and should prepare to take appropriate action (Suchman 1965). Thus, when the earliest signs of illness occur, the first person a married man usually turns to for exchange of information is his wife (Twaddle 1969). Decisions about what to do about the condition—whether to seek professional care or to treat the illness at home—are also negotiated largely within the family (Richardson 1970; Podell 1970).

There are two kinds of family influence at work. First, each family unit has a degree of autonomy and physical separation from other family units; this fosters *similarity* in medical care behavior among its members. The communication and influence exerted among family members operates to develop a common style of caring for illness among the members of a given family. There is a similarity in the frequency of medical consultations of fathers and sons, mothers and daughters, and husbands and wives (Pickens 1969), suggesting that family members develop common ideas about what constitutes sickness and when medical care should be sought. Members of a family are likely to go to the same doctor. One study disclosed that the longer a couple has been married the more likely they are to have the same doctor (Cartwright 1967).

Second, the role structure of family life brings about patterned *variations* in health care practices among the members; a person's distinctive role obligations within the family are reflected in his or her behavior concerning sickness. The man's role as provider may hem him in with more rigid time and performance restrictions than the woman's homemaker role. This may partly explain the fact that men use fewer medical services of all kinds and succumb to fewer disability days than women. The protective role of parents regarding their children is reflected in the higher rate of medical services obtained for children than for adult family members. These variations in sickness behavior emerge from a process of negotiations, in which each person attempts to carry out his or her responsibilities in the context of the demands for performance placed on him or her by the other members. The husband cannot afford to have his wife leaving her housework any longer than necessary, but neither can he afford to have her neglect health problems that would impair her functioning. For this reason, family members have considerable leverage in effecting the desired health care behavior (Booth and Babchuk 1972).

The health assessment process also reflects family role structure. It is the wife-mother who usually takes the lead in looking for particular clues that a member is not feeling well. The clues used even vary with the family role of the person under evaluation; for example, being quieter than usual may be regarded as a sign of illness in husbands, while leaving their food uneaten may be predictive of illness in children (Robinson 1971).

On summary, each family develops its own characteristic pattern of health practices, and the differentiation of roles within the family imparts a somewhat distinctive cast to the health behavior of each of its members. These two facts account for the strong influence that families have on their members' decisions about handling sickness.

CARE OF ILLNESS AT HOME

Illness and health defects are so common as to be a normal aspect of family life. About seventy-five out of every one hundred adults experience at least one episode of ill health or injury in an average month (White et al. 1961). A Cleveland study reported a rate of illness of all kinds of nine per person annually (Dingle et al. 1964). Family units necessarily experience illness at a higher rate than individuals. A study of low-income families calculated that individuals usually reported a symptom every thirteen days, while the families of these individuals reported a symptom once every three days. During the month of the study, 93 percent of the families reported one or more symptoms (Alpert et al. 1967). A panel study of 273 households reported that families generally deal with an acute illness on one of every four days (Knapp and Knapp 1972). A majority of families deals with a continuous state of illness, for one-half of the population have at least one chronic condition (HEW 1969).

Illnesses attended at home greatly outnumber illnesses attended in hospitals: About twenty acute illnesses or injuries involving reduced daily activity or medical attention are experienced outside a hospital for every one involving hospitalization (HEW 1971, 1972). These episodes represent a large amount of time requiring care at home. Acute conditions cause an average of 7.9 days of restricted activity per person in the population, including 3.4 days spent in bed (HEW 1969). Those hospitalized for surgery require convalescent care averaging from nine days for tonsillectomies to twenty-two days for appendectomies and forty-three days for hysterectomies (HEW 1963).

Many illnesses and disabilities are cared for exclusively by the family, without professional assistance. The study estimating that seventy-five out of every one hundred adults will experience some illness or injury during a month figured that fifty of these adults will take care of the problem without consulting a physician (White et al. 1961). The family's dominant role in caring for illness is brought out even more sharply in the previously discussed study of a month of illnesses among low-income families. Medical help was sought in only 12 percent of the 834 symptoms identified by the families, representing a 7:1 ratio of medically nonattended symptoms to medically attended symptoms (Alpert et al. 1967).

EXTENT OF FAMILY MEDICATION ACTIVITY

Taking medication is a major form of contemporary health care activity. During a thirty-week period, 95 percent of the households in a United States sample bought at least one drug. These households averaged almost fourteen drug purchases during the period, and they had over twenty-two drugs on hand. Drug products were used in over nine out of ten illnesses (Knapp and Knapp 1972).

Taking nonprescribed, or over-the-counter, medications is far more frequent than taking prescribed medicines. While prescribed drugs are used in about three out of ten cases of illness or injury, nonprescription drugs are used in over seven in ten, and nonprescribed drugs are used exclusively in six out of ten episodes (Knapp and Knapp 1972).

A significant amount of self-medication appears to be carried on as an alternative to professional care. A national survey found that about half of the sample self-medicated sore throats, coughs, head colds, and upset or acid stomach, and that 12 percent self-medicated for longer than two weeks for a variety of common ailments (HEW 1972). Families generally have routine procedures for caring for colds and other ailments and injuries which they judge to be too trivial and common to warrant professional attention, or which they feel competent to handle themselves. Home medication is not limited to a narrow range of common ailments. Over-the-counter preparations are used to treat a wide range of body systems, including the central nervous, respiratory, gastrointestinal, genital-urinary, and skin (Roney and Nall 1966).

A significant amount of home medication is supplementary to professional treatment. Eighty percent of a sample of physicians' patients were found to practice self-medication (Lader 1965). Even in the case of prescribed drugs, there is a significant element of self-medication. What is labeled by physicians as patient error and noncompliance is an alteration of the prescribed medication plan by the patient. For example, many diabetic patients deviate substantially from the medication regimen established by their physicians (Watkins et al. 1967). A significant amount of prescribed medication is rejected by patients; one study estimated a rejection rate of 50 percent (Linnett 1968). A British study estimated that only 2 to 5 percent of prescriptions were not filled at all, but 16 percent were thrown away before being used up, and 20 percent were not taken exactly as directed. Almost a third of a sample of persons who had had a prescription refilled said they usually did not see a doctor when refilling the prescription (Dunnell and Cartwright 1972). The practice of hoarding medications suggests that patients may use a medication prescribed for a particular episode for other episodes. One study discovered that over a fourth of the sample had taken a prescribed medication more than a year after it had been prescribed (Dunnell and Cartwright 1972). Family members may also exchange prescribed medications among themselves, although the extent of this practice is unknown.

The clearest cases of self-medication with prescription drugs occur when persons instruct physicians to provide them with prescriptions for medications, because the physicians are regarded as gatekeepers whose permission must be sought in order to carry out the desired self-medication (Pratt 1973).

CARE OF CHRONIC ILLNESS

Chronic illness is definitely a home care situation. Only about 4 percent of those who report activity limitation as a result of chronic disease or impairment reside in institutions; the vast majority live at home (American Hospital Assn. 1971). The professional health care system is not well equipped for handling diseases resulting from multiple causes, such as tissue wear, trauma, side effects of acute illnesses, and socioenvironmental conditions, which are less amenable to direct treatment and require long-term care. General hospitals treat chronically ill patients only for acute episodes and for important complications, terminating their responsibility when the emergency is over.

Even if professional services were adapted to the needs of the chronically ill, patients and their families would still take on the major share of care in order to permit patients to live at home, to maintain maximum independence, and simply to survive their illnesses. A diabetic patient, for example, may receive twelve hours per year of medical care from doctors and nurses, and the rest from family and patient. Diabetics must, in effect, become their own doctors, continually evaluating body needs, regulating food intake, and injecting insulin.

Certain types of long-term conditions require constant alertness to signs of deterioration and routine administration of special preventive measures. In dysautonomia, because of the failure of the eyes to tear, it is essential that the eyelids be bathed with warm water and that lubricants be administered at least four times daily (D'Amico 1972). In cystic fibrosis, it is continuously necessary to combat bronchial obstruction by attempting to liquefy the secretions and maintain pulmonary drainage; parents may be involved in administering therapy to children with the disease for three to five hours a day. One study found that when a homemaker herself was disabled, about four hours more were spent on household tasks than if she was not. While homemakers themselves spent 2.7 hours less, others contributed 6.7 hours more help (Manning 1968).

REHABILITATION

The family may become deeply involved in the rehabilitation of disabled and chronically ill persons, sometimes cooperating with professional rehabilitation services and sometimes undertaking the task themselves. The forms of disability that require rehabilitation cover a wide range, including skeletal impairments, visual impairment, cardiac defects, and tuberculosis.

Corrective therapy may involve physicial exercises to strengthen and co-ordinate functions and to prevent muscular deconditioning due to long con-valescence. After a person suffers a stroke, the family must both support and actively assist the patient in his or her efforts to restore speech, strengthen muscles, or learn to use a prosthetic device. Special training must be given to deaf children. The family must begin lip reading, auditory training, sense training, and language preparation, and must actively help the deaf child to learn how to use a hearing aid effectively so the child can learn to speak.

Therapeutic recreation may be provided for chronically ill and disabled persons, including arts and crafts, music, writing, dramatics, hobbies, games, and modified sports. The family's cooperation is essential in vocational re-habilitation, both in the case in which the patient must develop new skills for a different occupation, and in the case in which the patient must retrain for her or his former occupation. The home may serve as a sheltered work-shop for female patients, where they may retrain for homemaking tasks while protected and supported by the family (Angrist et al. 1972).

CARE OF THE DYING

Someone dies every sixteen and a half seconds in the United States (Lan-gone 1972). Unless the death occurs suddenly, the person requires that others help in caring for his or her physical needs during the terminal period. Although only about a fourth of American deaths now occur in the home, those patients who do die at home tend to be suffering from conditions that require care for a prolonged period of time—heart disease, malignant neo-plasms, vascular lesions, and accidents (Brim et al. 1970).

Care of the dying is extremely arduous work. It may include washing the patient who is confined to bed, helping the patient use a bedpan, giving enemas, changing bedclothes frequently, lifting and turning over the patient, taking measures to prevent bedsores, and applying surgical dressings. Many of these tasks involve a degree of physical effort to which family members may be unaccustomed, and may require long hours of attention that dras-tically interfere with the family's usual sleep and work schedule.

Even when the patient dies in the hospital, the family is called upon to participate in terminal care. Some hospitals make provisions for the mother to give the routine physical care for a terminally ill child. In all cases, the family must visit the hospitalized patient and develop modes of coping with the hospital, which has assumed control of their family member's care.

PROVISION OF PROFESSIONAL MEDICAL SERVICES

The use of professional services calls for selecting the appropriate medical services, negotiating the appointments and other arrangements, coordinating the services rendered by various professionals and agencies, expending time and travel to obtain the care, as well as undergoing the performance of these services.

SELECTING A MEDICAL SERVICE

The selection of practitioners and agencies to perform medical services is a complex matter, not only because medicine is so highly specialized and complexly organized, but also because the family's medical needs are constantly changing. The consumer must first determine what type of medical specialist is required, learn the proper criteria to employ in evaluating the practitioners available in this specialty, and then obtain the relevant information about each of the practitoners in order to make a choice. For example, to obtain surgical service, the very least that one should do is check out surgeons in the Directory of Medical Specialists to determine whether they belong to the American College of Surgeons, and to ascertain that they are certified by a surgical board and associated with a good hospital. After selecting and visiting a surgeon, the patient should check out the surgeon's recommendations with an internist.

Even when the consumer learns the appropriate technical criteria to apply in judging physicians and agencies, it is complicated to assemble the data concerning the physicians and services under consideration. One of the rare efforts to provide both basic guidelines and data on particular medical services is the series of guides published by *New York* magazine concerning various medical services in New York City. One of their guides provides information on emergency services of the major Manhattan hospitals, including the location, charges, hours of service, qualifications of staff, specialized services, usual waiting time, and accommodations (Smith 1972). A New York consumer research group prepared a guide to Queens doctors (that is, those willing to participate in the project), which lists office hours, billing practices, and hospital affiliations (Cerra 1974).

The intricacies of the selection process can be illustrated by the search for an abortion. This involves knowing the legal provisions of the state from which the patient seeks to obtain an abortion, including not only the grounds on which abortions are granted, but the duration of pregnancy within which abortions are authorized and the residency requirements. Specific decisions include the timing of the abortion, whether a referral agency will be used, the abortion procedure, the type of agency (outpatient clinic or hospital), and the particular agency.

Selecting the particular abortion agency calls for consideration of what services are provided (testing, counseling, aftercare, birth control, and type of anesthetic used); the costs of the service (in New York, from about $125 to $225 for an early abortion in a clinic, and from $300 to $500 for a late abortion in a hospital); and whether there are extra service charges (lab work, post-abortion checkup, and Rhogam injection for Rh-negative blood);

whether Medicaid is accepted; whether minors are accepted without parental consent; and the duration of pregnancy that is accepted (*New York* 1972).

Regardless of what kind of medical service is sought, numerous details must be negotiated, some of them highly technical. Many medical transactions turn out to be even more complex than the illustration used here.

MAGNITUDE OF MEDICAL CONTACTS

Consider now the total volume of all such medical services that a family must obtain. Almost nine out of ten families use a physician's services each year (Avnet 1967; Hassinger and Hobbs 1972). Americans average six physician visits per individual per year; the average for a family with a husband and wife and one or more children under age seventeen is almost twenty visits per year (HEW 1969, 1972). If we add in other medical services, such as laboratory, the average comes to a total of twenty-seven services per family of four members (Avnet 1967). In addition, each year one out of every two families hospitalize a member. Added to this is an average of almost eight dental visits per year per family (HEW 1969).

The task is complicated by the diversity of services. It is more common for a family to use more than one physician than to obtain all their care from a single physician: Three-fourths use the services of more than one, and more than a third use four or more different physicians during a year (Hassinger and Hobbs 1972; Avnet 1969). In most cases, this means that the family must relate to, and integrate the services of, different medical specialties.

EFFORT IN TIME AND DISTANCE

It takes time to investigate various sources of medical care, travel to the office or clinic, wait for the practitioner, and undergo the care. While this kind of family effort has mainly gone unrecorded, studies have found that patients commonly wait over an hour before being seen by a doctor with whom they have an appointment at a hospital outpatient department, and then wait additional time to obtain tests and other services. Many such visits require a half-day away from work by the patient, and sometimes by an escort as well (Houston and Pasanen 1972; Chenault 1971).

A study of medical care journeys in Cleveland reported for a sample of patients that the mean distance traveled one way was about 3.5 miles to both hospitals and physicians, about 3.4 miles to dentists, and less than 1.5 miles to pharmacies (Bashshur et al. 1970). The twenty physician visits and eight dentist visits made by a family of four average out to almost 200 miles per year.

CONCLUSIONS

A social system is what it does; it can be identified by its characteristic actions. The question posed in this chapter is whether the family can usefully be regarded as a personal health care system. Is personal health care an important area of family functioning, and do families perform a significant share of all societal health care activity?

The conclusions are: health care is a central focus of family life; health responsibilities of the family are prescribed by law; much of the household plant and equipment is dedicated to health maintenance; and the social life of the family—the mutual concerns, discussions, problem solving, decisions, collaborative behavior, and service activities—is oriented around health to a significant degree.

From a societal point of view, the family is a basic unit within which health behavior is organized and performed. Families pay most of the direct costs of health care and, in addition, contribute significantly to the support of the entire societal health care system through voluntary giving. Families maintain a societal network of health service plants within which almost all preventive health care and the major share of sick care is carried out. Families have principal responsibility for initiating and coordinating the health services performed by the professional sector.

The contemporary American family may be characterized not only by the personal health care tasks and activities it performs, but also by the degree of success or failure with which it performs these activities. The next chapter evaluates how effective families are in performing these health care activities and responsibilities for their members.

TWO

Effectiveness of Family Health Functioning

Magnum Photos, Inc. by Sepp Seitz

EVEN THOUGH FAMILIES CARRY on a wide variety of demanding health care activities, they do not necessarily perform all these tasks at a high level of proficiency. In a particular social era, the family system as a whole or large numbers of family units may be ineffective in the performance of certain tasks, or even many of the tasks, that its members and society require. Our objective is to assess whether the contemporary American family is generally functioning effectively as a personal health care system.

The criteria used to measure the effectiveness of family performance are: how well equipped are the homes for protecting health, and how adequate are families' personal health practices, medication practices, care of ill members in the home, use of professional medical services, appreciation of the importance of good health for personal functioning, and level of health knowledge.

The standards applied in evaluating each of these performance areas are those developed by various professional disciplines—medicine, health education, public health, architecture, and home economics. In general, these standards are in the public domain—in the accessible pool of publicly disseminated information. The resources and techniques for living up to these standards are currently available within American culture. Thus, they are standards that the health professions consider can be achieved by a hypothetical American family which sets out to do so. This does not mean that all Americans actually know the approved health standards, accept them as essential for maintaining their own health, and have easy access to resources needed for attaining them. The question at issue here is: To what extent do Americans know about, accept the importance of, actively seek out the necessary means, and fulfill in their own practices the standards of health care recommended by the health professions and regarded as potentially attainable within the contemporary societal context?

STRUCTURE AND EQUIPMENT OF HOMES

The structure and equipment of a home affects the health of the inhabitants by influencing the extent to which basic human physiological needs can be met, by affecting the occurrence and spread of disease among family members, and by influencing the risk of accidents.

PROVISIONS FOR PHYSIOLOGICAL NEEDS

Many families feel their homes are inadequate for their living needs. Complaints about housing focus on spatial dimensions and arrangements, such as inadequate storage space, through-traffic in work areas, poor location of laundry facilities and children's play areas, insufficient work space, and inefficient arrangement of kitchens or laundries. These housing defects impair housewives' performance; about a third of those with each of these undesirable spatial features reported that it greatly affected their workload, and that the time actually spent in housework tended to be significantly greater (Hall 1970; Rossi 1955).

Kitchen spatial arrangements have been found to be especially inadequate. In spite of the fact that more research has been conducted on the design of the kitchen than on any other room in the house, an analysis of 103 American kitchen plans revealed that a majority contained serious errors in basic design or in arrangement of facilities (Ranney et al. 1950). A majority of kitchens in one sample lacked good light at the kitchen work center, shelves for books and files, racks for dishtowels, and space for a small child to play and store toys. About half lacked storage facilities above and below the food preparation area and a convenient wastepaper basket, and at least one-fourth had inconvenient arrangements, such as incorrect height for work surfaces or lack of storage space for dish-washing tools at the sink (Daspit 1959).

One of the most productive attempts to evaluate the extent to which American homes provide sufficient space for healthful living used architectural sketches for ninety commonly used house plans (Mabry 1959). Thirty-one percent of two-bedroom houses had insufficient space for three-person families, and 97 percent were inadequate for six persons. Although all three-bedroom homes were spatially adequate for a three-person family, the proportion declined severely as size of family increased. Eighteen percent of the three-bedroom homes were inadequate for four persons, 35 percent were inadequate for five persons, and 62 percent were inadequate for six persons. Sleeping, dressing, and care of infants and ill persons were the activities for which the homes were most likely to be spatially deficient.

HOUSEHOLD CONTROL OVER DISEASE

Homes are expected to provide protection from such environmental hazards to health as extremes of temperature, excessive dampness or dryness, and air pollution. Yet not only may the home fail to protect the inhabitants against the dangers of the external environment, but environmental conditions may be produced within the home itself which are injurious to health.

Household cooking and heating fuels are an important source of pollution. A gas stove without a vent may emit carbon monoxide, which starves the body of essential oxygen. These emissions are especially dangerous to the elderly, the pregnant, the overweight, infants, the unborn, and those with respiratory difficulties (Hills 1973).

There is direct evidence linking household insecticides to body contamination. Autopsies performed on 271 deceased, hospital patients revealed that those who had used DDT extensively in their homes had levels in their tissues three to four times higher than those who had used a minimum of DDT (Radomski 1966). The aerosol dispenser is an effective means of distributing insecticides on all surfaces of a room; an insect landing on the surface days or weeks later can be killed. For the same reason, food may also be contaminated weeks after a room has been sprayed. Smoking, use of dry cleaning fluids, and parking cars in garages attached to the house also contribute to home air pollution.

Many homes fail to provide adequate facilities for preventing the spread of contagious diseases among family members. There is a marked relationship between crowding in the home and the frequency of contagion of various communicable diseases among both children and adults (Wilner et al. 1962; Britter and Altman 1941). Sharing a bedroom has been specifically implicated in the spread of streptococcal infections (Meyer and Haggerty 1962). Shared use of toilet facilities and inadequate ventilation also contribute to the spread of infectious diseases.

The increasing number of pets in American households create other home-based injury and disease problems. About 15 percent of children are estimated to have been bitten by an animal (Carothers 1958), and the risk of serious dog bites is increasing as the number of guard dogs maintained by urban families increases. A number of animal infections may be transmitted secondarily to humans. Dogs may harbor salmonellae and be immune to the pathogens, but may transmit them to humans. One outbreak of diarrhea caused by salmonellae was introduced into homes by children's Easter chicks. Psittacosis is endemic in many kinds of birds, and 60 percent of the cases in humans follow exposure to pet birds. Fleas, which are readily transmitted from pets to humans, are responsible for a common skin problem in young children and for notorious bites. Hairy pets may also cause allergic reactions in children, including eczema and asthma (Carothers 1958). The risk of disease transmission is enhanced by the common tendency for pet owners, particularly children, to live in intimate physical contact with their pets.

HOUSEHOLD ACCIDENT RISKS

At least one accident takes place in 40 percent of homes during a year's time. Forty-two percent of the accidents that require medical attention or restrict activity occur in the home, more than motor vehicle and workplace accidents combined (HEW 1970). Further, more people die from home accidents than work accidents, although there are more road fatalities than home accident deaths. While females are especially likely to experience accidents in the home—54 percent of all their accidents—males suffer 35 percent of their accidents at home, which is more than occur at work (Metropolitan Life 1973).

Evidence indicates that the condition of the home is an actual causal factor in accidents. One estimate has shown that a person living in a dilapidated dwelling unit is four times as likely to suffer a home accident death as a person living in a nondilapidated unit (Male 1968). Certain houses have been found to be accident-prone. In homes in which one person has had an accident during the year, the chance that a second person in the household will have an accident is twice as great as for other households (Macqueen 1960).

Specific housing characteristics have been implicated in accidents. More fatal home accidents occur as a result of falls than from any other form of injury (Metropolitan Life 1973). Household falls are frequently associated with defects in stairways, such as steep treads, poor lighting, and lack of railings. Falls are also associated frequently with tubs and showers that have slippery bottoms, lack handrails, or are too high for safely getting in and out (NEISS 1972).

Of course, other parties are also involved in creating dangerous conditions that result in home accidents, for example, those who manufacture defective and dangerous products, package poisonous products in unlabeled and seductive wrappings, or fail to maintain properties rented to families. However, the purpose of our analysis is to focus on the contribution by families to their own peril or safety.

PERSONAL HEALTH PRACTICES

There are significant defects in nutrition, exercise, smoking, and dental hygiene carried on in the home by large numbers of American families.

FOOD AND NUTRITION

The U.S. Department of Agriculture concluded from its 1965–1966 study of 7,500 families that:

"In a decade of economic expansion and rising incomes—even affluence—when Americans could choose from the greatest abundance and variety of nutritious food in history, U.S. family diets were not as good as they were in 1955. From this we must conclude that many of our people are making poor choices from our food abundance" (U.S. Department of Agriculture 1972, p. 4).

There is both a failure to consume essential nutrients and a tendency to consume unnecessary or harmful foods.

Twenty-one percent of household diets were poor in 1965, which was an increase from 15 percent in 1955. Moreover, the proportion of families with good diets dropped from 60 percent in 1955 to 50 percent in 1965. The nutrients in which household diets were most frequently deficient were calcium, vitamin A, and vitamin C. The calcium deficiency is accounted for by the declining use of milk, while the vitamin A and C deficiencies are attributable to insufficient consumption of fresh vegetables and fruits.

The tendency to skip some meals is partly responsible for these deficiencies. In our urban study sample, 35 percent of the adults and 12 percent of the children had not eaten breakfast the day before the interview.

Another important factor is the increased tendency to consume non-nutritious foods. The decline in fluid milk consumption is attributed to the increased use of soft drinks and other nonnutritive beverages. The growing tendency to consume "empty calories" is evident in the increased sugar consumption—from 77.4 pounds per capita in 1911 to 101.6 pounds in 1971 (Warren 1972). In addition to substituting for nutritious foods, the consumption of nonnutritive foods has direct harmful effects. Sugar contributes significantly to tooth decay. High-calorie snack foods are an important factor in causing overweight, which characterizes almost half of all American adults.

The increased consumption of meat by Americans has led to excessive amounts of animal fat in the diet; saturated fats have been implicated in cardiovascular disease. This higher meat consumption is not defensible on the grounds of supplying needed protein, for there is now twice as much protein in the diet as is needed (Brody 1973).

The family has a major influence on the dietary practices of all the members. An obvious factor is that most persons' diets are highly dependent upon whatever foods the family kitchen provides. The sanctioning of food behavior is largely a family-centered activity, with other persons exerting only a minor influence (Litman 1964). Consequently, there is a marked correspondence between the food patterns of family members (Brown 1967; Hellersberg 1946). Obesity tends to run in families. One study found that among one thousand obese persons one or both parents were generally obese also (HEW 1966).

EXERCISE

Some health experts have named lack of sufficient exercise as the nation's number one health care failure. This conclusion is certainly supported by the high rate of obesity found in groups of all ages and in the high rate of hypertension (Abbott 1972). An estimated seven million people are now being treated for backaches, the major cause of which is failure to get daily physical exercise (Warren 1973).

The respondents in our urban sample generally had very inadequate exercise habits. More than seven in ten of the men and well over eight in ten of the women reported that they never participated in any sports or physical games, and only 13 percent of the men and 6 percent of the women participated in sports or games regularly. Eight out of ten of the men and women never did any exercising, such as calisthenics, hiking, or bicycling, and only one in ten exercised regularly. Many more children than adults engaged in sports and exercising, but among these children, aged nine to thirteen, 14 percent never participated in any sports or physical games, and 45 percent did no exercising.

SMOKING

About half of the men and about a third of the women in the United States regularly smoke cigarettes (HEW 1969). Smoking patterns are strongly influenced by the family; in families in which both parents smoked, 23 percent of the fifteen- to sixteen-year-old boys smoked regularly, while in families in which neither parent smoked, only 9 percent of the fifteen- to sixteen-year-old boys smoked (HEW 1971).

The harmful consequences of smoking have been well documented. Smokers experience more chronic illnesses, more days lost from work, and more days in bed from illness than nonsmokers. A twenty-five-year-old man who never smoked regularly can expect to live 8.3 years longer than a heavy smoker (HEW 1969).

DENTAL HYGIENE

A national survey of oral hygiene concluded:

"In spite of wide acceptance as an essential safeguard for lasting dental health, oral hygiene was gravely neglected by a multitude of U.S. adults. While it is true that men and women on the whole observed a fairly good level of oral cleanliness, more than one out of four had substandard levels ranging from barely adequate to injuriously poor" (HEW 1966, p. 9).

And another report on a survey of children concluded: "Faulty oral hygiene, due primarily to the presence of soft foreign material loosely attached to teeth, was highly prevalent among U.S. children.... Two-thirds had moderate to heavy amounts of debris" (HEW 1972, p. 9).

A national survey found that about three out of five adults brushed their teeth at least twice a day, about three in ten only once a day, and almost one in ten less than once a day (Putnam et al. 1967). In our urban New Jersey sample 15 percent of the men and 9 percent of the women had not brushed their teeth even once during the previous twenty-four hours, and this was true of more than a fourth of the children.

The rule about brushing teeth soon after eating is clearly not practiced by most people. The national survey and our own study showed that the two most common times for brushing were before going to bed and after waking, and that very few persons brushed right after any meal.

There is a widespread tendency to use defective or inadequate equipment in teeth cleaning. A dentist evaluated toothbrushes used by families across the country, and concluded that 56 percent were unsatisfactory because they were worn out, caked with dentifrice, or had unsanitary deposits. One out of five toothbrushes was judged to be actually dangerous to the gingival tissue because the bristles were splayed to a great degree

(Bureau of Dental Health Education 1966). While a majority of families used a fluoridated toothpaste, four out of ten families did not (Cohen et al. 1967).

MEDICATION PRACTICES

People now consume so many medications, and so many of the medications are self-administered, that there are bound to be some ill effects due to consumer error, ignorance, or poor judgment. Patient errors can be of many types: medicine taken that was not ordered by a physician, ordered by a physician but not taken, or ordered by a physician but taken in incorrect doses, in the wrong way, or at the wrong time. A study of 178 elderly patients reported that only two-fifths were making no medication errors at all (Schwartz et al. 1962). A majority of diabetic patients were found to take improper doses of insulin, in some cases because they misunderstood how much they were supposed to take, and in other cases because they measured the amount of insulin in the syringe incorrectly (Watkins et al. 1967).

Another type of medication problem occurs because the drug should not have been consumed at all. The regular use of laxatives may be harmful and is, at best, unnecessary. Yet over $150 million is spent annually on over 700 laxative preparations (Altman 1973; Greenberg 1971).

About 822,000 nonfatal poisonings are reported annually in the United States, and one person per 100,000 population dies from accidental poisoning each year (Sunshine 1965). Aspirin, a drug that can produce gastrointestinal bleeding, caused more nonfatal poisonings than any other product. On the other hand, prescribed medications were responsible for 80 percent of fatal poisonings, with barbiturates heading the list.

One factor contributing to the risk of self-poisoning is the tendency to hoard medications. A household survey found that some people still had medications that had been used for children who had since grown up and left home, and one person inherited the mother's estate, including her medications (Roney and Nall 1966). Such drugs may undergo change over time, or lose their identifying labels, or the original purpose of the medication may be forgotten.

CARE OF ILLNESS

How capably are families caring for their members' illnesses? The scarcity of available information precludes a comprehensive answer. The sheer quantity of illnesses taken care of at home may suggest that families are capable of performing a vast amount of care. However, there are some particular illness situations that families tend to transfer to hospitals, nursing homes, and other institutions, rather than handle them at home. Terminal illness is a prominent example; although a majority of people say they would prefer to die at home (Vernon 1970), between two-thirds and three-fourths of the deaths now occur in hospitals and other institutions. Many chronically ill and elderly persons are also sent to nursing homes, even though doctors and nurses have estimated that perhaps 30 percent of the patients in nursing homes would have much better lives at home, if the families would have them and were capable of providing care (State of Florida 1971).

First aid is one of the specific forms of health care in which many families are unprepared. Fewer than 5 percent of the persons suffering an injury or sudden illness that requires first aid by a layman at the scene receive prompt and proper care (Brody 1973). One study reported that 79 percent of a sample of three generations would have failed a version of the CBS National Health Test. One-third did not know how to stop bleeding, about half did not know how to give artificial respiration either mouth-to-mouth or in the traditional manner, and almost half could not take a pulse (Litman 1971).

USE OF PROFESSIONAL MEDICAL SERVICES

The sheer magnitude of the use of medical services does not indicate the appropriateness of selection and use of services. We need to know such facts as the extent to which people obtain preventive examinations, tests, and immunizations before illness strikes, make wise and appropriate selections of services and practitioners, obtain care promptly when symptoms appear, and follow through with tests and treatment to completion.

Preventive Measures

An indication of a person's efforts to preserve health and prevent disease is whether or not the person obtains regular preventive medical checkups in the absence of symptoms. These examinations often discover disease that is still asymptomatic and amenable to successful treatment, they make it possible to avert some of the complications of disease and to prevent some diseases from developing, and they provide base line data which facilitate later diagnosis of disease that depends on recognition of changes in bodily states.

Over half of our urban sample of men, women, and children had not had a general physical checkup during the previous three years. Other studies found that about three in ten persons had not had a general physical examination during the previous five years (Hassinger and McNamara 1960; Haefer et al. 1967). There is a similar tendency to neglect preventive dental care. More than six in ten persons in our sample had not had their teeth cleaned by a dentist during the past three years. Just over half of the adults and a quarter of the children had not had an eye examination during the previous three years. No more than 40 percent of the women in the United States have ever had a PAP smear test, even though this simple procedure is effective in detecting cervical cancer in its incipient stage (Martin 1964; CBS Television News 1973).

Many people also fail to obtain immunizations that have been clearly demonstrated to be effective in preventing disease. A single vaccination against measles gives lifelong protection against the disease, yet only half of the children under age thirteen have had measles vaccinations. Only a third of the children have completed the whole series of immunizations against polio (*Family Health* 1973).

Delay in Seeking Care for Symptoms

Another criterion of how effectively a person uses medical services is the promptness with which he or she obtains advice and treatment when symptoms of disease appear. In our study sample, about six out of ten adults reported that they were currently in need of some dental or medical care, and three out of ten of these parents had delayed getting medical or dental care needed by their children.

There are many diseases in which delay in seeking treatment greatly increases the risk of fatality. An estimated two out of every four people diagnosed with cancer can be saved by current methods of treatment, but only one of those two will be saved, because the other one will delay seeking help until the disease has progressed too far to be helped (Blackwell 1963).

Compliance with Medical Advice

After having contacted medical personnel, how conscientiously will the person follow through on the recommended medical care regimen? Studies of appointment breaking showed that even after patients were diagnosed as requiring treatment for a dangerous disease, many did not return. For example, among people diagnosed as having glaucoma and referred to an eye clinic for treatment, only about half were under treatment a year later (Glogow 1970). A review of the literature on compliance with physicians' instructions reported that at least a third of the patients in most studies failed to comply with the physician's orders, with a range of 15 to 93 percent of patients failing to comply (Davis 1966). For instance, in a group of executives for whom recommendations for diagnostic follow-up study or therapy were made after a health examination, 23 percent did not comply at all, and 10 percent complied only partially (Gottlieb and Kramer 1962). When the medical regimen includes recommendations to change diet, smoking habits, and work activities, patients find the readjustment difficult, and noncompliance is especially high (Davis and Eichorn 1963). There is also a considerable amount of noncompliance with straightforward instructions to take medications.

Other Medical Service Behavior

Consumers' use of professional health services could be evaluated along other quality dimensions, but data are not available to permit sound appraisals. One of these dimensions is the extent to which patients make excessive and unnecessary use of medical services. Another dimension is how wisely and carefully patients select the particular practitioner and service. One indication of consumers' performance on this dimension is the fact that a majority of families fail to obtain professional advice in selecting a physician (Bishop et al. 1969); another indication is that in over half of the tonsillectomies, adenoidectomies, and appendectomies performed, the patients had selected physicians to perform the operation who did not have a special interest in surgery (Andersen and Anderson 1967).

Another measure of the quality of patients' performance is the extent to which they actively, systematically, and intelligently make use of the meeting with a physician to further their own health objectives. A study of patient-physician interaction reported that patients seldom make direct demands for information of the physician, particularly the sort that would give basic understanding of the disease (Pratt et al. 1957). Only about a third of American women have ever discussed with a physician how to examine their breasts to detect cancer, even though educational campaigns have stressed that this is the best method of early detection (Brody 1973).

Some analysts have concluded that Americans are more ignorant, uncertain, and inept as consumers of health services than as consumers of most other goods and services, that they cannot assess the quality of health services, and that they are unable to make effective use of the services they consume (Bowen and Jeffers 1971).

HEALTH AS A LIFE VALUE

Poor health care practices are caused by a variety of forces and circumstances, some of which are beyond the control of the family. However, it is important to determine the extent to which forces within the family tend to sustain or undermine health care behavior. The value placed on health and the level of knowledge about health and illness among family members represent important sources of family influence over health behavior.

While it is difficult to measure how much health is valued, available evidence suggests that good health is not generally ranked at the top of the American hierarchy of values. When mothers and fathers were asked to rate fifty-five values concerning child rearing, safety was ranked twenty-first and health thirty-eighth by mothers, while safety was ranked tenth and health twenty-fifth by fathers. The values receiving the highest mean scores among both mothers and fathers were independence, family unity, obedience, religion, getting along with others, responsibility, and morality (Stolz 1967). A national survey of high school students' values found that being healthful ranked fifth in a list of twelve personal values. Being healthful was outranked by being dependable, courteous and friendly, religious, and ambitious (Remmers 1965). When a group of children aged seven to eighteen were presented with a projective test called Health Ideation Pictures, the health-illness-safety content of the children's responses was generally low, and only a fourth of the children scored high in health ideation (Gochman 1971).

There may be a good deal of tolerance and acceptance of poor health. A majority of persons in a national sample agreed with the statement that "Some aches and pains you might as well get used to; they're not important." About half also agreed with the statement that "No matter how careful a person is, he has to expect a good deal of illness in his lifetime" (King 1962). Many people tend to regard good health as not especially relevant to successful job performance. When asked whether good health was essential to do one's work well, fewer than a third of a sample said that especially good health was required in their work, about half said fairly good health was sufficient, and almost a fifth said they could perform their work adequately if they were not very healthy (Borsky and Sagen 1959).

HEALTH INFORMATION

A high level of health information does not assure sound health practices, for factors other than knowledge have an important bearing on health behavior. But, incorrect and insufficient health information does influence behavior, because it prevents people from taking sound health care measures. Thus, we should determine if laymen's health knowledge has gaps or errors of a magnitude that would be likely to impede sound health care practices.

INFORMATION ABOUT DISEASE

A significant proportion of the public failed to absorb accurate or detailed information about common diseases, even the kind of information that is widely publicized in health education campaigns. A study reported that a sample of New York City clinic patients answered correctly only 55 percent of questions concerning tuberculosis, stroke, asthma, arthritis, syphilis, change of life, leukemia, diabetes, and coronary thrombosis (Pratt 1956). Similar results were achieved in a rural sample (Smith and Kane 1970). A national study conducted for Blue Cross reported that 30 percent of the population could not identify any of the seven danger signals of cancer, and only 13 percent could identify four or more of the signs (Miller 1971). The level of information about heart disease is also low. Over half of one sample were unaware that heart disease was the most important cause of death, about four in ten did not know that there was more than one type of heart disease, seven in ten had never heard of an electrocardiogram, and half did not understand the term heart failure (Hassinger and Anderson 1964). A significant proportion of the public failed to absorb information about measures that can be taken to prevent diseases such as cancer and tuberculosis, particularly the fact that tests or checkups can detect the disease before the appearance of symptoms. This is true in spite of the fact that this information has been disseminated for many years through intensive educational campaigns (Kirscht et al. 1966).

Many people are not very well informed about diseases which they have had themselves. Diabetics frequently lack knowledge of the fundamental principles of the disease, even though a major amount of medical responsibility is put on the diabetic person (Etzwiler and Sines 1962). A study of patients taking oral anticoagulants investigated their knowledge concerning the action, dosage, timing, and side effects of the drug. Half of the patients scored in the least informed category (Leary et al. 1971). The study which investigated clinic patients' knowledge of nine common diseases found that patients answered correctly only 63 percent of the questions about a disease they had had themselves (Pratt 1956).

PREVENTIVE HEALTH CARE MEASURES

The men and women in our sample were asked nine true-false questions about preventive health measures; the men averaged 51 percent correct answers and the women averaged 55 percent The proportions answering correctly are shown below for each of the nine questions.

When asked the meaning of fifty medical-health words that are commonly

	Percent Answering Correctly	
	Men	*Women*
Digestion is improved by a brisk walk to settle a meal (false)	20	21
A woman's fertile period—that is, the time at which she is able to become pregnant—is usually a day or two before, or a day or two after her menstrual period (false)	30	35
Having a drinking cup in the bathroom for everyone to use is a good health practice (false)	64	64
A major cause of hookworm is going without shoes (true)	34	26
The average adult human probably has a fever when his oral (mouth) temperature rises above 96.4°F (false)	40	48
An important thing to look for when choosing a doctor is that he have a medical degree and a state license (true)	85	87
The proper way to brush your teeth is with single strokes away from the gums (true)	63	62
Sleeping serves primarily to rest your eyes, which are easily strained (false)	67	67
Past the age of twenty-five, regular exercise is no longer needed (false)	53	84
Average (9 questions)	51	55

used by doctors in talking to patients, a group of patients gave adequate definitions of about 58 percent of the words. The only words known by at least nine out of ten persons were vomit, relieve, appointment, and constipated. Over half were unable to even attempt a definition of the words respiratory, malignant, secretion, and cardiac (Samora et al. 1961).

NUTRITION

A Food and Drug Administration study of two thousand consumers found that a significant percentage did not know what vitamins and minerals they need, the function of specific nutrients in maintaining good health, or the meaning of fortification (National Health Council 1972). Another study of mothers' basic knowledge of food and nutrition reported that the average score was more than two-thirds incorrect. Notably, three-fourths of these women had taken home economics in high school or college (Lund and Burk 1969).

CONCLUSIONS

A number of inadequacies have been documented in families' health care performance. Many homes are not structured and equipped to control disease, minimize the risk of accidents, and provide satisfactorily for the members' physiological needs. Several widespread deficiencies are found in the personal health practices carried on within households, including deficiencies in nutrition, exercise, and dental hygiene. Problems with medication are also fairly common for such reasons as consumer error, failure to follow professional instructions, and an inclination to take more medicines than are needed. Many families are not up to the task of caring for their members' long-term illnesses at home. A significant number of families fail to maximize use of professional medical services. In particular, they fail to take some preventive measures, delay in getting care for dangerous symptoms, decline to exploit their contacts with physicians to full advantage, and fail to comply with some important medical recommendations. The level of health knowledge and the value placed on good health are not sufficiently high to serve as a strong underpinning for sound health behavior. While some of the cited examples of faulty health care are trivial and may have an insignificant effect on health, the composite picture is one of fundamental failure in caring for health.

What accounts for the ineffectiveness of families in providing health care? The failures are so widespread among contemporary American families as to suggest that explanations must be sought in basic structural features of the society. Although various aspects of societal structure may be implicated, we propose that ineffective performance by families can be traced in part to the structure of the medical care system and in part to the structure of families themselves. That is, there may be some disparity between the functions the contemporary family must perform for its members and the structural resources that are available to the family for carrying out these functions effectively.

The next two chapters examine elements in the structure and functioning of the medical care system that may make it difficult for families to carry out their health care responsibilities proficiently. Later chapters will attempt to determine what aspects of family organization may hamper families in sustaining their members' health, and how widespread these inappropriate structural features are among contemporary families.

THREE

Problems in the Structure of the Medical Care System

CONTEMPORARY AMERICAN FAMILIES perform a complex array of health care tasks, and yet they do not generally carry out these responsibilities very effectively. We propose that some of these performance failures by families can be accounted for by characteristics of the medical care system that make it difficult for families to carry on health care activities effectively, as well as by some structural characteristics of families that limit their capabilities for maintaining their members' health.

The present chapter examines the structure of the health care system and the following chapter evaluates its performance. Our purpose is to ask why it may be difficult for families to cope effectively with the system and to carry on health care activities on their own.

The health care system is organized predominantly around the interests and objectives of its professional personnel, and minimally around those of its clients. While delivery of health care service is the publicly espoused function and goal, there are other competing functions and goals which tend to deflect the system from focusing on delivery of good medical service. In fact, national health policy has been dominated by medicine's professional interests rather than the interests of consumers. Medicine has achieved its authority to direct its own activities and to influence public policy by collaborating with the groups that dominate the central institutions. These groups jointly perpetuate the traditional social order on which their power is based (including such patterns as the traditional sex division of labor in the family), rather than adapting to the changing needs of families.

As a consequence of this structural pattern, medical care is in many respects unreliable and inadequate (as will be documented in the following chapter). The structure of the system impedes families in many ways, particularly by making it difficult to cope with the health care system itself, and inadequate services hamper families in attempting to provide good care for their members' health.

It should be clear at the outset that this is to be a highly selective analysis of the medical care system. It is neither a thorough description of the structure of the medical system nor a balanced appraisal of the successes and failures of its functioning. Our concern is limited to features that may present obstacles to families.

PROFESSIONAL AUTONOMY

An underlying structural characteristic of the medical care system in the twentieth century is the high degree of professional autonomy of physicians. This autonomy shapes the performance of physicians and all other personnel in the health care system, and it sets the tone for all relationships between the system and its clients.

Autonomous control over its own membership and working conditions is the essence of a profession (Freidson 1970), and American physicians have achieved this, *de facto* and *de jure,* to an extreme degree in this century. This includes a near-monopoly of the right to determine who is well and who is ill, for physicians officially exercise the right, on the basis of their evaluations, to permit or deny admission to school, passports, marriage licenses, many employment opportunities, life insurance, and death insurance benefits, as well as exemptions from work, military service, jury duty, and courtroom testimony. Physicians hold the licensed authority to practice medicine and to decide which people and health conditions will receive treatment and how and when a condition will be treated. For example, they may refuse to perform much sought after services, such as abortions; they may prohibit the use of certain forms of therapy, such as unorthodox cancer therapies; and they may decide who is to receive scarce and vital services, such as kidney transplant operations. They have the exclusive right to practice major forms of therapy, such as the use of potent drugs and surgery. Physicians determine who and how many will be admitted to and graduated from medical school. They establish the standards for medical education, carry out medical instruction, and serve as accrediting and review agencies of teaching institutions.

Physicians control hospital admissions. Although there are now dual lines of authority within hospitals, with administrators in charge of financial and housekeeping matters and physicians in charge of medical-patient care, the hospital is still unique among modern organizations. Technical experts in hospitals work without significant interference from, or control by, lay administrators. Strong physician dominance within hospital structure and the tendency for physicians to maximize status differentials between themselves and other personnel have important consequences for patients. One study found that rigid dominance by physicians was associated with poorer patient care, as measured by longer patient stays in the hospital; higher job mobility of nurses and auxiliary personnel; less use of psychiatric and social services, and other consultations by attending physicians; fewer explanations of medical treatments provided to patients or their families; and more errors in medication (Seeman and Evans 1961, 1961).

Physicians have achieved these wide-ranging rights to practice medicine by securing and enforcing drastic legal limitations on the jurisdictions of other health professions. For example, pharmacists may not prescribe drugs or substitute another manufacturer's brand of a drug for the brand named in a physician's prescription. Nurses may not diagnose illnesses or record observations in a patient's chart in the form of a diagnosis. A committee of the American Medical Association (AMA) serves as an accrediting agency for many of the allied-health educational programs, including medical technologists, occupational therapists, and physical therapists; similarly, the American Dental Association is the accrediting body for dental auxiliary personnel. This authority enables physicians and dentists to control the education, professional roles, and licensing of other health care personnel. They can also prevent new groups of practitioners from carrying on competing forms of care; for example, the practice of acupuncture by persons other than M.D.s has been prohibited.

There are two aspects of professional autonomy that have important consequences for patients and families: the right of the profession to monitor itself and the right to control technical information.

MONITORING PROFESSIONAL CONDUCT

The medical profession is permitted to monitor itself with little intrusion from outside control agencies. While the actual granting and revoking of licenses rests with state boards, professional licensing laws generally require that all board members be licensed practitioners, and board members are generally appointed from a list of names provided by the medical association (HEW 1971).

Licensing laws have been written and state boards behave to assure that once a physician's license has been granted, it is good for a lifetime. A physician's license is renewed automatically upon the filing of a form and payment of a fee, and in some states without even that. Only two states have enacted relicensure laws for physicians tied to compulsory continuing education and proof of proficiency, although several other states are considering doing so. Only fifteen states permit a license to be challenged on the ground of professional incompetence, and states do not commonly permit revocation even for gross negligence (Bowen and Jeffers 1971; HEW 1973). A Report on Medical Malpractice prepared for the Secretary of Health, Education and Welfare concluded that, "the law in most states permits conduct which, though it may not be criminal, nevertheless may result in needless harm to the patient" (HEW 1973, p. 52).

State agencies are very reluctant to take action against physicians. Twenty states took no disciplinary action against any physician between 1969 and 1973, and altogether only about seventy doctors' licenses are suspended or revoked each year among more than a quarter million physicians. Almost all involve serious law violations or moral turpitude—offenses involving drugs are the largest single category—and very rarely is the quality of medical practice involved.

A major instrument employed by the profession in monitoring its own members' conduct is the board of censors or mediation committees set up by the county medical societies of the AMA to hear grievances of patients against physicians. However, the existence of these grievance committees is not publicized. These review boards or committees are made up entirely of doctors, some of whom may be professional associates or friends of the physisian involved in the case. The hearings are closed, and the records are kept secret. In some jurisdictions only the physician appears in person, and the patient may not question the physician or present witnesses. There is no appeal to a higher authority except to go to court, and the outcomes of the hearings are not generally made public, even in the form of statistical summaries of actions taken during the year.

The possibility of impartial peer review is severely inhibited by the formal codes of ethics of the medical and dental professions. The American Dental Association's Principles of Ethics state: "The dentist has the obligation of not referring disparagingly, orally or in writing, to the services of another dentist, to a member of the public" (Denenberg 1973, p. 5). Public criticisms of peers bring about informal sanctions and professional reprisals.

There are also peer review committees within individual hospitals, which check admissions to ascertain whether they are medically justified and examine surgically removed organs and tissues to monitor for unnecessary surgery. These committees are composed entirely of insiders, and they do not disclose professional violations to consumers.

It is only recently that some hospitals have formally recognized patients' rights by drawing up a bill of rights for hospitalized persons. Only 27 percent of 1,040 hospitals surveyed had any kind of formal mechanism for handling patient grievances, and the systems that did exist were generally designed to handle petty complaints over red tape, billing, or the quality of food. The system usually consisted of only a single person, and that person generally did not have either the qualifications or the authority to deal with the medical aspects of patient care (HEW 1973).

Because the professional review mechanisms set up and operated by the medical profession itself have not adequately policed the profession, an amendment to the Social Security Act was passed in 1972 to provide for the establishment of Professional Standards Review Organizations (PSROs). This requires that medical care paid for by Medicare for the elderly or Medicaid for the indigent shall be reviewed for appropriateness by a review agency set up by doctors in a given locality. Even though PSRO membership is restricted to peers, in 1973 the AMA passed a resolution to oppose the system (Lyons 1973).

The failure of hospitals and physicians to provide effective mechanisms for bringing about equitable settlement in the early stages of disputes and for pinpointing those procedures and situations that lead to patient grievances has tended to drive patients to law courts to obtain relief. In 1972, 16,000 malpractice claims were filed against United States physicians, dentists, and hospitals (Hicks 1974), and about one out of every six physicians have had malpractice claims filed against them during the course of their practice (Greenberg 1971).

Yet a lawsuit is not a satisfactory mechanism for settling many patient grievances. About half of the malpractice claims brought by patients are not legally meritorious. This does not mean that the patient does not have a legitimate grievance, but only that it is not possible to prove fault on the part of the medical personnel involved. The victims of many other types of accident and injury are compensated without regard to fault. Travel, health, automobile collision, and life insurance operate in this way, and physically injured victims of criminal acts may be compensated from public funds in certain states. The lack of impartial and effective grievance systems for handling the wrongs done to patients leads them to resort to the courts, but the courts exclude from possible compensation all injuries except those in which a legally defined type of fault can be demonstrated.

It is difficult to satisfy the legal requirements for malpractice in a court of law. The law imposes no obligation on a physician to cure or even improve the patient's condition; the physician is required to exercise only that degree of care and skill which other doctors usually exercise (Holley). Malpractice requires a charge of negligence, assault and battery, deceit, or breach of contract. Negligence is the charge brought in about 85 percent of the cases. The courts hold that negligence on the part of the physician must be proven, and does not arise merely from the fact that the doctor's course of action failed to bring about the desired result (Forst 1972). The doctor is held liable only for injury which is the *proximate* cause of his or her lack of reasonable care; proof of a cause and effect relationship is required (Holley).

In addition, negligent malpractice behavior must be established by expert medical testimony, unless the negligence is so grossly apparent that a layman would have no difficulty in recognizing it (such as leaving foreign objects in the patient's body). In about nine out of ten cases expert testimony is required, but physicians tend to be reluctant to testify to facts which might involve another physician in legal liability or professional embarrassment. As long as a physician's performance is judged according to standards of care prevailing in his own locality, the only eligible witnesses are local colleagues. The trend now is toward accepting national rather than local standards, which widens the territory from which experts may be solicited, and thus facilitates the patient's chance of finding an expert willing to testify (HEW 1973).

A suit must be instituted at the initiative of the patient or the patient's family. The abrasiveness of the adversarial system which pits the patient against the physician in a costly and time-consuming legal contest deters some people with legitimate claims. One study found that of people who had had experiences with medical failure or negligence on the part of the doctors involved, only 8 percent considered seeking the advice of a lawyer, and of these less than one-half actually did talk to a lawyer. Further, law firms dealing with malpractice claims generally reject at least nine out of ten cases that are brought to them. As one malpractice lawyer teaches his students: "Don't accept the small malpractice case, or the doubtful malpractice case, unless you're interested in bringing your family closer together, because you will have to move into a smaller house" (*Medical Economics* 1970, p. 84).

Financial compensation is generally low for patients undertaking a malpractice action. These suits are usually pursued under the contingent legal fee system. This is an arrangement by which a patient does not pay the lawyer if the case is lost, but does pay the lawyer some fraction of the recovery amount, usually between 33 and 40 percent. The contingent fee system wipes out a substantial proportion of injured patients' recovery, but financial recovery is inadequate in other respects as well. Half of the settlements are for less than $3,000. In spite of the fact that physicians and insurance carriers complain that settlements have soared to astronomical figures, no more than seven claims recover $1 million or more per year, which is less than 1 in 1,000 settlements (HEW 1973).

It takes a long time to complete a malpractice claim. Only 50 percent are completed within eighteen months, and ten percent remain open more than six years after they are begun. This delays payment to injured persons beyond the time when they need it most—when they must pay medical and hospital bills, while they are unemployed, and while they are making readjustments and compensations in life due to the injury.

INFORMATION CONTROL

One of the most significant manifestations of the autonomy and dominance of a profession is the ability of its members to retain control over the information on which their expertise is based and over information generated in their work. It enables a profession to preserve its privileged position and its exclusive right to practice in the specialized field. So long as consumers are kept in ignorance, they are unable to perform the service for themselves, to evaluate the services they receive, or to interact assertively with professionals in order to influence their delivery of service. Monopoly of knowledge by a profession also prevents other professions from infringing on its territory. It enables the profession to protect its members by hiding mistakes, incompetence, and malfeasance. Practitioners can achieve high cost-efficiency by avoiding lengthy discussions with clients.

There is an integrated system of mechanisms and strategies through which the medical profession exercises control over medical information. Many of these mechanisms and strategies are formally established in law. Others are established in bureaucratic procedure and professional codes.

One of the basic means by which the medical profession holds onto trade secrets is through control over admission to and graduation from medical schools and licensing of physicians. Ethical standards adopted officially by the medical profession that preclude advertising and publicity also serve to maintain the information monopoly, for consumers cannot readily learn comparative costs and the merits of alternative practitioners.

The profession has established certain property rights to medical information. Medical records on patients are the legal property of the doctor or hospital maintaining them, and on this basis a doctor or hospital may refuse to disclose the contents to patients or their legal representatives in the absence of a special law or a court action (HEW 1973). In forty-one states the only way in which patients may even have access to their medical records is to bring a court action, such as filing a malpractice suit, and even in the remaining nine states there are limitations on patients' access to their records.

The Commission on Medical Malpractice concluded in its 1973 report that "We believe that the patient has a right to the information contained in his medical record—whether that be the hospital record or his doctor's office record" (HEW 1973, p. 76), and the commission recommended that the law recognize patients' interest in their medical records. The commission's evidence showed that the unavailability of medical records created needless expense for patients by requiring them to go to court, and it tended to drive patients into filing malpractice claims.

Hospital structure serves to restrict the flow of information to patients and their families. Authorized channels of communication are established to protect the rights vested in the various offices in the hospital hierarchy. Only physicians may inform patients about their illness and therapy, yet physicians are often the most elusive of all personnel, seldom being available for consultations with the family during visiting hours. The patient has greatest access to the lowliest ranks in the personnel hierarchy, yet these personnel are not sufficiently informed to communicate what the patient wants to know, and they are restricted from communicating what they do know.

But even the type of information that nonphysicians could be authorized to convey without infringing on physicians' professional functions—such as hospital routines—is not forthcoming. One study found that nine out of ten patients reported that no one at any time had bothered to explain hospital routine to them (Suchman 1965). In another sample, half of the patients were not informed about the hospital personnel to the extent that they could distinguish between medical students and physicians, and over nine in ten had no discussion of the cost of hospitalization with hospital personnel before or during the hospital stay (Houston and Pasanen 1972).

Over a third of patients were dissatisfied with what they were told about diagnosis, progress, and treatment while in the hospital (Houston and Pasanen 1972). Interviews with patients as they were discharged from a hospital disclosed that about half had one or more unanswered questions on discharge, and about two-thirds had been given no specific instruction about care after discharge. These patients disliked the casual responses to and evasions of their questions by physicians and nurses (Nickerson 1972).

There is also inadequate opportunity for feedback of information from the patient to medical personnel. A survey of thirty-six rehabilitation facilities showed that only one of the units had any formal mechanism by which to elicit patients' reactions to treatment programs or hospital services. That one unit had provided for a patient council in each ward, with a patient representative who attended weekly department head meetings, and who served both to voice patient views and to take views back from the meetings to the ward patients (American Rehabilitation Foundation 1969).

The restriction of information characteristic of medical care in hospitals has been found to have significant consequences for the physical well-being and recovery of the patient. A study of communication practices concluded:

"Under prevailing conditions the social environment of the hospital is likely to produce a great deal of stress for child patients and their mothers. For the children this stress is likely to result in elevated temperature, pulse rate and blood pressure, disturbed sleep, fear of doctors and nurses, a delayed recovery period, and other forms of behavior which deviate from the medical culture's norms of 'health' and normal progress of hospitalization" (Skipper and Leonard, 1968, p. 285).

Physicians have strenuously protected their exclusive right to communicate medical information to patients, yet the codes and customs of medical practice that the profession has developed restrain and obstruct the flow of information. One restraining factor is that the informal professional code does not favor physicians' telling patients the full extent of their illness, particularly the diagnosis of a dread disease, such as cancer, or the prognosis of imminent death. In the fee-for-service system of payment, physicians are also restrained by calculations of time-costs of discussing a dread diagnosis with a patient. The choices they entertain are to disclose the diagnosis and discuss it fully, which is too costly; to disclose the diagnosis and move to the next patient, which is insensitive; or to withhold the diagnosis, which is both economical and kind. Yet while physicians overwhelmingly withhold such diagnoses, nine out of ten cancer patients reported that they preferred knowing their condition. They worried more about the unknown, and knowing they had cancer removed the indefiniteness of the situation, and they would be more willing and careful to follow directions regarding follow-up examinations because they knew they had cancer (Kelly and Friesen 1950). The systematic tendency of physicians to withhold diagnostic information leaves many patients and their families poorly motivated and ill-equipped to cooperate in needed therapy and to make important adaptations in their family, social, and economic affairs.

Reticence is not limited to the diagnosis. Observations of fifty patient-physician relationships in a hospital clinic over the entire course of these relationships disclosed that most patients were never fully informed about the tests they were given. A third were told nothing beyond the fact that x, y, and z were to be taken, and only 14 percent received an explanation, with regard to even one test, of the type of evidence the tests would provide or what the test meant in terms of a possible disease. Physicians were even more likely to avoid completely discussion of the etiology and prognosis than they were to bypass the more immediately practical issues of tests and treatment, in which they required patient cooperation (Pratt et al. 1957).

Even when physicians do give information to patients, it is not generally presented in a form that is understood by many patients. A consistent complaint from patients is that they did not understand what the physician and other hospital personnel were telling them (Samora et al. 1961). Patients want direct answers phrased in language they can understand, with fewer medical terms. Physicians are also criticized for not letting patients tell exactly what is troubling them (Borsky and Sagen 1959). Thus, there is a restriction of information flow in both directions—to and from the patient—which effectively keeps the patient out of the action.

A study described the dynamics of the situation as follows: The vast majority of physicians tended to underestimate patients' knowledge, and, perceiving the patient as rather poorly informed, the physician

". . . considers the tremendous difficulties of translating his knowledge into language the patient can understand, along with the dangers of frightening the patient. Therefore he avoids involving himself in an elaborate discussion with the patient; the patient, in turn, reacts dully to this limited information, either asking uninspired questions or refraining from questioning the doctor at all, thus reinforcing the doctor's view that the patient is ill-equipped to comprehend his problem. This further reinforces the doctor's tendency to skirt discussions of the problem" (Pratt et al. 1957, p. 1281).

Those patients who did receive some explanation from the physician were more likely to increase their understanding of their problem and to ask slightly more questions than patients who were not given explanations. Thus, denial of information to patients perpetuates their inability to interact productively with the physician, for they fail to develop a framework of information within which to formulate questions.

BUREAUCRATIC REGIMENTATION AND CONTROL

A structural feature of modern medicine that has major consequences for patients' and families' ability to cope with the system and to obtain good service is the organization of the hospital as a formal bureaucracy. The basic structural characteristics of a bureaucracy are a hierarchy of ranked positions; specialization of functions and duties; standardized operating procedures for performance of duties (especially for the lower-ranking positions); precise definitions of rights and duties for each position; rules governing relationships among the positions and personnel; rigid discipline; exclusion of personal matters from the performance of duties and from official relationships with others; and secretiveness about the workings of the organization.

The bureaucratic form is a means of trying to cope with the problems of decision making and control in large-scale organizations, in which informal face-to-face resolutions are not possible. It is also a method of bringing coordination among the large number of specialized occupations and processes, assuring precision and reliability in the product or service created, rationalizing work procedures, and minimizing personal elements that distract from achieving the official goals.

Certain bureaucratic features of the modern hospital have a significant impact on patients and their families: specialization, stratification, control, and depersonalization of relationships.

SPECIALIZATION

As much as any modern organization, the hospital has been organized on the basis of functional specialization, with each group of specialists having highly distinctive duties and rights. Specialization follows professional-occupational lines, major ones of which are doctors, nurses, social workers, dieticians, occupational therapists, laboratory technicians, accountants, nurse's aides, cleaning maids, and laundry workers. Within medicine there is additional specialization based on professional subspecialties such as surgery, medicine, obstetrics and gynecology, pediatrics, and psychiatry. This specialization within the hospital has been strongly fortified by professional forces beyond the hospital—by the successful efforts of the medical profession to demarcate its own specialness from other health-related professions and occupations, and by the organization of professional education to prepare students for practice in subspecialties within the fields of medicine, nursing, social work, and other professions.

Any organization that divides up the work among a large number of diverse occupational groups necessarily has major problems coordinating the efforts of the various workers in order to meet the overall objectives of the organization. Various structural approaches are used to achieve this needed coordination, such as the clear definition of rights and duties for each position, combined with establishment of disciplined routines for performing the work and firm lines of authority. In contrast to private practice in the community, the hospital does succeed in bringing together various specialties around the patient's bed. In addition to mechanisms within the hospital, professionalism is counted on to assure that the personnel will be technically competent in their work and dedicated to the overall goal of patient care.

The needed degree of coordination has not been achieved. Fragmentation of patient care and responsibility among a variety of specialized personnel has resulted in various personnel working at cross-purposes with each other, to the detriment of the patient. In nursing, for example, the assignment of specific duties rather than specific patients to a given nurse means that patients have no one who focuses on pulling together their various needs and servicing them in an integrated fashion. They cannot get to know which particular person has what responsibility and, consequently, there are gaps in their care.

Barriers to communication between various occupational groups within the hospital affect patient care. One study concluded:

> "There are in the hospital certain tendencies which appear to set limits upon the degree to which integration of the organization's personnel can take place. It has been shown that communication tends to be for the most part channeled

within occupational lines, giving rise to a tendency for those who work together on the wards to know and associate principally with those of their 'own kind.' Associated with this tendency to isolation on the part of the various occupational status-groups is a set of disparate institutional ideologies. Each group expressed divergent ideas concerning hospital purpose and policy, and these attitudes point up areas of latent conflict between the groups" (Wessen 1972, p. 341).

This insulation limits the opportunities for members of one occupational specialty to be familiar with the technical viewpoints of other fields and personnel (Croog and Ver Steeg 1972), and it certainly works against a team approach to patient care.

Fragmentation of patient care is characteristic of private medical practice in the community as well as in hospitals. Since more than seven in ten practitioners now limit their practice to a specialty, there are relatively few practitioners who provide continuous care for the whole patient or family, or even coordinate the efforts of the various specialists who work on a given patient. For both general practitioners and specialists, the solo practice of medicine in the community physically separates doctors from their peers and fails to provide effective communication mechanisms among physicians about medical practice in general or about particular patients. The competitive business of solo practice restrains a physician from freely consulting with, or referring patients to, other physicians for fear of losing patients.

STRATIFICATION AND CONTROL

What is the client's position in relation to the stratification and control system of the hospital? In the rigidly stratified hospital system, the clients occupy the position of least authority and are subject to greatest control.

The clients' relationship with medical personnel has been described as *inherently* asymmetrical because of the professionals' expertise and full-time work at their roles, in contrast with the clients' weakness and inferiority due to illness and their amateur status—their ignorance concerning their health problems and their merely occasional acquaintance with the sick role. This view is questionable, for there are built into the hospital system a number of features that enforce subordination of patients regardless of their physical, intellectual, and social capabilities for active participation in the system.

A study of the patient's role in the hospital concluded:

> "Patient participation, as a member of the hospital community, is limited to submitting to the rules and regulations of the hospital and to the decisions of hospital specialists. ... he is expected to relinquish his real-life responsibilities even when he is capable of discharging them from the hospital bed. If he asks questions, refuses to do what he is asked to do unless he is told why, demands more attention than the staff thinks he needs, and if he tries to discharge his responsibilities to his family and his job, he is likely to be considered a 'bad' patient" (Taylor 1970, pp. 93; 65).

The personnel expect and demand submissiveness by patients, and patients acquiesce in order to avoid the imposition of sanctions against them. A British study found that a majority of nurses believed that "patients should be willing to accept prescribed treatment," "should try to obey hospital rules," and "should always respect the authority of the medical team." None thought that "patients should be allowed their own way while they are in hospital" (Stockwell 1972). An American study reported that fifty patients who were considered uncooperative by all categories of staff in an outpatient department were those who found it difficult to conform to the clinic routine (Schwartz 1958). Good patients are described principally as cooperative, appreciative, and accepting prescribed treatment (Ritvo 1963).

Various techniques are used for inducting patients into and then enforcing their subservience. The admissions procedure is calculated to establish the patient's position immediately and forcefully. A prominent part of the instruction of newly hired intake clerks by old-timers is to stress the importance of keeping control over patients so that they follow rather than give directions, and of making any patient wait who gets out of line (Roth 1972).

The physical confinement of patients to rooms and beds, which they generally may not leave without permission or escort, makes them subject to control even by the lowest ranks of hospital personnel. The removal of patients' street clothes further consigns them to their rooms and symbolizes that they are expected to remain lying down and quiet, if not actually unconscious or asleep. Under these conditions, in which patients are made dependent on hospital personnel for the satisfaction of the simplest to the most complex needs, an effective means of control is to ignore them or keep them waiting, and it is used by all types of hospital personnel in all phases of patient care.

Another device is to keep patients unfamiliar with, and inexperienced in, the workings of the hospital, its routines, and its personnel. The easy-going familiarity of the personnel with the hospital, in contrast to the feeling of strangeness of patients, inhibits patients from asserting themselves or even from seeking clarification. As previously noted, the hospital seldom provides this information to patients.

Still another method of enforcing patient cooperativeness and submissiveness is to call upon a moral ethic that the patient must not make demands because there are always other patients who are sicker and in greater need, so that a demanding patient is said to be denying attention to these others (Tagliacozzo and Mauksch 1972).

The hospital also severely limits patients' access to people of their normal family, social, and business life. All hospital routines are allowed to interrupt any work patients may try to do, and there are restrictions on when patients may be visited and by whom. The famiy relinquishes its right to control and care for the patient and to have free access to the patient. While presumably this transfer of control to the hospital is to be accompanied by a corresponding degree of access by the family to the hospital personnel, it turns out that the hospital expects to have access to the family whenever it is desired, but the family's access to hospital personnel is very restricted (Bell and Zucker 1968). Some analysts have interpreted that,

> "Families tend to perceive the hospital as a difficult organization to deal with, one which frustrates families' rights, requests, and needs. ... the family wants to be treated as a group with their own equally important rights and privileges. ... The hospital ... should be as ready to give as to request information. ... Personnel, including psychiatrists, should be available to family members at the latter's reasonable convenience" (Bell and Zucker 1968, pp. 73–75).

While visiting restrictions are instituted by hospitals for the manifest purposes of getting their work done and assuring that the patient will get rest, this device also achieves control over the patient and the family. As long as families are kept strangers to the hospital, with little freedom to move within it or to interact with their sick members, patients cannot use the families to intervene on their behalf and to manipulate the system for them.

This enforced submissiveness places patients at a distinct disadvantage. Since patients have almost no leverage over personnel, even when they are performing incompetently, patients cannot influence the care they receive. Two-thirds of the patients in a hospital sample indicated they had refrained from expressing their needs and criticisms at some time or other, and many viewed the hospital as having such power that patients could not risk endangering the nurse's or physician's view of them as considerate patients by asserting themselves. They expressed feelings of helplessness and fear of retribution in such statements as, "One is at their mercy" and "Trying to change things is futile," for they can refuse to answer your bell or make your bed. A fourth of the patients expressed resentment at their enforced helplessness (Tagliacozzo and Mauksch 1972).

DEPERSONALIZATION

There is an impersonality in the relationships of medical personnel with patients that derives from the way medical care is practiced by professionals, both within and outside hospitals. Neutral costumes worn by both professionals and patients during medical care activity serve to eliminate the individual personalities of the participants, technical language translates squeezing and poking of intimate body parts into diagnostic palpating and probing, and tools and gloves transform the doctor's human hands into technical instruments—these are all characteristic of medical practice, whatever the location, and they are designed to assure that the professionals will focus productively on their technical responsibilities. Additional sources of depersonalization are generated by the structuring of human relationships and work in hospitals.

There is a tendency for hospitals to reduce work to a series of mechanistic routines, including such work as feeding, bed changing, medicating patients, temperature taking, and filling out of charts. Routine procedures are attractive to management because they can be developed on the basis of rational analyses of cost efficiency, they facilitate supervision of the work of personnel, and they enable management to have concrete and precise measures of output and performance. Routinization overcomes problems caused by high turnover of personnel, because it makes possible the hiring of new personnel without careful screening, giving them brief but rigidly specific training, and putting them quickly to work on tasks of limited scope and under programmed supervision.

Routinization of tasks depersonalizes care of patients. Standardized routines enable the hospital to reduce the care of all patients to equivalent units. But since patients are not all alike and do not have the same needs at the same time, a rigid scheduling of work tasks is often ill-suited to particular patients or to many patients at certain times. For example, the bedmaking marathon of some hospitals, in which a certain number of beds have to be made before the day staff come on, entails waking patients early in the morning and subjecting all patients to disturbing bustle (McGhee et al. 1961). The rigidifying effect of the routines actually reduces the likelihood that some essential tasks of patient care are done when needed.

It is not only that some specific patient needs are left unmet, but that whole areas of need may be inadequately covered. For example, dying patients need more than anything to know that they are important to others; this means that they should not be left alone to the same extent as recuperating patients, and it may mean that they should have family members sharing in their care. The hospital's routinized organization of work serves as an obstacle to flexible patterning of care for patients with such special needs.

When work is broken down into small units, and specific task units are assigned to specific workers, care of the patient is split among various workers. There is no one person who looks after the patient, only a number of people who do specific things for or to the patient. This means that there is no individual worker who associates with the patient over a significant stretch of time in a number of activities, and who develops a sense of the needs of that whole patient.

Tasks that have been officially routinized take precedence over nonroutine activities. Performance of such routines as faithful and accurate recording in a chart or delivery of bed linen on schedule are readily measured, and tend to be used by management as the principal criteria for evaluating personnel. Routines are mainly technical performance routines (there are no tender-loving-care routines). Personal contact activities, therefore, get pushed out; they can be done only after the *real* work has been taken care of. This impersonal approach by the staff produces stress in patients, and the stress has been shown to increase a sick child's fever, unrest, blood pressure, and pulse rate, and to impede the child's recovery (Skipper and Leonard 1968).

ORGANIZATION FOR INTERNAL OBJECTIVES

The ideal of service to patients is the central ideological force in the medical profession and the hospital. Yet both the medical profession and hospitals have come to "organize their work in ways that protect the income, security, and well-being of their most valued personnel" (Wilensky 1964), rather than in ways that achieve maximum service to patients. The autonomy and power attained by the medical profession has been directed toward shaping not only their basic working conditions and the operations of medical schools, but also the broad societal arrangements for financing and delivering health services to the whole population, as well as national health priorities.

Work Arrangements

The medical profession has used its power to establish *time, place,* and *fee* arrangements of medical work to suit the convenience and work objectives of its members.

Doctors who reduce home visits to patients either to a minimum or none at all save time, increase earnings, and carry out work on their own terms within their own workshops, either private offices or hospitals. The few attempts initiated by government agencies to have mobile medical units that would travel into neighborhoods to serve clients have not succeeded in making a dent in the pattern of office-based practice (U.S. Senate 1972).

The pattern has significant effects on patients and families. The family relinquishes control over the transaction because it is carried on in unfamiliar territory rather than in the security of their own home. Family and patient also lose the benefit of the physician's insights into how home and family conditions may be involved in the illness or how household resources might be called upon to aid the patient, for the physician never sees the patient in his or her own social environment. The time and cost of travel shifts almost entirely to the client, and it is the sick person, rather than the healthy professional, who must submit to the weather and become fatigued from travel. The travel burden is magnified by the fact that, while insisting on office-based practice, the medical profession has also been determined to allow full freedom to individual physicians to locate their offices to suit their objectives, rather than to adapt location of physicians to the geographic distribution of clients. People living in low-income areas, smaller cities, and sparsely populated states are especially disadvantaged, because physicians are reluctant to locate in those areas.

Scheduling of medical care is also designed to obtain maximum use of physicians' time at the expense of long waiting times for patients, sometimes to make sure that physicians will never be kept waiting at any time. A system commonly used in hospital clinics is a Block Appointment System, in which all patients scheduled to be treated on any given day are given the same appointment time—the beginning of the clinic session (Soriano 1966). In other systems, appointment times are spread out over the clinic session, but patients are scheduled at a rate in excess of that at which the medical staff can see them, resulting in long delays for most patients. Scheduling of patients for office practice follows similar principles of stockpiling.

Physicians have been able to establish their own fees for services, keep fee schedules secret from the public, and resist pressures to regulate or lower fees. This combination of controls has made it extremely difficult for patients to practice intelligent consumership in the medical marketplace. It is virtually impossible to do price-comparison shopping.

The private practice of medicine is one of the best small businesses financially and the highest paid profession. In 1970 the average net income was almost $34,000 for general practitioners, over $40,000 for internists, and over $50,000 for surgeons (Cant 1973).

Medical fees have not generally been formulated on a rational basis, such as time spent with a patient or cost plus. Fees vary considerably from state to state and from one locality to another, and the variations are not accounted for by cost-of-living differences. For example, a gallbladder removal averages $900 in Manhattan, $750 in the other boroughs, and $550 in nearby counties of New York (Lyons 1973). Health insurance and government health programs might have been expected to bring about a rational fee system. Yet it has not worked out that way so far, because these agencies have accepted a formula devised by the AMA as the basis of paying doctors. A doctor's fee is considered reasonable if it is the usual fee an individual doctor charges patients for a given service, or the customary fee that doctors of a given specialty in a particular community charge (Cant 1973).

There is little that consumers can do about high fees because of medicine's success in keeping fee schedules secret from the public. The code of ethics in medicine and dentistry which forbids advertising provides a positive sanction for practitioners' reticence about fees. Fee schedules for physicians in a community, including specific doctors' fees and the distribution, range, and average for doctors, are not available to the public. Nor will individual physicians provide their own patients with a schedule of their fees.

Conflicts of Interest

Individual physicians and medical institutions have developed professional and business objectives that compete and sometimes conflict with their patient care functions. The increasing involvement of doctors in clinical research brings about situations in which the doctor's role as investigator may interfere with the role as therapist to the patient. For example, the research may require administration of drugs that have not been fully tested for safety, or an experimental design may call for arbitrary administration of a given therapy to one group and withholding it from a control group, without regard to the unique needs of individual patients.

The physician's businessman role may also conflict with the therapist role. About five thousand physicians own 128 private label drug repackaging firms. There are over two thousand physician-owned pharmacies, which the AMA allows, "as long as there is no exploitation of the patient" (Mintz, 1967). Such investments may encourage a physician to overprescribe and to prescribe by brand rather than the cheaper generic name, while patients pay for services selected solely on the basis of their welfare.

Some of the public stands taken on health issues by the AMA reveal that the business interests of the profession sometimes supersede their concerns about health benefits to consumers. The AMA frequently supports the interests of the pharmaceutical industry, which has proven to be a strong ally of the AMA in influencing national health legislation, has contributed funds for medical research, and has provided a large share of the advertising revenue for professional medical journals. Apparently in deference to the drug industry, the AMA board of trustees discontinued circulating a book prepared by its own Council on Drugs which evaluated drug products (Schmeck 1973). The AMA did not support a law giving the Food and Drug Administration authority to require evidence of drug effectiveness before granting permission to market a new drug product (Mintz 1967). It did support the tobacco industry's position in opposing a proposal by the Federal Trade Commission to require a health warning on cigarette packages (Harris 1966).

Compromises are made concerning patient services in hospitals and medical centers, for other important institutional objectives, particularly research and teaching, compete with service for patients. In large university medical centers, associated hospitals are used to provide subjects for medical research and for clinical training of students. The particular research concerns of a medical center have a dominant influence over what types of health care specialties are developed and, consequently, the health needs of the particular community in which the center is located may not be met. For example, psychiatric clinics established by a university medical center are likely to specialize in the very severe types of mental illness that staff members are interested in, or in military medicine for which research funds are available, rather than in needed community services, such as preventive mental health programs. In fact, fund grants obtained to provide health services to the community may be directed into research channels that fail to produce a service outcome for the community (Ehrenreich and Ehrenreich 1970).

When research interests dominate the planning and type of medical institute, clinics and programs tend to be set up on the basis of narrow academic specialties rather than on the basis of treatment needs of patients. This fragments the care of the patient among a variety of clinics, resulting in extra clinic visits, duplication of effort, additional diagnostic procedures, and lost medical records. Extensive research commitments make it desirable to annex small hospitals and community service programs in order to provide human subjects, clinical settings, and bases for obtaining grants. This results in increasing centralization of control by the medical center, thereby preventing the community from having control over its own health facilities (Ehrenreich and Ehrenreich 1970).

POLITICAL ACTION

The health professions and medical institutions do more than defend their interests; they aggressively assert them in the political arena. Their objectives are not limited to improving the quality of medical care, but extend to exercising decisive influence over the nation's health policies. Their techniques are not limited to informal persuasion, but include a full armament of professional public relations methods and campaigns backed up by strong financing. They do not rely on their own powers of influence, but form alliances with other powerful groups and legislators. Consumers of health services and families do not have this kind of political strength, nor do they have formal mechanisms for confronting organized medicine when their interests clash with those of medicine.

PROFESSIONAL MECHANISMS FOR POLITICAL ACTION

Medical professions and institutions are organized into professional or trade associations—American Medical Association, American Hospital Association, American Nurses' Association, American Public Health Association—as well as specialty organizations. The strength of such associations depends on having a grass-roots organization in local areas combined with a strong national leadership which can mobilize the entire membership. The strongest association is the AMA. It is made up of about two thousand county medical societies, whose members elect representatives to state medical societies, who in turn select representatives to the national house of delegates, which in turn names the AMA's board of trustees and its annual president.

These associations have developed formal mechanisms for exerting political influence. For example, the American Hospital Association has a Washington service bureau, which distributes to all affiliated hospital associations information on federal legislation affecting the health care field, the status of specific bills, and recommendations of actions that should be taken. Each state hospital association communicates with the congressmen from that state, and maintains a list of hospital trustees and other persons who may have influence with particular congressmen (American Hospital Association 1970). In 1964 the AMA had twenty-three professional lobbyists in Washington and seventy publicists in its headquarters in Chicago (Harris 1966). In 1974 the AMA spent more to finance political candidates than any group except the AFL–CIO (*New York Times* 1974).

The associations mount special campaigns for dealing with particular issues. The AMA hired the hard-hitting public relations firm of Whitaker & Baxter to prevent enactment of compulsory health insurance, and over the years the AMA spent $50 million for this purpose. They employed a variety of appeals, describing national health insurance as a threat to the sacred doctor-patient relationship, a product of nazism or communism, and a system to put medicine in the hands of bureaucrats. They participated directly in political campaigns to defeat or assist particular congressmen on the basis of their stands on health insurance. They mobilized a commercial boycott of Borden Company products, when the company chairman associated himself with a report endorsing national health insurance, resulting in a reversal of his stand on health insurance (Harris 1966). An indication of the influence of this long-term campaign is that in 1942 a *Fortune* poll found that 74 percent of the American public favored national health insurance (Harris 1966). Yet bill after bill was defeated in the Congress, and it was not until 1965 that the first national health insurance law was passed by Congress, and this covered only a small segment of the population.

POWER ALLIANCES

The health professions and institutions have been able to develop alliances with other powerful groups and to gain representation on public and private agencies that determine health policy. In this way they have extended their influence far beyond their own professional membership. In the long campaign to defeat national health insurance legislation, the AMA succeeded in lining up 1,829 organizations behind its position, including the U.S. Chamber of Commerce, General Federation of Women's Clubs, American Bar Association, American Farm Bureau Federation, National Association of Retail Grocers, National Grange, American Legion, Daughters of the American Revolution, and National Conference of Catholic Charities (Harris 1966).

Medicine has also cultivated the support of certain congressmen and other political figures. Congressmen from tobacco states were influenced to vote against Medicare by the AMA's cooperation in opposing the Federal Trade Commission's order that cigarette packages carry a warning about the hazards of smoking.

This power enables the medical profession and health care institutions to assert that their goals and procedures have higher priority than those of the family. Hospitals can restrict families' rights of access to their sick members, even to the point that patients' well-being may be adversely affected. While the contest goes on between physicians and pharmacists over control of prescription drugs—for example, whether the pharmacist will be allowed to make substitutions for the brands specified by the physician—the family finds itself with unidentified prescription bottles in the medicine chest and exorbitant drug bills. Because the family lacks information on drug prices and products, it cannot do comparison shopping.

In a broader sense, the family is a pawn in the fundamental power struggles of the society (Turner 1970). Various established power groups take advantage of the family's usefulness as a social resource for perpetuating their power and preserving the traditional social order. The major institutions—government, military, church, business, and the professions, including medicine and health-related industries—share certain concerns. These include maintaining the work ethic, ambition to rise through conformity to the goals and legitimate channels of social mobility, accumulation of material goods, patriotism and political obedience, religious obedience, sexual chastity, patriarchal authority in the family, differentiation of the roles of men and women, and subordination of children to parental and institutional authority. Since so much of this social order hinges on the family, the maintenance of a traditional and stable family system has been regarded as essential by those seeking to maintain the overall social order. Hence, the family is fair game.

Medicine and related health service groups play their role in enforcing social traditions within the family. Physicians have been instrumental in upholding the sexual codes on which the family-church-political order is based. In the nineteenth century doctors cautioned that masturbation causes blindness, fits, indigestion, idiocy, and paralysis; that sexual intercourse causes severe paroxysms of the nervous system and can be harmful if indulged in frequently by married persons; and that contraceptives cause many gynecological diseases (Comfort 1967). Twentieth-century physicians continue to enforce the conservative sex codes by refusing to deal professionally with problems of sexual malfunction (Lyons 1972; Vincent 1973).

Physicians have cooperated with schools in administering amphetamine-type drugs to alter the behavior of school children with minimal brain dysfunction, a problem that is identified by the child's tendency to be restless, inattentive, and uncomfortable with discipline. The official rationale for this drug program is to enable the individual child to make better adaptation at school. But perhaps schools also use the drug program to facilitate control and maintain discipline (Hentoff 1974).

When American prisoners of war were released by North Vietnam in 1972, they were not allowed to visit their families before undergoing a period of military debriefing, called Operation Egress Recap. The Navy's neuro-psychiatric research center administered Recap, physicians served as spokesmen with the press, the rationale was presented in health terms, and the men were confined to hospitals (Holles 1972). Medicine collaborated in controlling the ex-POWs and their families in the interest of military and political objectives.

Thus, medicine sometimes serves as an agent of social control, enforcing compliance by the family. It has been medicine's collaboration in perpetuating traditional authority and preserving the social order that has achieved for medicine its authority to direct its own activities and to influence public policy. All its expertise and the indispensability of its services would not have earned either adulation or power had the profession worked to upset the social order or threatened the established power alignments.

This is not the full extent of the family's vulnerability to outside manipulation, however. The family is called upon to act as an agent of social control on behalf of the dominant institutions by keeping its own members in line. Since the family is an integral part of the societal system, it is natural that this should be so. The problem arises when the overriding concern is the maintenance of order and control, irrespective of the costs to family unity or impairment of the family's ability to function. Abortion laws serve as illustration. All the major power elements, including medicine, cooperated in enforcing the antiabortion statutes, and they persisted in the face of mounting demand for abortions by individuals from all sectors of society. The family was held responsible for preventing abortion within the family circle, and was expected to condemn or even ostracize any member who might transgress. The fanaticism of the antiabortion forces succeeded in pitting parents and children against each other, and males and females against each other. Pressures on families to enforce the antimarijuana laws have similarly tended to alienate parents from their children. The costs for the family of maintaining the traditional social order have often been extremely high.

CONCLUSIONS

One can argue (and many do) that all these structural arrangements that vest autonomy in the professionals are essential to protect the consumer-family's health interests by preventing interference by laymen—government, community, families, and patients themselves—in the technical decision making of the experts. While the structure certainly has served to insulate the professionals from these types of interference in the practice of medicine, it has enabled the professionals' own business and power objectives to intrude upon service to patients and families.

In many important respects, the present structure of the health care system tends to impede families in their efforts to obtain essential medical services and to develop the health skills and knowledge needed for acting effectively on their own. Not only are families' interests generally neglected in the present structural arrangements but, in addition, the health care system tends to regulate and manipulate families in the interests of furthering medicine's business objectives and of preserving societal order, at the expense of families' needs to serve their own members' interests.

This chapter focused on structural deficiencies in the medical care system, for the objective was to try to locate the structural sources of families' inadequate health behavior. The structure is not locked in place, however. Structural innovations have been proposed or tried which are aimed at increasing the system's responsiveness and adaptation to the needs of consumer families, and some of these proposals will be discussed in a later chapter.

FOUR

Deficiences in Services
of the Medical Care System

Photo Trends by Arnold Kapp

THERE ARE SOME IMPAIRMENTS of physicians and some defects in the quality and reliability of medical service that hinder families in their efforts to preserve their members' health. Some of the defects in service can be traced to the present structure of medicine, especially the high degree of autonomy and lack of discipline over members of the profession, the rigid structure of medical institutions, and the organization of the system around achievement of objectives that compete with service to patients.

This review will focus only on those performance characteristics of the health care system that create problems for patients and families. Because of this limited objective, we will make no attempt to give a balanced picture of the overall quality of performance by the system. Nor will we discuss any of its spectacular achievements or outstanding performers.

PERSONAL IMPAIRMENTS OF PHYSICIANS

Physicians are subject to ailments and infirmities that may impair their professional functioning, as is the case with any occupation group. Physicians are more susceptible than many other population groups to certain types of problems, particularly emotional disorders, drug abuse, and suicide. The nature of medical practice may put physicians at greater risk and, in addition, the process of self-selection by which certain types of people decide to become doctors may bring more vulnerable people into this field.

There is evidence of a relatively high rate of psychiatric morbidity among physicians. In a seven-year period, 5,925 patients were admitted to the psychiatric service of the Mayo Clinic, of whom ninety-three were physicians. This represents a ratio of one physician to every sixty-four admissions, which is disproportionately high (Duffy and Litin 1967). Another long-term study of men who were sophomores in the same college in 1942 compared forty-seven men who became physicians with seventy-nine who entered different fields. Thirty-four percent of the physicians had visited a psychiatrist ten or more times compared to only 19 percent of the nonphysician classmates. In addition, 47 percent of the doctors had experienced bad marriages compared to 32 percent of the nonphysicians. The researchers claimed that the differences are traceable to unhappy childhood experiences of the physician group, and these same experiences also led them to the field of medicine (*Occupational Mental Health* 1973). Related to this high risk of emotional illness is the excessively high suicide rate among physicians. Suicide is the cause of death for one out of every fifty physicians, which is two hundred times the rate for the general population (Lewis and Lewis 1970).

Between 1 and 2 percent of the nation's practicing physicians are addicted to narcotics, and at least another 1 or 2 percent are habituated to amphetamines or barbiturates. Altogether, at least 5,700 physicians may be habituated to drugs. This rate is from thirty to one-hundred times greater than that of other population groups (Emshwiller 1972). On top of this, there is a higher than average rate of excessive alcohol consumption among physicians. Addiction problems have been recognized as an occupational hazard of medical practice by the AMA's house of delegates, and this professional body has developed guidelines to aid the profession in dealing with the problem (*New York Times* 1972).

These particular types of personal problems exhibited by physicians pose danger for patients, for doctors' emotional problems and addiction may cause impaired judgment and careless work. The present organization of medical practice fails to protect patients adequately from these potential dangers. In the case of drug abuse, physicians can hide their own consumption behind their legal authority to write prescriptions. The decentralized pattern of solo practice permits physicians to shield themselves from the scrutiny of peers as long as they limit themselves to office practice. In addition, peers may be more ready to cover up for the physician than is the case in less solidary occupation groups. If the physician chooses to seek professional help, that help will be discreetly given. If the physician's problem becomes flagrant and comes to the attention of the state medical board, the board may allow the physician to continue to practice to facilitate his or her rehabilitation.

INADEQUATE MEDICAL CARE

An indication of the level of performance of the medical profession is available in evaluations made by patients. Physicians, however, consider patients' level of knowledge and experience insufficient to make valid judgments about their technical performance. Perhaps it is partly due to the fact that patients have been kept uninformed about the technical intricacies of medical practice that the American public have remained fairly uncritical of doctors' performance. However, there is evidence that many families feel they have had at least one exposure to what they consider incompetent or inappropriate care by a physician. In a sample of patients in a large New York health plan, about half said that they or their spouses had stopped going to a physician (either before or after joining the plan) because they were not satisfied with the physician, and almost two-thirds reported having had a doctor who seemed to be incompetent (Freidson 1961). Just over two-fifths of the persons in another sample reported that they or a dependent had had a negative medical care experience, but very few reported more than three such incidents. Among those with negative experiences, four-fifths felt the experience had caused unnecessary pain and suffering and two-thirds needed additional medical care afterward (HEW 1973).

Technical appraisals of physicians' performance by professionals have been more critical. A study of rural general practitioners in North Carolina judged 44 percent of the physicians to be performing below standard, and most of the deficiencies were gross and striking. The deficiencies can be traced to the patterns that typify medical practice, for those who had obtained additional training after being licensed, who had access to laboratory services and other professionals, and who maintained appointment systems for their patients were likely to perform better (Peterson et al. 1956).

DIAGNOSIS

Medical care hinges on the accuracy of diagnosis. Yet one hospital found that a fourth of the patients in the surgery service and over half of those in medicine were misdiagnosed (Duff and Hollingshead 1968). Most of the errors were underdiagnoses—failure to detect a condition. In a mass screening test, 60 percent of chronic conditions reported by patients themselves were not reported by physicians who examined those patients (HEW 1965). Another attempt was made to evaluate physicians' effectiveness in detecting disease in a group of patients examined periodically by the doctors. When these patients were examined after death, the disease that caused death had been correctly identified by the physicians in only 51 percent of the cases (Schor et al. 1964). There are also problems of overdiagnosis. For example, in a mass screening test for heart disease among schoolchildren, out of 161 children with a previous report of heart disease, 145 actually had no signs of heart disease, and the screening project found it necessary to *delabel* these children (Cayler et al. 1969).

TREATMENT

Emergency care and hospital emergency services have been found to be notably deficient. A survey of one busy Baltimore emergency room revealed that less than a third of the noncritical cases had received adequate care. Another study of a large metropolitan emergency room concluded that over half of the auto accident victims who died from abdominal injuries after admission would have had a reasonable chance for survival if there had not been an error in diagnosis or treatment. By every criterion used in the study, the medical care was both inefficient and inadequate (Brook and Stevenson 1970).

Another problem with emergency services lies in the inadequate response before the patient gets to the hospital. Twenty-six percent of the ambulance attendants in New York have no recognized training, and only 13 percent are trained as medical emergency technicians, including training in cardiopulmonary resuscitation, emergency childbirth, and extrication of victims from traffic accidents. Four-fifths of the country's ambulances are not real ambulances. Half are hearses operated by morticians who do not even know first aid (Andelman 1973; *Family Health* 1973). The response time for ambulances in New York City is reported to be thirteen minutes, but in some other areas, such as Suffolk County, the response time is almost three times as long (Andelman 1973). Few towns have emergency telephone numbers that can be called twenty-four hours a day, or have coordinated police and fire departments, local hospitals, medical societies, and ambulance services into a single community-wide unit. The significance of these failures is indicated by the estimate that 20 percent of the emergency cases who die could have been saved by adequate emergency services (*Family Health* 1973).

SURGERY

Not all surgery is performed skillfully. A study of the medical care received by a Teamsters group concluded that a fifth of their operations were poorly performed (Langer 1970). One reason is that about half of all surgery is done by physicians who are not certified as specialists (Greenberg 1971), and this is a reflection of the lack of discipline within the profession concerning the competence of its members and the withholding of professional evaluations from the public.

Some operations are performed unnecessarily. Physicians tend quite consistently to err on the side of performing surgery that may not be needed rather than on the side of withholding surgery that might turn out to be warranted. About a million tonsillectomies are performed annually, accounting for a fourth of all surgery and two-thirds of the operations on children under age ten. It is a significant operation for the patient, for it is now thought that tonsils play a part in the body's immunity system. About 300 children die annually from this surgery, usually from anesthesia accidents and hemorrhaging. Factors other than the health needs of the patients prompt many of these operations, for some physicians now estimate that 95 percent or more of the tonsillectomies are unnecessary (Graham 1973). United States and Canadian surgeons perform about twice as many operations proportionate to population as do British surgeons. Yet the greater use of surgery in the United States and Canada does not provide better health results. Death rates from cervical, uterine, and breast cancer in the United States, Canada, and Britain are similar despite the differential use of surgery. The death rate among the elderly from gallbladder diseases is much lower in Britain, probably because of the lower rate of surgical intervention (Bunker 1970; Vayda 1973; Sedgwick 1974).

One of the factors prompting unnecessary surgery is the fee-for-service system, which gives the physician an economic incentive to operate. This was demonstrated by a medical audit in a California hospital. When the entire staff of gynecologists were on salary they performed 26 hysterectomies, but later when the doctors were on a fee-for-service basis they performed 130 hysterectomies (Tunley 1966). Big money is at stake. About $375 million is spent annually on tonsil and adenoid surgery alone (Graham 1973).

A fee-for-service system of paying physicians would seem to require a well-developed system of checks on physicians to see that they are not carried away by greed or eagerness to operate. It was, in fact, found in a system set up by the United Store Workers Union health plan that when the first physician's recommendation for surgery was reviewed by a second physician before an operation was permitted, there were 19 percent fewer operations than had originally been recommended (Hicks 1973). Yet the system of solo practice puts physicians in competition with each other and decentralizes the network of physicians so as to inhibit them from consulting each other on their cases. The surgical review committees within hospitals are clearly not very effective in preventing unnecessary surgery.

MEDICATION

Physicians write prescriptions in two-thirds of all patient visits (Stolley and Lasagna 1969) for a total of over a billion prescriptions a year (Stolley et al. 1972). A significant number of these prescriptions are issued in a manner that fails to meet the standards of rational prescribing—the appropriate selection of the right drug for the right patient at the right time (Greenberg 1971). Many of these drugs are ineffective or cause adverse effects in the patients.

There are about a million and a half annual admissions to hospitals due to adverse drug reactions, with an average length of stay of eight days, and hospitalization expenses of about $900 million. The incidence of illness due to drug therapy is about 10 percent of all admissions to hospitals (Brodie 1971). There are a wide variety of diseases that are induced by drugs. Digitalis, diuretics, and other drugs can produce cardiac rhythm disturbances. Other drugs produce dermatologic diseases, such as eczema, urticaria, and acne; gastrointestinal problems, such as hemorrhage; and hemotoxic reactions, such as total bone marrow suppression and coagulation abnormalities (Moser 1964).

The greatest concern is the use of antibiotics because they are the most frequently dispensed type of drug, and when used with abandon have great potential for harm. About 95 percent of physicians issue prescriptions to patients with a common cold, and almost 60 percent of these prescriptions are for antibiotics, even though these drugs are not effective for colds (Stolley et al. 1972). In fact, over half the antibiotics given to patients are not medically indicated. In addition, they may cause toxic reactions, for seventeen to twenty million persons in the United States are hypersensitive to antibiotics. They are one of the major causes of fatal adverse drug reactions, many of which were avoidable; a review of fatalities due to penicillin revealed that the drug was not medically justified in over half the cases (Moser 1964).

Another widespread pattern of drug abuse is prescribing drugs for pregnant women. Forty-one percent of a sample of Houston women had been given antibiotics during pregnancy (Brody 1973). This pattern persists in spite of the thalidomide tragedy and the body of research indicating the adverse effects on the unborn of a variety of drugs, including some usually harmless ones, such as aspirin and sedatives.

Many of the defects in physicians' drug prescribing practices are rooted in the structural conditions of medical practice. What is regarded as unnecessary medication from a medical-therapeutic standpoint is not ineffective from the viewpoint of the independent practitioner or hospital personnel. By prescribing medication, the physician can demonstrate decisive action to the patient. In addition, seeing and treating a patient in one fast motion conserves doctors' time and enables them to handle more patients than using another more time-consuming method. An alternative method would include a history, physical examination, and laboratory tests, and then deciding on proper therapeutic measures, which might or might not include drug therapy. Time-saving considerations often impel physicians to prescribe drugs on the patient's first visit, even though about half the time the physician is unable to reach a definitive diagnosis on the first visit.

Factors other than the patient's well-being are important in the extensive dispensing of psychoactive drugs by physicians. Nearly one-half of United States adults have used one or more kinds of psychoactive drugs (Stolley et al. 1972), and the 225 million prescriptions for these drugs in 1970 ranks them second only to antibiotics in frequency. Since the average physician sees over ninety patients a week and devotes about twenty minutes to each patient, any factor that affects the productivity formula has a direct impact on the doctor's income. One of the most threatening factors in modern medical practice is the extent to which psychological and social factors are coming to be regarded as important contributors to disease. It is time-consuming to talk with a patient in order to diagnose the psychosocial factors affecting her or him, much less to advise the patient concerning these problems. Rather than dealing systematically with the patient's underlying problem or ignoring it entirely, the physician chooses to prescribe a psychoactive drug, usually a tranquilizer, hoping it will aid the patient to cope with her or his emotional problems. But the routine prescribing of these drugs is shortcut medicine that is encouraged by the present structure. In one medical care program so organized that physicians had a limited caseload of patients to serve as family doctor, physicians gave more supportive care to patients, and prescribing of tranquilizers was uncommon (Muller 1972). Hospital use of psychoactive drugs is also fostered by practical considerations, for sedation of patients helps in restraining patients from making demands on the personnel and in subduing the restlessness created by early bedtime.

Much of physicians' misuse of drugs is currently uncontrollable. A study concluded that there is no organized mechanism for drug use review in the private sector of medical care (Brodie 1971). Moreover, physicians continue to resist review of their prescribing practices. The New York State Medical Society has denounced a law mandating a computerized review of the prescribing and dispensing of narcotic and other addictive drugs by the state's physicians, dentists, and druggists (Clines 1973). Physicians even objected to the Food and Drug Administration's publication of lists of drugs found to be ineffective or unsafe, because this would reveal to the public that some physicians are continuing to prescribe faulty drug products (*Consumer Reports* 1971).

In hospitals, also, the distribution of medications is often lax. The pharmacist has a part-time position in all but the very large hospitals, and this has forced nurses to assume the responsibility for getting and distributing drugs. This, in turn, has fostered the system of stocking drugs on every ward, with a resulting lack of professional control over drug use (Brodie 1971). A computer analysis of drug dispensing in one large hospital found a significant amount of inappropriate prescribing, including giving too much of the drug, allowing patients to have too much of the drug in their possession because of multiple prescriptions, and giving two or more drugs concurrently that were inappropriate to have in combination (Maronde et al. 1967).

Physicians generally are inadequately trained to cope with the complex and fast-changing array of modern drugs. The traditional pattern of medical education places a relatively low priority on pharmacology, and once a physician is licensed to practice, relicensing does not depend on the physician's keeping abreast of developments in the field. In order to maintain a busy practice, physicians rely more on detail men of pharmaceutical companies as their source of information about drugs than on professional views of peers or medical journals. Thus, physicians tend to prescribe expensive brand name drugs rather than less-expensive generic products. They also prescribe combination drug products, which are profitable for the company but are often irrational medications, since usually only one of the elements in the combination is effective against a given disease (Brodie 1971).

CONCLUSIONS

Chapters Three and Four have examined some structural characteristics of the medical care system that make it difficult for families to cope with the system, and deficiencies in medical services that hamper families' efforts to care for their members' health.

Since families are highly dependent on the professional system for services, health care failures of families may be traced in part to these problems in the structure and functioning of the professional system.

Family health care failures may also be traced in part to problems in family structure. What type of family structure is needed for dealing effectively with health matters generally and for coping with the medical care system particularly? The next several chapters are devoted to proposing a family model—the energized family—which might have the required capabilities. The model is tested to determine whether it works—whether this type of family is able to get better health services, practice better personal health care, and have healthier members than other types of families.

PART TWO

A Study of How Family Structure Affects Health Behavior

Part Two will examine the general hypothesis that family structure is related to the level of health and the effectiveness of health behavior within families, and specifically, that the energized family achieves better results than other family forms. We conducted a field study to test the hypothesis. We will first describe the mechanics of the study.

THE STUDY METHOD

We based the study on information obtained from detailed personal interviews conducted in 1969 in a northern New Jersey city, of about 150,000 people, with a representative cross-sectional sample of families having a husband and wife in residence and at least one child aged nine to thirteen. Since this was a study of the structure of relationships within families, it was essential that the sample consist of nuclear families with the full complement of personnel—a father, mother, and at least one child. It was also important to obtain separate interviews with each of the three members; it was not considered good enough to have one person report on another.

The interview instruments designed for the study consisted of fixed questions with structured response categories. The interviews with the husband and wife each lasted approximately an hour and a half, and the child's interview about forty-five minutes.

The final sample consisted of 510 families. The evidence presented here is based on 273 of those families in which the wife, the husband, and one child were interviewed separately. In the remaining 237 families only the wife and a child were interviewed (because of cost considerations), and these families have been used to check reliability.

More detailed information concerning the method of research is supplied in the Appendix.

CONCEPTS AND MEASURES

The basic concepts used in the study are concerned with family structure and with health and health behavior.

Family Structure Concepts

Extent and variety of interaction among family members
Extent of family links to other social systems
Extent of active coping effort by family members
Extent of freedom and responsiveness to individual members of the family
Flexibility-rigidity of family role relationships

These family concepts constitute the dimensions or components of the energized family concept or model.

Health and Health Behavior Concepts

Level of health and illness
Quality of personal health practices
Extent and appropriateness of use of professional medical services

These concepts are all fairly abstract and cannot, therefore, be measured directly by respondents' answers to particular questions in the interview. Respondents do not think in terms of sociological concepts, and can be expected to report accurately only when asked about specific experiences, such as whether or not they had an eye examination in the past three years or whether they went to the movies with their children. A two-fold problem in social research is to formulate concepts that describe a significantly broad form of behavior to be socially significant, and then to devise accurate measures of the concept out of the concrete pieces of information produced in an interview. The challenging research task is to bridge the gap between the general concepts, which give the research its significance, and the specific data obtainable from interviews, which permit accurate measurement. This usually calls for combining several specific types of behavior reported in the interview into a composite measure, which will represent the broad concept.

In this study, we constructed measures to represent each concept in the following way. We broke down each concept into specific components, and then designed questions for the interview to represent each of the specific elements. For example, in the case of the concept "extent and variety of interaction among family members," we asked husbands and wives how frequently they engaged in eleven different types of activity together (parties, church, meetings, cards, and so forth). This made it possible to construct a composite measure or index to represent "the extent of husband-wife interaction." In the same way, we constructed an index of father-child interaction and an index of mother-child interaction. We then constructed an even more general index for the whole family by combining husband-wife, mother-child, and father-child interaction indexes. We called this overall index the "family interaction index." These indexes constitute the measures used in the study to represent the various concepts.

We devised a formula for computing each index by assigning weights to the answer categories of the various questions (for example, never = 0, occasionally = 1, often = 2). We obtained an individual person's score on a given index by summing that person's weighted answers to the group of questions which comprised that index. An index constructed to represent the wife's behavior is based on her own report, the husband's on his own report, and the child's on his or her own report. A family index combines the individual indexes for the father, mother, and child in the family. We constructed one hundred different indexes for wives and husbands, forty-two for children, and thirty-seven for the combined family, although only selected ones of these will be reported on here. The interview questions used in constructing the principal indexes are presented in the Appendix.

Thus, three levels of abstraction are involved here:

The interview question is the most concrete or least abstract level, as illustrated by "Have you had an eye examination in the past three years?" Since the items of behavior reported in the individual questions are of limited significance in their own right, the questions have been used mainly to construct composite indexes, and have then been relegated to the Appendix.

The index or composite measure represents a broader form of behavior than the question: for example, the extent of use of preventive medical services. Yet the index is limited to the specific items of information that comprise it (for example, the twelve types of preventive medical services included in the index), so that it is more concrete than the concept.

The concept is the abstract or general statement of the social behavior that is of basic concern. The goal is to have the concepts accurately represented and measured by the indexes. Examples of concepts include appropriateness of use of professional health services, and the extent and variety of interaction among family members. The energized family represents an even higher level of abstraction, because this concept combines the various family structure concepts into a multidimensional model.

FAMILY STRUCTURE CONCEPTS AND INDEXES

On the next page are the major family structure concepts that make up the energized family model, together with the indexes or composite measures used to represent each. A notation after each index indicates whether the index was constructed for men (M), women (W), children (C), and combined family (F).

Family Structure Concepts	Indexes Used to Represent the Concepts	
Extent and Variety of Interaction Among Family Members	1. Husband-wife interaction (frequency and variety)	(M,W)
	2. Mother-child interaction	(W,C)
	3. Father-child interaction	(M,C)
	4. Man's emphasis on father role vs. job role	(M)
	5. Combined family interaction	(F)
Extent of Links to Other Social Systems	1. Extent of community participation (membership and attendance in clubs and organizations)	(M,W,C)
	2. Number of towns used	(M,W,C)
	3. Extent of cultural participation (lessons, performance, attendance)	(M,C)
	4. Variety of child's activities	(C)
	5. Combined family extramural participation	(F)
Active Coping Effort	1. Health training efforts by parents	(M,W,C)
	2. Household health facilities	
	3. Child's health care equipment	(C)
	4. Child's exercise equipment	(C)
Freedom and Responsiveness to Individual Members	1. Aversive control of child by parents	(M,W,C)
	2. Obstructive conflict between husband and wife	(M,W)
	3. Supportiveness of child by parents	(M,W,C)
	4. Child's autonomy	(M,W,C)
	5. Autonomy of members	(F)
Flexibility-Rigidity of Family Role Relationships	1. Conjugal division of tasks (segregation or flexibility in major task areas)	(M,W)
	2. Conjugal division of task of child health care	(M,W)
	3. Conjugal division of task of wife health care	(M,W)
	4. Conjugal power (shared or unilateral decision making)	(M,W)

These concepts are defined and discussed in subsequent chapters, and the questions used in constructing the indexes are shown in the Appendix.

HEALTH AND HEALTH BEHAVIOR CONCEPTS AND INDEXES

Three major health-related concepts were investigated. Following is an outline of these concepts and the indexes or measures used to represent each in the research.

Health/Health Behavior Concepts	Indexes Used to Represent the Concepts	
Level of Health and Illness	1. Extent of health problems (self-rating)	(M,W,C,F)
	2. Level of present health (self-rating)	(M,W,C,F)
Use of Professional Medical Services	1. Use of preventive medical services (tests, examinations, immunizations)	(M,W,C,F)
	2. Use of specialized medical services	(M,W,C,F)
	3. Use of medical services for illness	(M,W,C)
	4. Total use of professional medical (preventive, specialized, restorative) services	(M,W,C)
Personal Health Practices	1. Personal health practices (sleep, exercise, elimination, dental, smoking, alcohol, and nutrition combined)	(M,W,C,F)
	2. Sleep (regularity and effectiveness)	(M,W,C,F)
	3. Exercise (regularity and amount)	(M,W,C,F)
	4. Elimination (successful functioning)	(M,W,C,F)
	5. Dental hygiene (regularity and appropriateness of timing)	(M,W,C,F)
	6. Smoking (quantity)	(M,W,C,F)
	7. Alcohol (frequency and quantity)	(M,W)
	8. Nutrition (regularity and nutritional adequacy)	(M,W,C,F)

The next three chapters present the rationale and test results for the three parts of the hypothesis—that the energized family pattern fosters personal health practices (Chapter Five), effective use of professional medical services (Chapter Six), and sound health (Chapter Seven). Chapter Eight assesses how typical the energized family is in contemporary American society.

A considerable amount of statistical evidence is presented so that readers may learn how the data were analyzed and how the conclusions were reached. Some readers may wish to skip over the detailed statistical material and rely on the verbal descriptions of the results.

FIVE
The Energized Family
and Personal Health Practices

Photo Trends by Ed Scully

Our hypothesis is that the energized family form will foster, develop, facilitate, and reinforce sound personal health practices among its members to a greater extent than a nonenergized form. This chapter first discusses how this is presumed to come about and then it presents a research test of the hypothesis.

THE RATIONALE

The rationale is, briefly, that the various aspects of energized family structure are expected to foster personal health practices by developing the competence of members for taking care of themselves and by assisting the members to perform competently by backing them up with the social and physical resources of the family group. Since we propose that personal health practices are based on competence, this concept must be defined.

"Competence denotes capabilities to meet and deal with a changing world, to formulate ends and implement them," and "to estimate and evaluate the meaning and consequences to one's self of alternative lines of conduct" (Foote and Cottrell 1955, pp. 49, 56). Competence includes capacity for self-direction and self-governance, the ability to conduct oneself satisfactorily in handling important issues in life, and the capability of handling critical situations in a flexible, versatile, spontaneous, and resourceful fashion (Farber 1962). It is mastery over oneself and one's life situation (Olim 1968). Competence is a social ability, the effectiveness of one's performance within social settings. It is a social product as well, an achievement reached within social groups.

Personal health practices reflect the competence with which the members of families care for their health; this type of personal competence is developed largely within the family. Families can develop the capabilities of individual members for taking care of themselves, and can provide group resources to back up their efforts to cope and tend to their physical needs (Pratt 1973).

The following discussion concerns how each of the features of the energized family model is expected to contribute to personal health practices.

Freedom and Responsiveness to the Individual

A feature of energized family structure that is proposed as having an important positive influence on health practices is the tendency to provide autonomy and to be responsive to the particular interests and needs of individual family members, as contrasted with the tendency to require conformity to prescribed patterns and to thwart movement toward individuality. This includes the tendency not only to accept but to prize individuality and uniqueness, and to tolerate disagreement and deviance. Respect and acceptance are given unconditionally, without continuous comparison of the person to others or to prescribed standards. The family does not insist that family roles supersede all other aspects of self, and may assist members to

84

construct escape hatches so that no member is confined by family responsibilities (Goffman 1971, 1961). Family members are encouraged in their various endeavors, especially in seeking new areas of growth and in developing their creativity, imagination, and independent thinking. This pattern represents, then, an orientation toward individual fulfillment through autonomy, as contrasted with an orientation toward conformity and family stability through control.

Other sociologists have also focused on the family's responsibilities for enhancing the individual's opportunities for personal development. Stott (1951) proposed that a central criterion of family success is whether it fosters and facilitates individual functioning and progress toward fulfillment of one's potential. Otto (1963) cited as a criterion of family effectiveness the ability to be sensitive to the needs of family members and to provide support and encouragement. Olim proposed that in the fully functioning family, each person is given unconditional positive regard and is not punished for differing, for being human; wide latitude is given to the person "to discover and construct reality for himself, to find his own values, his own beliefs, his own moral code, what he wants to do with his life" (Olim 1968, p. 145).

It should be noted that sociologists have not generally espoused this structural pattern of autonomy and responsiveness to individual uniqueness. There has been a tendency to emphasize the need for a type of family structure that would assure societal and family stability and integration, rather than the need for a structure that contributes to personal growth and physical and psychological well-being.

There is a considerable body of child socialization research which supports the proposal that children raised by parents who stress democratic relationships, give unconditional personal regard, and encourage individuality and personal development show greater competence and resourcefulness in taking care of themselves than children raised by parents who emphasize discipline, punishment, and conformity to prescribed patterns.

Punishment is less likely than positive encouragement to develop the child's inner resources for evaluating and correcting his or her own conduct, for punishment generates resentment and resistance which are restrained only when the fear of authority is maintained (Aronfreed 1961, 1968; Eron et al. 1963; Becker 1964; Sears et al. 1953; Sears 1961; Clausen 1968). Thus, while parents may obtain superficial social conformity by using punishment, they may not achieve their long-term socialization objectives, because children orient themselves to the external sources of authority rather than develop their own internal capacities for self-correction. On the other hand, encouragement and support provide enjoyment which becomes associated with the behavior itself, thus reinforcing the behavior and fostering the development of the child's personal resources.

Various studies have reported that granting autonomy to children is associated with competence, self-control, self-reliance, outgoing social behavior, intellectual growth, and differentiated cognitive functioning—types of effects on children that indicate ability to take care of themselves. On the other hand, restrictive, controlling, or power-assertive parental behavior has been found to be associated with dependency, inhibition, and obedience in children (Baumrind 1967; Strauss 1964; Witkin 1969; Becker 1964). The fact that power-assertive parental behavior produces obedience might lead one to entertain the possibility that our hypothesis should be reversed—that parental control is more effective than autonomy in producing good health practices—through obedience to parental dictates. Yet restrictive control by parents also tends to produce hostility, aggression, and noncooperative be-havior in children "because it frustrates not only the act but also the child's need for autonomy" (Hoffman and Saltzstein 1967, p. 54). For this reason, children of power-assertive parents maintain an uneasy balance between con-formity and defiance; since they are hostile and aggressive as a result of this parental pattern, they tend to conform superficially but remain in readiness to resist control.

The evidence suggests, therefore, that encouragement and autonomy are more likely to produce in children the self-management capacities needed for caring for their own health than are punishment and control. Although re-search evidence concerning adults is lacking, the same rationale can be ex-pected to apply to them. Men and women whose family arrangements pro-vide opportunities for autonomy and personal growth are more likely to assume full personal responsibility for caring for their own health, to seek out the best methods of health care, to strive for maximum development of their physical capacities, and to be resourceful in responding to the changing health needs of their bodies, than are persons whose families seriously limit and constrain their modes of being and acting.

ACTIVE COPING EFFORT

A second feature of the energized family form that is thought to foster members' personal health practices is the tendency to actively and energeti-cally attempt to cope with life's problems and issues. This consists of an openness to new ideas, information, techniques, opportunities, and resources; taking the initiative by actively seeking out such new resources; and apply-ing them to the solution of family and personal problems. It entails creatively developing original solutions in response to changing needs, tailoring solu-tions to one's unique needs, analyzing the implications of alternative courses of action, rationally selecting among alternatives, and planning with long-term consequences taken into consideration. This is a problem-solving approach to life. It requires striving for full development of one's capacities and capa-bilities, and for mastery over oneself and one's life situation.

This approach can be contrasted with a fatalistic tendency to passively accept the world and life as given, perhaps complaining but not assertively attempting to attain mastery, a tendency to use conventional, standardized solutions to problems when those solutions are often based upon simplistic formulas, and to deal with immediate crises on a day-to-day basis.

Other researchers have stressed the importance of families' coping capabilities. Kieren and Tallman (1972) have viewed marriage as a relationship that requires competence in problem-solving. This consists of the ability of both partners to deal effectively with problematic situations by changing strategies on the basis of new assessments of their situation. Stott (1951) proposed that the criterion of family effectiveness should be the extent to which the unit fostered the increasing functional effectiveness of its members.

The family pattern of providing freedom to each member and encouraging individuality is closely related to this pattern of coping energetically with life's problems. Both involve encouraging individuals to develop to their fullest potential and supporting their efforts to function fully and effectively. Encouragement of autonomy and individuality fosters the person's efforts to develop his or her capacity for effective functioning. Fostering efforts to cope effectively strengthens individuality and a person's capacity for autonomous functioning.

Some evidence supports the notion that family coping effort fosters health practices by developing the members' capability for action. Rainwater (1968) suggests that the reason people brought up in poverty have less adequate personal health practices than persons in higher socioeconomic levels is that lower-class people's experience of themselves and their world is crisis-dominated and pervaded by barely managing to cope with daily problems of existence. They develop little sense of ability to affect significantly the course of events through personal action. Consequently, lower-class people tend to neglect basic health care in favor of pressing immediate concerns, and attend to health problems only when they reach crisis proportion. This rationale can be applied to explain differences among families as well as differences between classes.

Parents who use printed materials such as books, bulletins, and newspapers for information to aid in child rearing have significantly better child-rearing practices, including health care practices concerning eating, sleeping, and toilet training, than do parents who do not seek out such information (Hoeflin 1954). This activist approach by parents contributes to the development of their children's capabilities, for parents who give reasons for their directives, provide information, and encourage their children in verbal give and take, succeed in developing the children's ability to solve problems and to behave competently (Baumrind 1967). Parents who actively and successfully cope with their dental health needs stimulate children to develop the ability to care for their own teeth (Richards and Cohen 1971). The same holds true for tobacco, alcohol, and psychoactive drug use, for children whose parents are nonusers are more likely to abstain than children whose parents use the drug (HEW 1971; Smart and Fejer 1972). These varied pieces of evidence suggest that what is being developed within the family is not simply certain specific forms of health behavior, but a more complex behavioral pattern consisting of active efforts to deal with health within the family through discussion, attention to information in the media, evaluation of behavior, and deliberate modification of family routines and individual behavior in accordance with health objectives.

FLEXIBLE AND EGALITARIAN STRUCTURING OF RELATIONSHIPS

An egalitarian distribution of power and a flexible division of tasks and activities among family members contribute to the members' personal health practices. These two structural concepts will be discussed jointly, because they have so often been combined in a single concept, such as division of labor, role specialization, or power.

Distribution of power concerns the extent to which the power to make decisions in the several major areas of family life is concentrated in a particular member or members of the family—an authoritarian pattern—or is distributed and shared—an egalitarian pattern.

Division of tasks and activities concerns the extent to which there is a sharp differentiation between the tasks and activities of the various family members based on conventional definitions of age and sex roles, or the extent to which there is interchangeability and flexibility in task performance among family members. Some labels used to express this idea include: flexible as opposed to rigid or conventional task assignment or division of labor, and overlapping role pattern or nondifferentiation as contrasted with age or sex role specialization, differentiation, or segregation.

The flexible and egaliurian role pattern is closely related conceptually to a family pattern discussed earlier—freedom for and responsiveness to the individual. The role pattern concept refers to the tendency for persons to have latitude to shape their family roles to themselves rather than to have rigid role prescriptions foisted on them; the concept of freedom and responsiveness pertains to the opportunity for indivduals to choose among alternative life-styles and to develop their unique qualities. Thus, both are concerned with the extent to which the family fosters individuality or constrains and limits individuality.

Some sociologists have suggested that an egalitarian, nondifferentiated family form may have functional advantages, primarily because of its greater adaptability and attention to the needs of individual members. Pollak (1967, p. 199) has argued that, given the fact that the modern family must above all fulfill the need for understanding, the traditional sex and age divisions are likely to appear absurd, "for in the realm of intimacy there are only equals." In fact, these divisions may be highly disruptive. A father who performs a specialized disciplinarian role "becomes an alien intruder to his children" (Slater 1961, p. 305), and empirical studies have shown that strict parental role differentiation is associated with poor emotional adjustment of the child (Manis 1958). Slater (1961, pp. 307–308) concluded:

"It may be that the more highly differentiated family, despite its prevalence, is simply too unsophisticated a structure for a technologically advanced industrial society such as ours. Its apparent dependence on a stable social context imparts to it a rigidity analogous, in its effects on the family system, to the greater rigidity of inherited as opposed to learned responses in the individual organism."

Hobart (1963, p. 410) has maintained that changes in the social structure have tended to make the traditional form of family obsolete.

"It follows from this that the family of the future must not be defined in terms of more structure, but in terms of less explicit structure. It must at once be flexible enough for increasingly individuated people, yet a stable basic unit for human life. The family as a commitment implies freedom in the definition of the marital relationship in order to meet the demands of the particular way of life of the two people involved."

A flexible organization of family tasks in combination with egalitarian decision making may foster sound personal health practices by enabling the family to mobilize for maximum productive effort. A flexible work pattern, evolving on the basis of skill, interest, and availability of persons, rather than springing from traditional age and sex preconceptions, is likely to produce greater dedication to performing the task well, responsiveness to the unique needs of the various members of the household, and spontaneity in pitching in to do a job when emergencies arise; for example, taking over tasks and providing care when a member is not feeling well. Family members are more likely to pitch in and share a variety of tasks if they participate in decisions concerning such matters as kitchen design, selection of health care equipment for the household, schedules for meals and use of bathrooms, food preparation, and standards of health practice to be maintained in the family. This rationale seems strongest when applied to those health maintenance activities that depend on having the family work together cooperatively, such as in setting bathroom schedules, feeding activities, and exercise.

In contrast to the position presented here, there is a considerable body of literature, based largely on psychoanalytic theory, which contends that clear sex differentiation in tasks and power is an almost universal feature of the family, and a pattern which functions best for members. Parsons and Bales (1955) have proposed that male and female areas of responsibility within the family are clearly differentiated on an "instrumental-expressive" axis, with the male specializing in instrumental functions—relating to external social systems and external goal-objects, and the female specializing in expressive functions—handling the internal affairs of the family, maintaining integrative relations between the members, and regulating tension levels.

The rationale for this position, as stated by Westley and Epstein (1969, p. 32), is:

"The family with a culturally approved type of organization (division of labor and pattern of authority) is one in which the members feel culturally approved and rewarded." Further, "The family, like other parts of society, profits from the specialization permitted by a division of labor, and also from the clarification of responsibility and the greater motivation to work incidental to this kind of organization."

On the basis of this reasoning, the failure of parents to maintain their gender-linked roles has been proposed, variously, as a central feature in the etiology of schizophrenia in the offspring (Mischler and Waxler 1968), of juvenile delinquency (Pollak and Friedman 1969), of emotional problems in adults and children, and of sexual maladjustment in adults (Westley and Epstein 1969).

Regular and Varied Interaction Among Family Members

A fourth element in the energized family model that fosters personal health practices of the members is a pattern of regular, frequent, and varied forms of interaction among all the members, specifically including father-child as well as mother-child and husband-wife interaction. This encompasses joint participation in tasks and in leisure, structured and unstructured events, and physical activity as well as verbal and nonverbal communication. This concept is the core of what has been described as the companionship family by Burgess and Locke, a form which is distinguished by "emphasis on intimate interpersonal association as its primary function" (Burgess et al. 1963, pp. 525–526).

Price (1968) stated as a fundamental rule of organizational functioning that organizations which have a high degree of communication are more likely to have high degrees of effectiveness than those which have a low degree of communication. This proposition can be applied to the family's capacity to foster its members' health practices.

Some health maintenance practices are essentially social behavior in that they are acted out with other people in a social setting. This is most characteristic of feeding and exercise. Feeding requires that planners, buyers, cookers, servers, cleaners, and eaters interact if human nutrition is to be adequate. The family serves as the essential team for much of its members' regular exercise; for example, hunting and fishing have specifically been found to be family sports (Sofranko and Nolan 1972).

Most health care activity is performed on the shared premises and with the common equipment of the household. This requires awareness of the schedules and needs of other members, which can come only from regular give and take. Many practices rely on exchange of technical information. Encouragement and support are needed to sustain the individual's constancy in carrying out monotonous, rigorous, and even unpleasant health routines. In these several ways, a dynamic family network serves as a social partnership for carrying out personal health care practices.

It is possible that a high level of family interaction is not in itself a sufficient positive force for promoting members' health practices without other aspects of the energized family pattern. Slater (1962) has pointed out that a high degree of mutual involvement of family members can turn out to be "intrusiveness." Thus, a high degree of family interaction is likely to have the strongest positive effect on members' health practices within a context of individual freedom, for the members' contacts are then supportive and facilitating rather than overwhelming and limiting.

Regular Links with the Broader Community

An essential feature of the energized family model is the dynamic ties that the family maintains with the broader community through participation by all family members in external groups and activities that bear on the family's needs. This includes membership, leadership, and active participation by all family members in clubs, organizations, and community groups; extensive use of the society's varied resources; and exposure through travel to alternative ways of life, activities, and resources.

The rationale is grounded in systems theory. Any social system must have a movement of information and activity into and out of its boundaries if it is to perform its functions or accomplish its goals. Interchanges between a system and its environment are an essential factor underlying the system's viability, continuity, and ability to adapt (Buckley 1967). Thus, open systems, in which inflow and outflow may be rather freely conducted by any member of the system, are more adaptive than closed systems, in which the system's gatekeepers rigidly limit and screen exchanges across the boundaries.

The family alone cannot serve all its members' needs without enrichment from other sources. The self-enclosed unit cages its members; if it feeds on itself incessantly, it deteriorates to an ineffectual unit (Birdwhistell 1966). To be effective, a family needs to initiate and promote growth-producing relationships in the neighborhood, town, and wider society (Otto 1963). Thus, we propose that social participation can contribute to family health practices by developing awareness of alternative courses of action, increasing the flow of information into the family, encouraging receptiveness to new ideas, and increasing understanding of the importance of sound health and the value of self-directed action for promoting health.

There is little research evidence concerning this proposal. Apparently, active community participation fosters sound nutritional practices. Boek (1956) reported that men who were active in the formal organizational life of a community had diets containing greater amounts of calcium and a greater variety of foods than those who participated less. Less food aversion was found among children with extensive contacts and activities outside the home (Smith et al. 1955).

While participation in the broader community is viewed here as an aspect of family structure and functioning, more typically, social participation has been regarded as *nonfamily* activity, as separate or distinct from and sometimes competitive with the family. This frame of reference is reflected in the literature which attempts to demonstrate the loss of influence of the family to other social institutions and to peer groups.

The rationale for the importance of family links to the broader community will be discussed more fully in connection with the use of professional medical services, where it is thought to exert a major influence.

ENERGIZED PATTERN OF FAMILY HEALTH CARE

The composite pattern of health practices performed in a given family constitutes an essential part of the living arrangements in that family, and is experienced by members as an integral aspect of their life in the family. In some families, in which all members tend to be conscientious, resourceful, careful, and enlightened in their personal health practices, the composite picture can be called an energized pattern of family health care. Members experience this climate of energized health behavior in somewhat the same way that they experience various elements of the energized pattern of family structure.

For example, a member of such a family experiences the way in which the others integrate teeth cleaning after meals into their activity pattern, pack a good lunch to avoid vending machine food, practice restraint in eating fatty foods, and exercise faithfully. A member can see that the others are actually able to accomplish these things and that these practices produce some desired effects, such as muscle tone or desired body weight. Members also pick up practical tactics for eliminating obstacles to good health practices; for example, how a stopped-up drain is cleared or how nutritious snack foods are made more accessible than sweets.

Thus, persons who live in families with generally energized patterns of personal health care will have better personal health practices than those living in nonenergized health care environments.

RESEARCH RESULTS

We will now present the research results concerning the hypothesis that personal health practices of members of energized families are significantly better than the practices of members of nonenergized families. The analysis is based on the sample of 273 families of mothers, fathers, and children. A considerable amount of statistical evidence will be presented for the benefit of readers who wish to learn how the conclusions were arrived at.

MEASUREMENT OF PERSONAL HEALTH PRACTICES

As defined here, personal health practices comprise all body care activities, including protection and development of the body's capacities and resources. Health care performed by medical professionals is excluded from personal health practices and will be examined separately. The principal measure of personal health practices is a composite index of practices in seven health care areas: sleep, exercise, elimination, dental hygiene, smoking, alcohol, and nutrition. There are also separate indexes for each of the seven health care areas. (These are described in the Appendix.)

THE DIMENSIONS OF FAMILY STRUCTURE AND HEALTH PRACTICES

The first objective in the analysis is to determine whether each of the separate family structure dimensions is related to the personal health practices of family members as hypothesized. The statistical technique used to accomplish this is the correlation coefficient (r). A positive correlation indicates that a relationship was in the direction hypothesized—a highly energized family pattern associated with sound health practices, while a negative r tends to refute the hypothesis. In this sample, a correlation coefficient of .10 is statistically significant at the .05 level, which is the level of confidence accepted for use here. Table 5–1 shows the correlations between each of the family structure indexes and the health practices of children, men, women, and the composite practices of the three family members.

The various dimensions of family structure were generally found to be related to the personal health practices of family members as hypothesized, although some aspects of family structure were more influential than others.

Regular Interaction Among Members Although the correlations are not extremely large, there is a consistent and statistically significant tendency for regular and varied interaction among family members, including interaction between husband and wife and between both parents and the child, to be associated with sound health practices of all family members.

The extent of the man's interaction in the family was especially important. In fact, the rates of husband-wife and father-child interaction were more important to women's health practices than women's own interaction with children. Father-child interaction had more influence on the overall health practices of the combined family than did mother-child interaction. This suggests that deep involvement of the man in family activities supports the wife, for she then does not have to bear by herself the responsibility for internal family operations, as tends to occur in traditional family structure.

Freedom and Responsiveness A high degree of autonomy and a high degree of support for the child were both associated with good health practices in children. Indeed, support for the child also showed a positive relationship to parents' health practices. The index of aversive control, or punishment, was not related to children's health practices. It appears that positive fostering of autonomy and individuality has the constructive effect hypothesized, but the amount of punishment does not have the negative effect on children's development of sound health behavior that was hypothesized. The one measure of freedom-control for adults—extent of obstructive conflict between husband and wife—was significantly related to women's health practices but not to men's.

Table 5–1.   *Relationship of the Dimensions of Family Structure to Personal Health Practices of Men, Women, Children, and the Combined Family**

| | Personal Health Practices | | | |
Dimensions of Family Structure	Men	Women	Children	Combined Family**
Interaction				
Husband-wife interaction	.26	.22	.20	.20
Father-child interaction	.23	.26	.26	.26
Mother-child interaction	.11	.14	.26	.18
Combined parent-child interaction	.23	.21	.30	.26
Freedom and Responsiveness				
Child autonomy	.12	.05	.34	.22
Support (by parents)	.14	.14	.24	.19
Aversive control (by parents)	.01	−.10	.00	−.01
Obstructive conflict between husband and wife	.10	.19	.13	.22
Coping Effort				
Health training efforts by parents	.26	.13	.21	.25
Household health facilities	.15	.19	.24	.22
Child's health care equipment	.10	.15	.18	.16
Child's exercise equipment	.10	.19	.22	.19
Links to Community				
Man's/woman's community participation	.05	.16	.14	.11
Child's community participation	.11	.14	.35	.21
Cultural participation by family	.22	.13	.18	.19
Combined family extramural interaction	.17	.26	.26	.33
Role Structure				
Conjugal power	.13	.13	.02	.15
Conjugal division of tasks	.22	.12	.04	.17

* Correlation coefficients of .10 are significant at the .05 level. A positive correlation indicates that the relationship was in the direction hypothesized: an energized family pattern associated with sound health practices.

** The combined family health practices index is a composite of the three family members' health practices scores.

Active Coping Effort   Parents' health training efforts were related positively to the health practices of the parents, as well as to those of the children. This is in line with the rationale of our study, for it is the energy which is directed toward problem-solving that contributes to the development of sound health practices. Thus, the parents' efforts to assist their children not only express this problem-solving tendency, but also nourish the parents' efforts to cope with their own health needs. Since the fathers' health training efforts have an especially strong influence on their own health practices, this suggests that it is the involvement of men in internal family functioning which is the underlying reason that their health habits are favorably affected. Women, on the other hand, who are inevitably deeply involved in internal family operations, do not require further deepening of their participation in order to have sound health habits.

Family Links to the Community The extent to which the members of a family participated in activities and organizations outside the home was significantly and positively related to the personal health practices of all three members. The effect of external social participation was somewhat different for men than it was for women and children.

All types of extrafamilial participation were positively related to women's and children's health practices. But men's participation in community organizations was not significantly related to their own health practices. It is likely that the normal, job-related participation of men provides sufficient expansion of their horizons so that additional participation in voluntary organizations would not contribute further to their health practices. Whatever men might gain from community participation to bolster their health practices is redundant of the employment experience. On the other hand, extensive *cultural* participation, which represents a type of enrichment not found in jobs, was found to be significantly related to men's health practices.

The usual social situation for women and children is quite different from that of men. Since women and children have generally tended to be more homebound, the energizing that they require is to get into appropriate external systems, away from the restrictiveness of home and family. The energizing required by men, on the other hand, consists of becoming more involved in internal family functioning. Thus, interaction with family members and active coping with internal family health matters were found to be more critical for men's than for women's health practices. Participation in external social systems was more crucial for women's and children's health practices than for men's.

Role Structure Both flexible division of tasks and egalitarian power were correlated with the health practices of men and women. Though statistically significant, the correlations are not large. Conjugal role structure was not related significantly to children's health practices.

RELATIONSHIP OF FAMILY STRUCTURE TO SPECIFIC HEALTH PRACTICES

The measure of personal health practices employed in the analysis so far has been the composite index of practices in sleep, exercise, elimination, teeth, smoking, alcohol, and nutrition. Examination of the relationships between family structure and each of the separate health practice areas showed that it was in the areas of exercise, elimination, and dental hygiene that family structure had the strongest influence.

Interaction among family members and links of family members to the community were the aspects of family structure most closely related to exercise habits. Of all the health practices, exercise may be the one that is most dependent on stimulating and reliable companionship, within as well as outside the family.

Elimination and dental hygiene practices, on the other hand, are not companionate activities, but they are social nonetheless. These practices require convenient and efficient facilities, considerate sharing of the facilities, exchange of technical information concerning problems and procedures, and encouragement. Thus, active coping effort and interaction among family members were the dimensions of family structure found to be most closely associated with good elimination and dental hygiene practices.

We had thought that nutrition practices would be significantly influenced by interaction among members, active coping effort, and flexible role structure, but found very little support for this in the correlations.

RELATIVE IMPORTANCE OF VARIOUS FAMILY STRUCTURE DIMENSIONS

Another objective of the analysis is to determine the relative influence of the various aspects of family structure on personal health practices. We used stepwise regression analysis to determine this. The results are shown in Table 5–2 for men, women, children, and the combined family trio.[1] This table ranks the family structure indexes in order of their influence on health practices.

It can be seen that the rank ordering of the indexes is different for children, men, and women. The most important influence on children's health practices is their community participation, followed by their autonomy and parent-child interaction. For women, the most important influence is father-child interaction, followed by obstructive conflict between husband and wife and community participation. For men, the first ranked variable is husband-wife interaction, followed by coping effort, the child's autonomy, and father-child interaction.

This statistical evidence reveals the interdependence of family members. Personal health practices depend upon the structure of relationships among all the members. The influence of a particular structured relationship reverberates beyond the person or persons directly involved; for example, father-child interaction influenced women's health practices, and the child's autonomy was bound up with men's health practices. The findings also show that

---

[1] Each regression coefficient represents the amount of change in the dependent variable (health practices) that is associated with a change in one of the independent variables (husband-wife interaction, for example), with the remaining independent (family structure) variables held constant (Blalock 1960). See the column headed *Standardized Regression Coefficients*. The *p* (probability) column indicates the level of statistical significance for each coefficient.

it is truly family structuring which is at work rather than simply the interdependence that might occur in any intimate group. The influence that a structural pattern has on health practices differs depending on the person's family role. Thus, men's health practices are best when men are drawn deeply and productively into the internal operations of the family—through interaction with wife and child and through coping with family health matters. Men's habits, however, are not affected substantially by community participation. On the other hand, emancipation from the confines of house and

Table 5–2. *Stepwise Regression Analysis of the Relationship of Family Structure to Personal Health Practices of Men, Women, Children, and the Combined Family*

Independent Variable	Multiple R	R^2	Changes in R^2	Standardized Regression Coefficients	F Ratios	p	Simple r with Dependent Variable
Men							
Husband-wife interaction	.26	.07	.07	.11	20.1	.001	.26
Health training by father	.34	.11	.04	.09	13.2	.001	.26
Father's encouragement of child's autonomy	.36	.13	.01	.12	4.5	.01	.14
Child's autonomy	.37	.14	.01	.12	3.6	.01	.12
Father-child interaction	.38	.15	.01	.07	2.7	.05	.23
Women							
Father-child interaction	.26	.07	.07	.77	20.0	.001	.26
Obstructive conflict between husband and wife	.31	.09	.03	.14	7.7	.001	.19
Women's community participation	.34	.11	.02	.13	6.0	.001	.16
Parent-child interaction	.35	.12	.01	−.95	1.6	.ns	.26
Mother-child interaction	.37	.13	.02	.45	4.7	.001	.14
Husband-wife interaction	.37	.14	.01	.07	1.7	.ns	.22

Table 5–2. *Continued*

	Children						
Independent Variable	Multiple R	R^2	Changes in R^2	Standardized Regression Coefficients	F Ratios	p	Simple r with Dependent Variable
Child's community participation	.35	.12	.12	.19	38.2	.001	.35
Child's autonomy	.44	.20	.07	.24	24.6	.001	.34
Parent-child interaction	.48	.23	.04	.15	12.5	.001	.30
Participation in community groups and organizations	.50	.25	.02	.13	6.6	.001	.12
Supportiveness of parents	.52	.27	.02	.12	6.8	.001	.24
Obstructive conflict between parents	.53	.28	.01	.10	3.7	.01	.13
Health training by father	.54	.29	.01	.06	2.7	.01	.18

	Combined Family						
Independent Variable	Multiple R	R^2	Changes in R^2	Standardized Regression Coefficients	F Ratios	p	Simple r with Dependent Variable
Parent-child interaction	.26	.07	.07	.12	20.2	.001	.26
Child's autonomy	.34	.11	.05	.14	13.9	.001	.22
Health training by father	.39	.15	.04	.15	12.2	.001	.25
Obstructive conflict between husband and wife	.44	.19	.04	.21	12.4	.001	.22
Supportiveness by father	.44	.21	.02	.16	5.9	.001	.18
Health care facilities	.48	.23	.02	.12	6.5	.001	.22
Child's health equipment	.48	.24	.01	.09	2.6	.01	.16
Conjugal power	.49	.24	.01	.07	2.5	.05	.15
Supportiveness by parents	.50	.25	.01	.08	2.4	.05	.19

family through links to the broader community are important influences on women's and children's health practices.

The structural patterns that have the most important positive influence on health practices are all in sharp contrast to the structural patterns of traditional families. Ties of women and children to the broader community have a more favorable influence on their health practices than does restriction of women and children to house and family. Deep and productive involvement of men in internal family operations has a more favorable influence on all members' health practices than does the traditional pattern of greater isolation of men from internal family functioning. A high degree of autonomy for children and a tendency to encourage their individuality is more favorable to children's health practices, and to their fathers' as well, than the traditional tendency for children to be clearly subordinated to adults and constrained to conform to prescribed codes. Creative problem-solving and active coping contribute more to all members' health practices than the application of traditional formulas in family operations.

The stepwise regression analysis also reveals that conjugal power and division of tasks did not exert a significant influence on the health practices of men and women after the influence of the other indexes had been taken into account, even though the correlations show both to be related to men's and women's health practices. This is not to say that power and division of tasks have no influence; it means that whatever influence they may have is reflected in the other structural measures.

Combined Influence of the Energized Family Dimensions

The stepwise regression analysis also reveals the *combined* influence of the several dimensions of family structure on the health practices of men, women, children, and the composite family group. The R^2 column in Table 5–2 indicates the proportion of the total variance in health practices that is accounted for by the family structure indexes. The first figure listed in this column indicates what proportion of the variance in health practices is explained by the family structure index that ranked first, and each subsequent figure in the column shows cumulatively what proportion of the variance is accounted for by the combination of structure indexes. Thus, the last figure listed in the R^2 column indicates that the whole combination of energized family indexes accounts for about 29 percent of the total variance in children's health practices, 14 percent of women's, 15 percent of men's, and 25 percent of the total variance in the family group's combined health practices. This means that differences in family structure account for one-fourth of all the variance in the health practices of family groups, while three-fourths of the variance is due to other factors.

We are clearly able to account for more of the variance in health practices with the combination of energized indexes than by any one index alone. This lends support to the energized family model.

The data also indicate that the pattern of family structure is significantly related to the composite health practices of the *family group,* as well as to the health practices of individual members. The energized form tends to work more effectively for the whole family unit than a nonenergized pattern. The consistent influence of the energized pattern on all members may come about not only because this type of structure develops the capabilities of the individual members, but also because the resources of the family group serve the members as a unit. Such group resources as the pool of skills, the household plant and equipment, and the communication network are at the disposal of all members of the family.

It is notable that men's health practices are influenced by family patterns to as great an extent as women's. Much of the research literature suggested that women are more subject to family influence than men (for example, problems in family relations have been reported to have a greater bearing on female crime and delinquency than is true for males), and that work is a more important source of influence on men.

The greater overall relationship of family structure to children's than to men's or women's health habits probably reflects the fact that children have not been exposed to various sources of influence outside the family over a long time period. Adults' practices have been molded by sources other than their present family, including their family of origin, and they have been subject to such influences over an extended period.

Family Health Behavior: An Energized Pattern of Health Care

This evidence that an energized pattern of family structure tends to affect favorably all the members' health practices suggests that the *combined health behavior* of all family members may be regarded as a further dimension of the family's pattern of living. Families in which all the members tend to care for their health in a conscientious and enlightened manner may be viewed as having an energized pattern of family health care.

By analyzing the data in this way, we found that the health practices of each member are related to those of the other members. We can account for 11 percent of the total variance in women's and children's health practices and 14 percent of the total variance in men's health practices by the health practices of the other two family members. The health practices of the members of a family apparently do constitute a dynamic aspect of the living arrangements within the family.

Let us then extend the concept of the energized pattern of family life to include an energized pattern of health behavior, as well as an energized structuring of relationships. When the family health practices environment—the health practices of the other two family members—is combined with the structure of family relationships, there is a significant increase in the variance explained in each member's personal health practices. The increase is from 15 to 23 percent of the explained variance in men's health practices, from 14 to 18 percent of the explained variance in women's health practices, and from 29 to 31 percent of the explained variance in children's health practices.

Percent of Total Variance
Accounted for by Family Structure
and Family Health Practices

Men	23
Women	18
Children	31

A favorable health practices environment in the family makes a particularly important contribution to men's health practices. Both their wives' and their children's health behavior contribute to men's health practices. The health care environment in the family also influences the personal practices of women and children, but it is the men's practices that are the most significant aspect of that environment. Fathers' health practices have more of an impact on children's practices than do mothers' health practices; and husbands' health practices are more important to wives than their children's health habits. These findings reinforce the earlier findings on family structure which showed that a crucial aspect of the energized form which distinguishes it from traditional families is the deeper involvement of men in internal family functioning.

We conclude that an energized style of family life, including both an energized structuring of family relationships and an energized mode of family health behavior, functions more effectively to support members' efforts to care for their health than does a nonenergized life-style.

CONTROL FOR SOCIOECONOMIC STATUS

The relationships found between the energized family pattern and health practices of family members were not due to the influence of socioeconomic status (SES). We had to suspect this possibility because SES is often related to health behavior, as well as to such aspects of family organization as marital conflict and child-rearing practices.

By using an index of SES which combined husband's education and family income, we found that SES correlated with personal health practices:

	Correlation Between SES and Personal Health Practices
Mothers' practices	.14
Fathers'	.21
Children's	.09
Total family's	.12

But when SES was held constant, every family variable that was related to the personal health practices of fathers, mothers, and children remained significantly correlated. In fact, SES contributed nothing to the total explained variance in health practices beyond what was already accounted for by the family structure indexes alone.

ALTERNATIVE INTERPRETATIONS

While our research results tend to support the hypothesis that an energized family form is associated with a higher level of personal health practices than a nonenergized or traditional form, the analysis can be pressed further in order to interpret how this influence operates. The rationale proposed that the energized family accomplished this because it developed the competence of members for taking care of themselves and backed them up with the social and physical resources of the group. But there are competing explanations of how the family affects health behavior. One explanation is based on the idea that high family integration prevents alienation and thereby reduces the tendency to self-destructive health practices. A second explanation is that certain family forms are more successful than others in socializing members to adhere to health behavior norms. Some limited tests were made of these alternative interpretations, using data available in our study.

FAMILY INTEGRATION AND MINI-SUICIDES

In the early stages of our study, we made an attempt to apply the body of theory concerning social integration and suicide to account for the relationship between family structure and health practices. This model proposed that a low degree of family integration is associated with a high degree of alienation among family members; and poorly integrated families fail to provide members with a sufficient coefficient of preservation against self-neglectful and self-destructive health practices—what can be termed *mini-suicide* behavior. In this rationale, some of the family structure measures (such as high interaction and low conflict) are interpreted to be measures of level of family integration, and the health practices measures to represent the extent of self-destructive or self-preservative behavior.

Evidence to support this interpretation would have to show, first, that high scores on the family integration measures were associated with low alienation among family members; second, that alienation of members was related to poor health practices; and third, that alienation was an intervening variable which accounted for some of the relationship between family integration and mini-suicide behavior.

The first step in our test did show, as required by the rationale, that the family integration measures were related to an index of alienation of family members. A low level of parent-child interaction, husband-wife interaction, and egalitarian power, and a high level of husband-wife conflict and role segregation were all significantly related to a high level of alienation of family members.

But we did not find alienation related to any type of health practice in the manner required by the model—not even to smoking or alcohol consumption. In order for the mini-suicide model to be supported, it was essential to find that smoking and high alcohol consumption were associated with a high level of alienation, because these practices can plausibly be regarded as active self-destructive behavior, more plausibly than, say, inadequate dental hygiene or failure to exercise, which appear to reflect passive neglect to a greater extent than active self-destruction.

Since the evidence failed to support in any way the notion that alienation is associated with harmful health practices, the mini-suicide model cannot account for the relationship found between the family structure measures and personal health practices.

Another competing explanation of how family structure affects health practices is based on the conception that faulty health practices are a reflection of inadequate socialization and constitute a form of deviant behavior. Such an approach has commonly been taken with regard to use of psychoactive drugs and alcohol. Within this framework it has been proposed that the form of family structure which results in a low risk of drug experimentation by children is one characterized by firm parental discipline and conventionality (Blum 1972).

Although no information is available in our study on use of psychoactive drugs or alcohol by children, our data do permit a test of the relationship between a disciplinary-conventional style of parenthood and a variety of other types of health practices. Much of the relevant evidence has already been reported in the present chapter. We found that granting autonomy to children, parental responsiveness to the child's uniqueness, and a tendency to use reasons and explanations in relations with children were associated with a higher level of overall health practices among children, including a lower tendency to smoke cigarettes, than were parental control and firm adherence to conventional standards.

Thus, there are data from other research which indicate that a disciplinary-conventional style of parenthood serves to insulate children against drug use, and our data which indicate that this style of parenthood is associated with poorer health practices of various sorts. The disciplinary-conventional family form may succeed in preventing drug experimentation precisely because it tends to produce children who are more conformist, less likely to explore, and more dependent and responsive to authority, as are their parents. For these same reasons, children from disciplinary-conventional families may also be less likely to care adequately for their general health and physical development. They lack both the required personal commitment to goals of full personal development and the capability of assuming responsibility for their own performance. Regardless of what family forces result in drug abstinence, our findings on health practices cannot be adequately interpreted in terms of socialization of children to behavioral norms, for the disciplinary-conventional family is not the form that results in a high level of personal health care.

CONCLUSIONS

We found that an energized pattern of family structure worked more effectively to foster members' efforts to care for their health than a nonenergized, traditional pattern. The family form that fosters members' health practices may be characterized as follows: All members are actively engaged in varied and regular interaction with each other; the family has ties to the broader community through the active participation of its members; there is a high degree of autonomy and a tendency to encourage individuality; and the family engages in creative problem-solving and active coping. The superiority of this form over the traditional form in fostering health behavior is evident by the fact that it is precisely in those dimensions in which the energized family diverges most sharply from the traditional form that it provides its most significant contributions to members' health behavior. It is men's deep involvement in internal family functioning, rather than the more traditional deep involvement of women and children, that contributes most significantly to the health practices of the whole family. It is women's and children's health practices, rather than men's, that are fostered by autonomy and community participation, another nontraditional structural pattern.

SIX

The Energized Family and Use of Professional Health Services

OUR HYPOTHESIS IS THAT members of energized families will use professional medical services more effectively than members of nonenergized or traditional families. This chapter first discusses the rationale and then presents the results of an empirical test of the hypothesis. Tests of two alternative interpretations of the data are also reported.

THE RATIONALE

The energized family form is expected to foster the effective use of professional medical services by family members by enhancing the capability of the individual members and the whole unit for taking care of their needs, particularly by equipping them to deal effectively with formal technical systems and by encouraging active coping effort.

The process by which the energized family fosters the effective use of professional medical services is the same, in certain respects, as the process for personal health practices, for both require competence in taking care of personal health needs. But the dynamics differ somewhat because the use of professional services entails negotiations with formal agencies and professional personnel.

REGULAR LINKS WITH THE BROADER COMMUNITY

The dimension of the energized family model that is expected to have the greatest bearing on the effectiveness of members' use of professional medical services is the systematic and extensive ties between the family and the broader community through the participation of all members in groups and activities that bear on the family's needs. This includes membership, leadership, and active participation by all family members in clubs, organizations, and community groups; extensive use of the society's varied resources; and exposure through travel to alternative ways of life, activities, and resources. Such links between the family and other social systems are considered essential if the individual members and the family unit are to develop and maintain the capability and resources that are needed for successful transactions with technical and formally organized systems, such as the modern health service system.

Inkeles (1966, pp. 280–281) has described the kind of competence that is required to perform effectively in a highly differentiated social structure:

"Effective participation in modern industrial and urban society requires certain levels of skill in the manipulation of language and other symbol systems, such as arithmetic and time; the ability to comprehend and complete forms; information as to when and where to go for what; skills in interpersonal relations which permit negotiation, insure protection of one's interests, and provide maintenance of stable and satisfying relations with intimates, peers, and authorities; motives to achieve, to master, to persevere; ... a cognitive style which permits thinking in concrete terms while still permitting reasonable handling of abstractions and general concepts; a mind which does not insist on excessively premature closure, is tolerant of diversity, and has some components of flexibility; a conative style which facilitates reasonably regular, steady, and persistent effort."

For the individual, opportunities for expanded social experience through exposure to heterogeneous groups of people, varied activities, causes and ideas, and various styles of social relationships provide greater scope for self-actualization, greater tolerance for ambiguity, and greater capability in handling oneself (Hausknecht 1962). Active participants can develop an understanding of social processes—how the community and its institutions operate, how things are done, how power is exercised, and who has power. Community participation also develops the ability and readiness to manipulate social agencies for achieving one's own ends. Persons who participate in organizations are more likely to report being competent to influence their government than nonparticipants. Active participants also attempt to influence local government by organizing a group; arousing friends and neighbors and getting them to write letters, protest, or sign petitions; or independently contacting political leaders or the press (Almond and Verba 1963).

Participation in the organizations and affairs of the broader community is, in important respects, a matter of *family* participation, rather than simply participation by separate individuals; and the consequences of that participation are felt both on the family group and on individual members. The family serves to mobilize and direct the participation of its members, encouraging some types of activities and memberships, and discouraging others. The social participation of an individual is to a considerable degree a function of the participation of the family, for if husbands participate, wives usually do; and if husbands and wives participate, children usually do. In many organizations a participant represents the family. The whole family may jointly take part in certain community activities. Thus, participation of members in community organizations and activities can be considered a dimension of family structure in the sense that, in varying degrees, families structure and mobilize their relations with other social systems.

The consequences of these family ties to the community constitute an integral part of the family's resources and capabilities. It is not only that the behavior of individual members is affected, but also that the family unit functions differently when its members are deeply involved in the community than when they are not. The family achieves a network of contacts with community resources through its members' participation, which the whole family can draw on. The know-how of negotiating with particular organizations can be shared. The confidence in having the ability to manipulate successfully the community's agencies, and the realization that personal needs can be satisfied by transactions with community agencies create a feeling of assurance that pervades some families, just as a feeling of impotence and resignation in the face of a seemingly hostile and intractable social structure spreads through other families. A family that has developed expertise and assertiveness in community affairs can, by using its united influence and skills, manipulate a variety of organizations on behalf of its members. Its power to influence far exceeds that which its separate members would have if acting independently.

This is not to suggest that most families systematically plan and develop their participation in the broader community to enhance their power to stand up to outside agencies on behalf of their members. Vincent (1966) has pointed out that the family has typically *adapted* to the demands of other institutions by taking on tasks they refused to perform, responding to demands as to how to socialize and control its members, and adapting its own schedules and ways of organizing daily life to the time and organizational patterns of other agencies. Vincent concluded that families have no alternative except to adapt, for they have no power to assert their own demands vis-à-vis other institutions. But Sussman (1972, p. 127) proposed that the family need not respond so passively and, indeed, that it is the family's basic responsibility "to socialize its members for competence in handling the normative demands of bureaucracy, the most central task for the individual in modern society."

Pollack (1967, p. 197) also charged the family with the task of preparing its members for active confrontation with community agencies.

> "The time has arrived when the bureaucratic jungle of government offerings of service in the fields of health, education, and welfare will either produce its professional scouts or force the family to develop these scouting skills in its own membership. From this viewpoint it may be much more important for a father to take his children to a district health office, to a department of welfare, to a large city clinic...than to take him fishing or camping. The fun may not be quite so obvious, the air not so fresh, the father's skill not quite so obviously superior, but the growth in coping capacity and the relevance of information and orientation to our world derived from such expeditions are likely to be considerably greater."

The evidence tends to substantiate that extensive ties between the family and the community do contribute to the members' capacity for negotiating with the formal health system. The use of health services was found to be positively related to organizational membership (Cornely and Bigman 1963; Moody and Gray 1972). A study of poor women, for example, found that failure to obtain postpartum checkups and immunizations for new babies is significantly associated with social isolation (Bullough 1972). Several writers have attempted to account for the more inadequate and irregular use of medical services by the lower socioeconomic group than by higher SES groups on the basis of the narrower range of experience and lack of penetration into community structure by the poor, and their consequent inability to deal successfully with bureaucratic organizations (Rainwater 1968; McKinlay 1973; Cohen and Hodges 1963; Irelan 1965). Pomeroy concludes that "medical utilization is but one manifestation of overall utilization and 'participation' in the larger society and its personal and social resources" (Pomeroy, 1970, p. 87).

ACTIVE COPING EFFORT

The family's community participation contributes to, and is reinforced by, another feature of energized family structure—active coping effort. This is the tendency of families to approach life by creative problem-solving and by efforts to develop mastery and control over events, rather than by application of standardized formulas and passive submission to events.

There are bits and pieces of evidence which indicate that the active coping tendency is related to effective use of medical services. One concrete indicator of coping effort is possession of tools needed to make a preliminary diagnosis of illness. Families that possess a clinical thermometer use professional health services significantly more than families that lack this tool (Pomeroy 1970). Persons who have a general motivation to exert control over their environment by their own resources are more likely to seek out and accept medical care, specifically, influenza inoculations, than persons who are not strongly motivated to exert control (Dabbs and Kirscht 1971). A study of Aberdeen families also concluded that families who use maternity care services tend to have control over their lives and to plan for their future lives, while families who underuse the services sustain a crisis existence (McKinlay and McKinlay 1972).

Hospital patients with a sense of personal mastery obtain more information about their condition (tuberculosis) from medical personnel than patients with a sense of powerlessness (Seeman and Evans 1962). Patients who feel powerless are inhibited from seeking and getting information because of their orientation that life is uncontrollable, that those in power run things, and that average people don't have much influence. This tendency is accentuated in highly stratified hospital wards, for patients who feel that their progress could be managed by themselves rather than by some external control or by fate have a particularly great advantage in dealing forcefully with a highly stratified system.

A number of writers have attributed the relatively inadequate use of medical services by the poor to the more passive life orientation of this group compared to higher socioeconomic groups. As Irelan (1965, p. 6) interpreted:

> "The diffuse fatalistic feeling of powerlessness which informs so strongly the relationships of the poor to the rest of society is embodied most pathetically in resignation to illness. It is often regarded as unavoidable . . . For example, one finds very often the idea that total loss of teeth is ultimately inevitable."

This tendency to cope actively or to submit passively, which has so frequently been regarded as a feature that distinguishes various social classes, also distinguishes various families.

REGULAR AND VARIED INTERACTION AMONG MEMBERS

Taking care of one's health is a social matter in the sense that it requires dedication, effort, skill, determination, and perseverance, which can be sustained only in a context of supportive social relationships. Second, it is social in the sense that it entails complex and sometimes perilous transactions with service agencies, which require the backing of family or other close associates. Family members may help in decision making about whether and when to seek service, selecting an appropriate source, scheduling appointments, transporting and chaperoning, and generally negotiating and transacting the service relationship.

Life in a family does make a difference in the quantity of medical services used. Married persons in a comprehensive health plan average a larger number of medical visits than single, widowed, divorced, or separated persons (Avnet 1967). To be sure, many factors other than sound health care practice may be involved in this difference, but one factor may be that the married have the advantage of supportive family interaction. These comparisons of the married with the nonmarried only suggest that interaction is what makes the difference. Unfortunately, there appear to have been no direct studies of the effect of level of interaction among the members of intact families on their use of professional health services.

FLEXIBLE AND EGALITARIAN STRUCTURING OF RELATIONSHIPS

A flexible division of labor and shared decision making within the family are also expected to facilitate the family's transactions with the professional health care system. The potential advantages of structural flexibility were discussed in some detail in connection with personal health care practices in the home. Briefly, we think this pattern produces greater responsiveness to the special needs of each member and fosters spontaneity in pitching in to do jobs that need to be done.

These advantages apply with special relevance to the family's use of professional services, because transactions with health agencies require cooperation and mutual assistance of a high order. In the flexible pattern, various members at different times are able to make the arrangements for medical care—selecting the service; making appointments; transporting; coping with medical personnel, forms, procedures and machinery, and with financial and insurance arrangements; and securing and administering medications and other therapy (Pratt 1972). Such adaptability facilitates efforts to obtain routine health care, but it may be of overriding importance when care is urgently needed for a seriously ill family member. In contrast, rigid adherence to traditional sex and age patterns of task assignment and decision making stand in the way of having the woman handle the financial aspects of medical care, or having the man or the child tend to the physical needs of ill members of the family.

RESEARCH RESULTS

We will now present the research results concerning our hypothesis that members of energized families use professional medical services more effectively than members of nonenergized families. The procedures used are the same as those employed in testing the influence of family structure on personal health practices.

MEASUREMENT OF USE OF MEDICAL SERVICES

Use of professional medical services consists of applying one's knowledge, skill, energy, will, and effort toward selecting and securing appropriate professional medical advice and services for the purpose of protecting and developing one's bodily capacities and resources, and for promoting healing and rehabilitation for illness or injury. In designing measures to represent the quality of use of medical services, we made an attempt to measure the tendency to obtain appropriate services and the tendency to protect and develop the body in the absence of illness. Sheer quantity of service consumed is not a satisfactory index of quality, because some use may be unnecessary or inappropriate, and because a high consumption of services reflects the tendency to be ill a great deal, as well as careful protection of the body. The index of use of *preventive health services*—the extent of immunizations and examinations in the absence of illness—is our most satisfactory index, and it is the principal measure used to test the hypothesis.

In order to represent discriminating selection of services, a second index measures the extent to which various *specialized* medical services were used when service was needed. A third index represents the extent to which medical attention was obtained for *illness;* it is based on the number of health problems needing care for which medical care was obtained. A fourth index represents *total use* of professional medical services; it combines the extent of use of preventive services, specialized services, and services for health problems.

THE DIMENSIONS OF FAMILY STRUCTURE AND USE OF SERVICES

The first objective is to determine whether the various dimensions of family structure are related significantly to use of medical services, as hypothesized. The correlation coefficients between each of the family structure indexes and use of preventive medical services are shown in Table 6-1.

Family Links to the Community   Participation of men, women, and children in community organizations and activities was associated with a high level of use of preventive medical services, specialized services, services for health problems needing care, and all kinds of services combined, by all family members. This held true for a variety of different indexes of community participation: number of memberships in organizations, participation in cultural activities, and number of different towns traveled to in carrying on various activities. While the correlations are not large, they are statistically significant and form a consistent pattern.

Not only was a given family member's level of outside activity related to

Table 6–1. *Relationship of the Dimensions of Family Structure to Use of Preventive Medical Services by Men, Women, Children, and the Combined Family**

Dimensions of Family Structure	Use of Preventive Medical Services by			
	Men	*Women*	*Children*	*Combined Family***
Links to Community				
Man's community participation	.24	.14	.08	.19
Woman's community participation	.20	.21	.16	.24
Child's community participation	.17	.24	.16	.26
Number of towns man uses	.18	.01	.03	.06
Number of towns woman uses	.20	.30	.15	.27
Variety of child's activities	.19	.20	.18	.25
Cultural participation by family	.21	.22	.28	.31
Combined family extramural participation	.30	.23	.19	.29
Interaction				
Husband-wife interaction	.21	.15	.05	.20
Father-child interaction	.23	.14	.10	.22
Mother-child interaction	.07	.18	.14	.17
Combined family interaction	.14	.14	.03	.14
Coping Effort				
Health training efforts by man	.16	.11	.08	.12
Health training efforts by woman	.16	.11	.18	.19
Health training efforts by both parents	.03	.18	.11	.20
Role Structure				
Conjugal division of tasks of child	.10	.12	.19	.20
health care	.18	.06	.13	.14
Conjugal division of tasks (overall)	.08	.05	.11	.16
Conjugal power				
Freedom and Responsiveness				
Child autonomy	.06	.03	−.01	.05
Support of child by parents	−.05	.06	.07	.05
Aversive control by parents	.01	−.08	−.11	−.03
Obstructive conflict between husband and wife	.06	−.01	−.04	.01

* Correlation coefficients of .10 are significant at the .05 level. A positive correlation indicates that the relationship was in the direction hypothesized: an energized family pattern associated with high use of preventive services.

** The combined family use of preventive services index is a composite of the three family members' use of services scores.

Table 6–2. *Relationship Between Combined Family Extramural Participation and Combined Family Use of Preventive Medical Services*

Family Use of Preventive Medical Services	Percentages *Family Extramural Participation*				
	Almost None	*Low*	*Medium*	*High*	*Total*
Low	53	37	25	3	34
Medium	22	43	37	44	36
High	25	20	38	53	30
Total (Percent)	100	100	100	100	100
(Number)	(81)	(86)	(72)	(34)	(273)

that member's own use of preventive medical services, but the level of each member's activity was also related to the use of services by each of the other members and by the family as a whole. The relationship of children's activities to their own and to their parents' use of services is especially interesting. While parents' community participation could be expected to contribute directly to their proficiency in negotiating services for children and themselves, children do not negotiate independently for services. Yet children's community experience apparently contributes to the general capability of the family for dealing with the health service system. This is further indicated by the fact that the family's *combined* participation in the community was more closely related to the use of medical services by each individual member than was that member's own community participation. The community participation of each member contributes to the family's pool of resources, and each member benefits from the family's overall resources, as well as from the member's personal community activity. Table 6–2 shows that over half of the families with almost no ties to the community scored low on use of preventive medical services, while only 3 percent of the families with many ties scored low.

As we found in personal health practices, the community participation of women and children had a greater influence on the family's use of preventive medical services than did men's community activity. Since men have traditionally tended to be active in the broader community through their occupational responsibilities, as well as through representing the family in civic affairs, it is the tendency for women and children to become active in community affairs that provide the family with its critical advantage in dealing with service agencies. Unlike the findings for personal health practices, men's community participation was found to have some influence on the family's use of preventive medical services. This might be expected, since the use of medical services requires a distinctive kind of competence; that is, the capability of dealing with a formal and technical system. Thus, the more of this type of expertise that a family develops in all its members, the more proficient it is in such dealings.

Extent and Variety of Interaction Among Family Members   The frequency and variety of activities engaged in jointly by fathers and children, mothers and children, and husbands and wives was consistently related to the effective use of medical services by family members. The correlations are not large, however.

When interaction between a particular pair was high, the preventive services used by both members of that particular pair was consistently high. The remaining member was not necessarily affected, with one exception: the higher the father-child interaction, the greater the use of preventive services by the mothers, as well as by the fathers and children. The broader impact of the father's interaction with his children on the health behavior of the whole family corresponds with the findings for personal health practices. It indicates that a crucial feature of the energized family form that distinguishes it from the traditional pattern is that there is a *balanced* interaction pattern, with high activity between father and child as well as the traditionally high mother-child activity.

Active Coping Behavior   When parents exert much effort to train their children in health matters, use of professional medical services by family members is more effective. Women's health training efforts had more influence on children's and total family use of services than men's health training efforts. In order to engage in extensive health training activity, women must secure materials and information from sources outside the family, for example, pamphlets, books, lectures, films, courses, and consultations, and then apply this information to the satisfaction of family needs. This represents a breakaway from the traditional pattern of dealing with problems by conventional wisdom circulated within the family and the female friendship network. It is this greater involvement by women with the resources and information agencies of the broader community that provides the family with advantages in dealing with the professional medical system.

This interpretation might at first glance appear to contradict the interpretation regarding personal health practices. Men's health training efforts had more influence than women's on personal health practices. This indicated that men's health training efforts represented a greater involvement in *internal* family affairs than is found in the traditional family, and that this internal involvement was responsible for the greater influence of men's health training efforts on family health practices than women's health training efforts. Extensive health training efforts by men and women have different effects within the family because they represent different types of divergence from the traditional roles of men and women. For men, it means more responsible involvement with their children. For women, it represents the use of external sources of information in handling family problems. Hence men's greater involvement in health training is important in fostering personal health practices within the family, while extensive health training efforts by women enhance the family's capabilities for dealing with the formal medical care system.

Flexible-Egalitarian Role Structure Both flexible division of tasks and egalitarian decision making are significantly related to the family's use of preventive medical services. While the correlations between the indexes of general role structure (all types of tasks) and use of preventive services are small, there are consistent relationships with the role structure in health care tasks. Thus, the use of preventive services by all family members tended to be better when there was a flexible role patterning in these tasks: teaching children the proper foods to eat; toilet training; teaching children how to brush their teeth; buying medicines; staying up with sick children; knowing what to do when children are ill or injured; and taking children to the doctor or dentist.

Freedom and Responsiveness This aspect of family organization was not related significantly to the use of medical services. Since the child's autonomy and the parents' support for the child were significantly related to personal health practices, it can only be assumed that this aspect of internal family relationships is not relevant to the family's capability in dealing with formal agencies, but that it is directly relevant to the family's health behavior within the household.

RELATIVE IMPORTANCE OF VARIOUS FAMILY STRUCTURE DIMENSIONS

The results of stepwise regression analysis are presented in Table 6–3 to indicate the relative importance of the various family structure indexes. They also reveal which indexes continued to have an independent influence under control for the others. Only those indexes that made a significant contribution beyond the contribution of the others are listed.

The extent of the family's ties to the community was clearly the dimension of family structure with the strongest influence on the use of preventive medical services by men, women, children, and the combined family. Some one of the indexes of community participation ranked first for each family member's use of services.

For women, extent of family ties to the community took precedence over all other dimensions. Women's health training effort, which indicated the extent to which women use external technical resources, also had an influence on women's use of preventive services. After the influence of these measures had been taken into account, other dimensions of family organization did not have further influence on women's use of services. This does not mean that family interaction and role structure were irrelevant, but only that their influence was reflected in the other, more powerful, family structure measures.

Table 6–3. *Stepwise Regression Analysis of the Relationship of Family Structure to Use of Preventive Medical Services*

Independent Variable	Multiple R	R^2	Changes in R^2	Standardized Regression Coefficients	F Ratios	p	Simple r with Dependent Variable
Men							
Man's community participation	.23	.06	.06	.14	15.8	.001	.24
Father-child interaction	.29	.09	.03	.17	9.0	.001	.23
Woman's community participation	.33	.11	.02	.12	6.6	.001	.20
Variety of child's activities	.34	.12	.01	.11	3.1	.05	.19
Women							
Number of towns woman uses	.30	.09	.09	.24	26.3	.001	.30
Child's community participation	.35	.12	.03	.13	10.6	.001	.24
Cultural participation by family	.38	.14	.02	.15	6.4	.001	.22
Health training efforts by both parents	.40	.16	.01	.12	4.0	.01	.18

For men, the extent of father-child interaction had an influence on use of preventive services in addition to the influence of community activity. Thus, both family penetration of the community and deep involvement of men within the family contributed to men's use of medical services.

Children's services were also influenced by the parents' efforts to provide health training to children. This suggests that parents' attempts to obtain useful information for their children aids the parents' general efforts to cope with technical health agencies on behalf of their children. The flexibility of the parents' arrangements for performing health care tasks in the household

Table 6–3. *Continued*

	Children						
Independent Variable	*Multiple R*	*R^2*	*Changes in R^2*	*Standardized Regression Coefficents*	*F Ratios*	*p*	*Simple r with Dependent Variable*
Cultural participation by family	.28	.08	.08	.22	22.3	.001	.28
Health training efforts by woman	.31	.10	.02	.12	6.8	.01	.18
Conjugal division of task of child health care	.33	.11	.01	.09	2.6	.05	.19
Woman's community participation	.33	.11	.01	.08	1.6	n.s.	.16

	Combined Family						
Independent Variable	*Multiple R*	*R^2*	*Changes in R^2*	*Standardized Regression Coefficents*	*F Ratios*	*p*	*Simple r with Dependent Variable*
Cultural participation by family	.30	.09	.09	.18	27.7	.001	.31
Woman's community participation	.38	.14	.05	.19	16.0	.001	.27
Health training efforts by both parents	.41	.17	.03	.12	8.5	.001	.20
Child's community participation	.43	.19	.02	.14	5.8	.001	.26
Father-child interaction	.45	.20	.01	.10	3.9	.01	.22

had a significant influence on the extent of medical services obtained for children.

The influence of family structure measures on the family's combined use of preventive services provides a summary of these effects. Extensive and varied ties to the community had the strongest influence. The extent of parents' efforts to cope effectively by providing health training to their children and the extent of men's interaction with children also contributed significantly to the family's use of preventive services.

COMBINED INFLUENCE OF THE ENERGIZED FAMILY DIMENSIONS

The cumulative figure in the R^2 column of Table 6–3 reveals that the combination of family structure indexes accounts for about 16 percent of the total variance in women's use of preventive services, 12 percent of men's, 11 percent of children's, and 20 percent of the total variance in the family group's combined use of services.

The combination of indexes accounts for a larger proportion of the total variance in the family's use of preventive services than is accounted for by any one variable alone. The relationship of the energized pattern to the combined family's use of services is much stronger than the relationship to a particular member's services. This lends support to the idea that an energized family model represents a family form with capability for working effectively on behalf of its members' needs.

While our hypothesized family model accounts for a significant amount of the variance in the family's use of preventive health services, a large amount of variance remains unaccounted for. Next, the combined health behavior of the family will be examined as a further dimension of the family's pattern of living to determine whether this contributes further to explained variance in the use of preventive services.

FAMILY HEALTH BEHAVIOR:
AN ENERGIZED PATTERN OF HEALTH CARE

Up to this point the use of medical services has been regarded as the dependent variable, and our objective has been to measure its dependence upon family structure. But the effectiveness of a family's use of medical services and the adequacy of personal health practices can be considered to represent the extent of the family's organized coping effort, and families who cope effectively with health matters could be said to have an energized pattern of health behavior. Thus, family health behavior becomes the independent variable in this hypothesis: the more energized the overall health behavior in a family, the more adequately the individual members will use preventive medical services.

The simple correlations in Table 6–4 indicate that the extent of each family member's use of medical services is significantly related to other family members' utilization pattern. The most significant relationship was between mothers' and children's use of services, indicating, not surprisingly, that mothers obtain services for their children in the same way they obtain services for themselves.

While the level of personal health practices in the family had only a small influence on *individual* use of services, the relationship between family health

Table 6–4. *Relationship of Pattern of Family Health Behavior to the Use of Preventive Medical Services by Family Members*

Pattern of Health Behavior Among Other Family Members	Use of Preventive Medical Services by			
	Men	*Women*	*Children*	*Combined Family*
Man's use of preventive services		.21	.14	
Woman's use of preventive services	.21		.31	
Child's use of preventive services	.14	.32		
Man's personal health practices	.19	.03	.05	.18
Woman's personal health practices	.05	.10	.10	.12
Child's personal health practices	.10	.15	.10	.11
Combined family's health practices				.15
Combined family exercise habits				.22

practices and the combined use of preventive services in the *family* was significant. In particular, exercise was significantly related to the family's use of medical services. Unlike some personal health practices, which are carried on entirely at home, exercise is likely to take family members into community athletic and recreational facilities, and such activities can contribute to the members' capabilities in dealing with external agencies for health care purposes.

A stepwise regression analysis shows that by extending the concept of the energized pattern of family life to include the use of services by other family members and the personal health practices of all family members, we can increase our ability to account for variance in the use of preventive services from 12 to 15 percent of the variance in men's use of services, from 11 to 17 percent for children, and from 16 to 22 percent for women. The proportion of total explained variance in the family's combined use of preventive services changes from 20 to 23 percent when family exercise is added to family structure indexes.

Use of Services by	Percent of Total Variance Accounted for by Family Structure and Family Health Behavior
Men	15
Women	22
Children	17

RELATIONSHIP OF SOCIOECONOMIC STATUS

A vast amount of research literature has documented the generally less adequate use of professional health services by the lower socioeconomic group than by higher groups (Pratt 1967; McKinlay and McKinlay 1972; Green 1970). The correlations between SES and use of preventive medical services in the our study sample are $-.28$ for men, $-.14$ for women, $-.07$ for children, and $-.17$ for the combined family. Differences among the socioeconomic groups have also been reported for various aspects of family structure, including discipline and support of children, marital conflict, division of tasks, power, and community participation (Komarovsky 1964; Bott 1957; Blood and Wolfe 1960; Rainwater 1965; Rainwater et al. 1959; McKinley 1964). We had to make sure that SES was not the underlying variable that accounted for the relationship found between family structure and use of medical services.

Control for SES had no significant effect on the relationships for women and children. It diminished slightly the relationship between community participation and the use of medical services by men, although that relationship did persist to a significant degree. Further investigation revealed that it was men's level of *education* which was the aspect of SES that overlapped with their community participation. Since education represents broad exposure to the ideas, procedures, and institutions of the society, it contributed to men's use of professional services in much the same way that extensive community and cultural participation contributed.

ALTERNATIVE INTERPRETATIONS

There are other possible interpretations of the relationship found between family structure measures and use of medical services than the proposed explanation. One alternative is that a parochial or cosmopolitan life-style, which the family indexes could be considered to represent, influences people's response to scientific medicine. A second alternative is that the person's level of community participation represents that person's degree of social integration, and this influences that person's conformity to social norms, such as acceptance of scientific medicine.

Parochialism-Cosmopolitanism

An alternative interpretation that merits serious consideration is that a close-knit family restricts the life experience of family members and inhibits acceptance of scientific medicine, whereas emancipation from family ties expands the social and intellectual horizons of family members, leading to greater acceptance of professional medical care. The close-knit family has been viewed as part of a parochial life-style, and emancipation from family ties as a vital aspect of a cosmopolitan life-style (Suchman 1964, 1965). This parochial-cosmopolitan hypothesis is in accord with the proposal made here that ties to the community foster effective use of professional medical services. It differs in that the energized family hypothesis proposes that a high level of exchanges among family members enhances, rather than restricts, their tendency to deal effectively with the medical care system, and that a high rate of internal family interaction and a high rate of interaction in the community by family members are mutually supportive.

Providing general support for the alternative interpretation is the research literature which cautions that families whose members feed only on each other cage themselves, breeding stagnation and conflict (Birdwhistell 1966). The death of the family has been predicted on the grounds that the family is a form of social existence which can never leave a person alone and destroys autonomous initiative (Cooper 1970). More specifically, members of parochial networks were found more likely to hold a nonscientific orientation toward medicine, including low factual knowledge about disease, suspicion of outside professional medical care, and reliance upon one's own group for help and support during illness (Suchman 1964, 1965). Significantly, however, that study did *not* find any consistent relationship between parochialism-cosmopolitanism and measures of preventive medical *behavior,* such as getting check-ups and immunizations. Other studies found that women who underused professional medical services were more likely to rely on a narrow network of readily available relatives, especially their mothers, as lay consultants, than were women who actively used medical services; but, notably, they were less likely to consult their husbands than were active users (McKinlay 1973). Thus, while close-knit extended kin groups may impede use of medical services, close-knit *nuclear* relationships apparently encourage use.

Data from our study showed, first, that interaction *within* the family was positively related to family members' interaction in *outside* activities. Hence, these two forms of interaction are compatible. Second, internal as well as external family interaction were associated positively with members' tendencies to cope actively and rationally with health matters rather than to rely on conventional wisdom. Internal as well as community interaction were related positively to a measure of competence. (The available measure of competence was a self-assessment of whether or not "I can do pretty much anything I set my mind to.") This supports the idea that family interaction generates a flow of ideas which fosters competence.

The most critical test is whether or not there was a negative relationship between internal family interaction and use of medical services, as the parochial concept of family interaction would predict. No negative relationships were found and, in fact, when all members of the family interacted with each other at a high rate—the situation in which any tendency toward caging would be most likely to manifest itself—the use of preventive medical services for the whole family group was especially high.

Another possibility is that in the absence of energizing links to the community, close internal family relations may tend to be caging. The data indicated that among men and women with very restricted community activities, those with high family interaction were much more likely to make active use of preventive medical services than were those with low family interaction. High internal exchanges need not be combined with external exchanges in order to have a positive effect on use of medical services.

This is a crucial finding. It may be recalled that stepwise regression analysis performed on the whole sample of women showed that after taking account of the influence of women's community participation on their use of medical services, women's level of internal family interaction made no further contribution. The parochialism conception encouraged the suspicion that when women's activities are restricted mainly to the home, an intense pattern of interaction within the family might compound their caging and result in even poorer use of medical services than would be found among women who are active neither in the community nor in the family. Since this was not found to be the case, it can be concluded that while a high rate of interaction within the family does not influence women's use of professional services to the extent that external participation does, it certainly has no negative influence. Among women with little community exposure, a high rate of interaction within the family is the saving grace that stimulates some use of professional services.

The evidence is consistent with the parochialism-cosmopolitanism notion that participation in community organizations and activities has a positive influence on use of medical services. But contrary to that hypothesis, a high rate of interaction within the family was found to be a liberating rather than a restricting influence, as expressed in more effective use of preventive medical services.

SOCIAL INTEGRATION

Another possible interpretation of the relationship found between the energized family measures and the family's use of preventive medical services is that the level of community participation represents the degree of one's social integration. A high level of community participation produces a high degree of conformity to social norms, and this is what accounts for the greater use of preventive medical services. (This contrasts with our interpretation that community participation develops capability for coping with formal agencies, such as the medical care system.) A study (Moody and Gray 1972) reported not only that high social participation was associated with high use of preventive health services, but also that low alienation (high social integration) was related to high use of preventive services. This suggests that integration into the social fabric may induce people to cooperate with health agencies.

If it is, indeed, the level of the individual's social integration that fosters cooperation with and acceptance of medical care agencies, then low alienation should be found to be positively associated with high community participation; and the relationship between community participation and the use of preventive services should be diminished or eliminated under control for alienation.

The first test rules out this possible explanation, because alienation was not related to extent of community participation in our sample. Alienation was not related to women's use of preventive services, although it was related negatively to men's use of services. The social integration-alienation-conformity rationale concerning the use of professional services does not, therefore, turn out to be a satisfactory explanation for the relationship found between community participation and use of preventive services.

CONCLUSIONS

We found that an energized pattern of family structure provides the family with advantages over a nonenergized, or traditional, form in obtaining professional medical services. The most important aspect of family structure was the extent of family links with the organizations, activities, and resources of the broader community. It is particularly by having women and children actively engaged in the community that the energized family achieves its advantages over the traditional pattern. As was found for personal health practices, men's use of services was enhanced by their active involvement in internal family matters.

An energized pattern of family health behavior—a tendency for the whole family to cope effectively with health matters—also contributed significantly to the individual family members' capabilities for securing professional medical services.

SEVEN

The Energized Family
and Health/Illness

Photo Trends by Dan S. Nelken

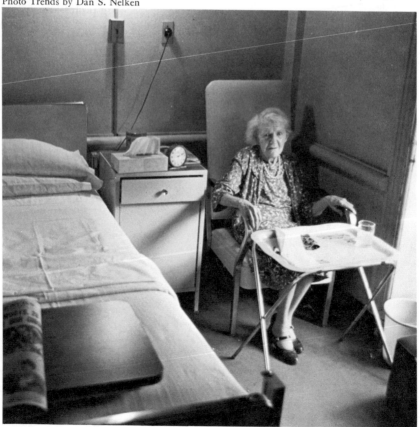

MEMBERS OF ENERGIZED FAMILIES have a higher level of health than persons living in nonenergized families. This chapter will develop the rationale of this hypothesis concerning how family structure affects health, and then will present the results of an empirical test of the hypothesis.

HEALTH AND ILLNESS

The level of health or illness is the extent of a person's capacity to use all his or her physical faculties, including strength, energy, dexterity, endurance, coordination, sensory acuity, recuperative power, and immunity (Foote and Cottrell 1955). Health is based not only on a person's ability to function at one moment in time, but also on that person's tendency to develop capacities, or to maintain them at a low level, or to allow them to deteriorate; the tendency to move toward or hold back from full physical functioning; the tendency to persevere toward recovery from illness or to prolong illness; and the tendency to think or to behave as though sick or healthy.

While our work does not investigate the physiological processes by which disease develops and health is maintained, we did make some assumptions about this process that affected the formulation of our study. Illness is not a simple matter of exposure to a disease agent; only a small minority of persons who are exposed actually develop a given disease. The reason for the occurrence of disease must be located in the condition of the person and in the environmental circumstances in which the person lives, as well as in the person's exposure to a disease agent.

Human beings are in a constant interplay with the external environment, both physical and social, and this environment is constantly varying. The human organism must respond adaptively to the environment in order to survive and remain healthy. Disturbances in the environment and failure of the organism to maintain a satisfactory relationship with, and adaptation to, the environment can cause disease directly, or can set in motion a chain of effects that ultimately damage the organism (Dubos 1959). In human beings, the social and symbolic environment is as great a source of threat to health as the physical environment. Our study concerns itself with attempting to comprehend and conceptualize some of the forces or situations in the social environment that are associated with good and ill health.

THE RATIONALE

The reasoning is that the level of health will be greater in families which support their members' personal needs and interests, assist the members' efforts to cope and function, and tolerate and encourage members' moves toward self-actualization. A higher level of illness will be associated with a family's tendency to impede or block members' efforts to function and to act independently.

Other researchers have proposed various explanations of the social condi-

125

tions associated with health and illness, including family conflict, loss of a family relationship, migration and change, job dissatisfaction, and excessively demanding life situations. Although these varied explanations of the social causes of illness are quite different from the one we propose, many of these formulations turned out to be consistent with, and to lend support to, the proposal that family structure affects health by supporting or blocking members' efforts to function.

OBSTRUCTIVE CONFLICT

Numerous studies have reported an association between family conflict and higher levels of illness. A review of family dynamics in relation to illness concluded: "A consistent element is that the patient is in a family situation which is ... often tense and conflictual" (Meissner 1966, p. 150). Another review cited conflict between parents, parental rejection of children, and hostility as important aspects of family relationships associated with illness (Croog 1970). Other researchers found that the better a boy got along with his parents, the fewer somatic complaints he had (Bachman 1970), and that boys from unhappy unbroken homes were much more likely to have poor health than were boys from broken homes (Nye 1957). Family conflict has been implicated in specific types of illness, including streptococcal infection (Meyer and Haggerty 1962), allergy (Miller and Baruch 1950), asthma (Rees 1964), accidental injuries (Husband and Hinton 1972), and myocardial infarction (Croog 1970).

Family conflict has often been viewed in psychological terms—as the conveyance of a hostile attitude or negative affect, resulting in unhappiness or tension in the participants. But for our purposes it must be defined as a type of social relationship. Thus, we view family conflict as the blocking or impeding of the efforts of family members to cope, function, and work toward personal objectives and fulfillment. The essence of the relationship is *obstruction* or, as Cohen (1968, p. 146) phrased it, "Conflict involves deliberate attempts to prevent the attainment of goals by others." It encompasses a wide range of physical restraints; physical assault; withholding of essential materials, services, or information; refusal to perform functions; and denial of accustomed rights of action or expression. Blocking can be physical and direct, or symbolic and indirect. For example, children may be overpowered and confined to their rooms to prevent them from carrying on certain activities. Or parents may ridicule activities that children wish to engage in, or disparage the kind of people who engage in those activities as a means of blocking their children's pursuit of the activity. The blocking may be practiced unilaterally by one member against other members, or it may be mutually practiced.

It is this range of obstructive behavior within families that holds promise to explain how family conflict serves to impair health. Some of the available evidence concerning the influence of family conflict on health fits this description. The type of family conflict associated with asthma is the child's struggle for independence from a mother who tends to be overprotective and to demand capitulation from the child (Rees 1964). Boys experience a higher rate of asthma than girls because they are expected to achieve greater independence than girls, and thus pay a greater cost when they must capitulate to the control of the mother (Nathanson and Rhyne 1970). A feature in the etiology of eczema is the mother's effort to keep the child dependent and the child's inability to assert himself or herself for fear of losing the mother's approval (Knight 1967).

PUNISHMENT

Another aspect of family behavior that might have a bearing on health is punishment, or aversive control. This is the application of an unpleasant stimulus to or withdrawal of a rewarding stimulus from a person for doing something or for failing to do something, and the punishment is given to suppress that behavior. The forms of aversive control employed within families range from beating, in which physical violence puts an explicit stop to the victim's actions, to complex symbolic forms, in which the aim may be to achieve far-reaching control over the subject's character and way of life. A distinguishable feature of punishment is that it simply blocks the person's course of activity without providing positive redirection or assistance toward an alternative course of action. It is this obstruction of the person's efforts to function and cope that is thought to have a bearing on health. In this respect punishment has much in common with conflict.

Wolf (1971, p. 5) made this general appraisal of the relationship between blocking the human being's efforts to function—to have satisfying activity, power, prestige, and love—and illness: "Threats to his ability to perform in all of these spheres constitute the important everyday stresses that are apparently behind so many states of disability and disease." The little available evidence tends to support the proposal. It was reported that arthritis patients frequently perceived one or both parents as strict and uncompromising in discipline and the mother as dominating (Scotch and Geiger 1962). Parental punitiveness was associated with a higher level of somatic symptoms in boys (Bachman 1970).

RESPONSIVENESS AND SUPPORTIVENESS

While impeding family members' efforts to function through punishment and conflict impairs health, active support and responsiveness to members' efforts to function and cope sustain health. Particularly important are the family's tendencies to encourage and foster autonomy, self-expression, and personal fulfillment; to assist and encourage members in their various endeavors, especially in seeking new areas of growth; and to tolerate and appreciate differences in the members. Such support gives a forward thrust to life that contributes to sound health. It must be the family that serves as the principal refuge for unconditional acceptance and support, because most other social groups are too specialized and impersonal to fulfill this function for the person.

Data on recovery and rehabilitation suggest that families which tend to give general support, affection, and acceptance to an ill member facilitate recovery, and families which fail to provide such support impede the return to full physical functioning (Hoberman et al. 1951; Litman 1962; Gray et al. 1964).

There is impressive evidence that the absence or loss of supportive family relationships increases the risk of mortality and morbidity. Single, widowed, and divorced persons generally have higher mortality and sickness rates than married persons (HEW 1970; Berkman 1969; La Horgue 1960). In particular, married persons are less likely than nonmarried persons to die of influenza and pneumonia. Since these are nonfatal diseases when treated promptly, it is likely that the mutual care of hubsand and wife reduces mortality risks. The married also have lower death rates than the nonmarried from suicide, accidents, and tuberculosis; perhaps the supportive social bonds of the married are responsible (Chen and Cobb 1960).

Studies of widows show that the medical consultation rate for physical symptoms increases radically from before to after the loss of the spouse, and remains elevated for some time (Parkes 1964). Widowhood also brings about a significant increase in death rates (Cox and Ford 1964; Young et al. 1963). Men admitted to homes for the aged are more likely to die within the first year after admission than the same population on a waiting list for institutionalization (Lieberman 1961). Studies show that loss of a parent or other key relative is associated with arthritis (Scotch and Geiger 1962), and may be a factor in the onset of leukemia and lymphoma (Taylor 1968; Kasl and Cobb 1966), ulcerative colitis (Lindemann 1950), and perhaps of disease in general. It appears to be the loss of an important supportive relationship that is the underlying influence on health in these various situations.

RIGIDITY-FLEXIBILITY OF ROLE STRUCTURE

Rigid role structuring in the family may adversely affect recovery from illness. Where families' usual pattern is sharing tasks and flexibility in their internal adjustments to illness, the care of the ill person is performed more effectively and the families are more self-sufficient in handling the illness, relying less on external resources. On the other hand, families with a usual pattern of rigid specialization of task performance become greater users of back-up structures, shifting many tasks to extrafamilial resources, and leaving many tasks undone (*Nursing Research Report* 1971).

Among families with a child afflicted with polio, an egalitarian style of family relations was related to the family's tendency to try to normalize their relationships and activities within and outside the household, while a traditional family pattern was associated with a tendency to disassociate and to insulate themselves from various contacts and situations.

> "The equalitarian atmosphere, with its looser differentiation of family roles and greater tolerance of pluralistic demands, offers a more fertile medium for the cultivation of normalization techniques than does the traditional family atmosphere. By comparison, the latter, with its stricter demarcation of age-sex roles and harsher standards of acceptable performance, is less capable of accommodating the 'slippage' from conventional normative standards that normalization entails" (Davis 1963, p. 161).

While it is anticipated that flexible role structure contributes to health principally through facilitating care of illness and promotion of recovery, it is possible that flexible structure may also contribute to the maintenance of sound health.

OTHER FORMS OF OBSTRUCTED FUNCTIONING

Although our concern is focused on obstructed functioning in the family, evidence concerning other types of situations and relationships that tend to obstruct the person's efforts to function successfully can shed light on whether this type of social environment is generally associated with poorer health than social environments that encourage or facilitate the person's efforts.

Mobility and Change Almost as many studies show that major changes, such as migration and war, produce no increase in illness as show an increase. But one type of change that is systematically associated with increased rates of mental and physical illness is migration in which the receiving society expects the immigrants to adapt to the new culture, but those in power employ deliberate efforts to block the adaptation (Murphy 1961). This interpretation of migration effects suggests that it is the frustration of the migrants' coping efforts that is associated with illness rather than change *per se*.

Job Conflicts and Dissatisfaction A type of job situation that has a significant bearing on symptoms of physiological strain is overload. This is a situation of temporally incompatible demands, in which the person is unable to meet the demands simultaneously or within the required time limits (Kahn 1973). Role ambiguity is another such occupational situation. This occurs when there is a discrepancy between the amount of information the person has and the amount the person needs to perform effectively (Kahn 1973). The lack of influence and control over the work process and conditions of employment are also related to illness (Gardell 1971; Taylor 1968). On the other hand, persons' feelings that their work is useful and that they are performing meaningful social roles, proved to be an excellent predictor of longevity (Palmore and Jeffers 1972). These studies suggest that blocking efforts to cope and to function fully are attributes of work environments which have injurious consequences for health.

Excessively Demanding Life Situation   Hinkle and Wolff (1957, p. 131) conclude that ill health tends to occur "when an individual exists in a life situation which places demands upon him that are excessive in terms of his ability to meet them or which fails to satisfy his own peculiar needs and aspirations." Life situations characterized by failure are associated with a high tendency to respiratory illness (Jacobs and Spiken 1970). Social inadequacy and feelings of inferiority are associated with rheumatoid arthritis (Scotch and Geiger 1962). In one study of a group of women with cervical dysplasia, those women with a high degree of general hopelessness about life were more likely to develop cervical cancer than those with a hopeful outlook (Schmale and Iker 1971). Finally, coronary disease patients, when compared with healthy controls, were found more often to have undertaken work that was too difficult for them and to have failed in achieving their life goals (Cathey et al. 1962). These findings suggest that people whose social situations or relationships impose demands that exceed their capacity to cope successfully will be more likely to suffer ill health than persons whose backgrounds and opportunities have equipped them to meet the demands of their lives.

The thread that runs through these diverse findings concerning the family, work, and other social relationships is that a basic structural situation which tends to impair health is the failure of the social relationship to provide adequate support or the tendency even to block individuals in their efforts to function and cope with their life situations.

Family Health as a Social Environment

A family's general level of health or illness can be regarded as an important aspect of the social environment for the family members. A family whose members are in robust health is capable of full and effective functioning, and can provide vigorous and consistent support for each of the members in their efforts to develop their full powers and to function effectively. A healthy family can also serve as a strong service structure for each member. On the other hand, a family pervaded by illness or disability cannot as readily support its members because some of its resources are drained off by the debilitating physical effects of illness, as well as by the depletion of the family's time, money, energy, and emotional reserves.

This proposition involves us in two questions. To what extent is illness transmitted within families? What effects does illness have on the functioning of the family?

Interdependence Among Members' Illnesses   There is convincing evidence that persons who live in families with a significant amount of illness are more likely to become ill than those who live in relatively healthy families. Families develop their own characteristic level of health and illness that has persistence over time; some have consistently high levels of incidence and others have consistently low levels (Dingle et al. 1964). Various transmission processes are at work, including genetic transmission, infection, and social diffusion of illness behavior.

Diseases that can be transmitted genetically to offspring include hemophilia, sickle cell anemia, and Cooley's anemia. Another is phenylketonuria (PKU), a metabolic disease in which the body fails to produce one of the liver enzymes, causing brain deterioration if untreated. There is a hereditary component in diabetes mellitus. A genetic defect known as Type II hyperlipoproteinemia results in a high cholesterol level, which predisposes the person to a higher risk of heart disease.

A pregnant woman can transmit certain of her own health problems directly to her unborn child. In New York City in 1971, about 550 children were born addicted to narcotic drugs because of their mothers' addiction (Kihss, 1972). A baby can be born with syphilis if the mother is infected with the disease. Women's health practices during pregnancy can also affect their unborn children; for example, pregnant women who smoke increase the risk of stillbirth and low birth weight (Schmeck 1973).

The family can also serve as a social network of infection. For example, when one family member introduces a respiratory disease into the home, an average of 25 percent of other family members quickly develop respiratory illness (Dingle et al. 1964). Tuberculosis, typhoid, and dysentery have a strong tendency to spread through families, because family relationships involve bodily contact and close interaction in confined physical space. Within families the risk of infection varies with the closeness of relationship between particular members, with the highest rate of transmission occurring between mothers and children (Dingle et al. 1953; Kellner 1963).

Certain noninfectious diseases, such as some types of gastrointestinal dysfunction, essential hypertension, and obesity, spread through families (Dunn and Gilbert 1956). Faulty nutrition and food aversions are learned within families, and this may be one mechanism through which obesity is transmitted (American Academy of Pediatrics 1965). While alcoholism may be partly a hereditary matter, the social role of the family in transmitting the drinking pattern is evident. Alcoholic men with alcoholic fathers are much more likely than alcoholic men with nonalcoholic fathers to have had their first drink at home and to have been offered that drink by a parent (Cseh-Szombathy 1972). There is also a marked relationship between parents' and their adolescent children's use of mood-altering drugs and cigarettes (Smart and Fejer 1972; HEW 1971), and this could produce a familial tendency to develop health problems caused by those practices.

The disposition toward certain kinds of ailments may also be communicated among family members as a result of sharing experiences and views concerning body function and pursuing common health practices. In this way, families may come to favor certain types of dysfunction, for example, insomnia or constipation (Wilson 1970).

Other social contagion processes that occur within close social groups have not yet been clearly identified. Animals tend to become more alike in physiological response when living in a group, and this tendency has also been found in humans (Cassel 1970). For example, girls' menstrual cycles come to coincide with their mothers' and close friends' (McClintock 1971).

Effects of Illness on Family Functioning   Medical sociology has tended to regard illness as having potentially highly disruptive consequences for the family. Parsons and Fox (1952) proposed that the resources of the family for coping with illness are relatively weak. Illness upsets role relationships, impairs task performance, and generally disturbs family equilibrium. But there is remarkably little documentary evidence concerning the effect of illness on task performance and role relationships.

The ability of the family to survive and to function may be threatened by certain forms of illness. Cystic fibrosis has been described as a family-shattering disease. A study of families with a cystic fibrosis child reported that 75 percent of the families were broken, 5 percent of the parents had attempted or committed suicide, and the siblings tended to be socially poorly adjusted and to feel themselves stigmatized as potential carriers of a bad gene (McKey). Another study reported that diabetes in a child is associated with lower marital integration and greater marital conflict among parents (Crain et al. 1966), for the hereditary basis of the disease fosters conflict between the parents over who is to blame for the child's disease. Other diseases and disabilities have their own distinctive social and emotional components that can disrupt family relations: radical mastectomy, colostomy, cardiovascular ailments, paraplegia. The depressive reactions accompanying hepatitis and mononucleosis or the irritability of severely burned persons may make them hard to live with, inducing the rest of the family to respond in kind, which may lead to a snowballing of family strife (Vincent 1967). Types of illness that impair sexual functioning can have a profound effect on the marital relationship.

A study of the impact of the illness of one spouse on the emotional balance of the other spouse found that the impact was greater when the illness was severely disabling, especially when the patient's ability to perform his or her usual family and work roles was impaired (Duff and Hollingshead 1968). Similarly, in families in which a child afflicted by polio remained severely handicapped, disturbances in family functioning were still evident eighteen months later (Davis 1963). But the child's disability did not result in major alterations in the family's style of living, meanings, or purposes; in fact, there appeared to be a tenacious sameness of life in the midst of these disturbances.

A study of English adolescents with a history of chronic illness found that relationships between these adolescents and their parents tended to improve rather than to deteriorate when the children were ill. Furthermore, these changes in relationship occurred only during episodes of illness, for when these adolescents were not ill, there were no significant differences between the chronically ill group and healthy adolescents (Peterson 1972). This evidence fails to support the idea that families with histories of chronic illness evolve a distinctive climate of interpersonal relations.

Coping with the fatal illness of a child has been interpreted as a crisis that endangers family equilibrium, but the evidence fails to indicate a long-term maladaptive outcome for the parents. A study reported that "The fatal illness of a child leads to an emotional crisis for parents characterized by marked internal turmoil, temporary interpersonal disequilibrium and the triggering of coping as well as defensive measures to deal with the danger" (Futterman and Hoffman 1973, p. 5). Some parents achieved personal growth through the experience, for example, increased empathy for others or a greater capacity to live every moment.

In general, the limited evidence available indicates that severely disabling and stigmatized illnesses disrupt roles and relationships in many families, at least during the crisis stage of the illness, although the strenuous coping efforts that are stimulated by illness in the family often result in new patterns of adjustment within the families.

RESEARCH RESULTS

We will present research results from the study of 273 families concerning the hypothesis that members of energized families will have better health than members of nonenergized families and, in particular, that the tendency to provide freedom and to support and respond to—rather than to restrict or block—their members' efforts to cope and function fully is a pattern which contributes significantly to health. We will also present results concerning the extent to which a high level of family health is an aspect of family life that supports the health of individual members.

Measurement of Health and Illness

The measures of health and illness used in the study are based on each person's self-evaluation and not on medical reports. We wanted to obtain the most direct expression of the individual's and the family's experience of good or poor health. While health data obtained by this method have limitations, weaknesses in physicians' reports have also been documented. Significant differences were found in the symptoms reported and diagnoses made by two physicians examining the same patient (Elsom et al. 1960; Schor et al. 1964), doctors and patients were found to disagree about what symptoms are significant (Koos 1954), and physicians failed to diagnose as many as 60 percent of the chronic conditions that patients themselves reported in interviews (HEW 1965).

The measure used most extensively in our analysis is an index of *extent of health problems*. It is based on a series of questions which asked the respondent, "Have you ever had ... ?" and "Has this happened in the last two weeks?" The health problems included constipation, skin rash, unexplained nosebleeds, seeing double, earache, stiff joints, fever above 100 degrees, sore or bleeding gums, shortness of breath, stomachache, nausea, backache, dizziness, sore in the genital area, swelling in the legs or feet, and others. For each problem, individuals were scored 0 if they had never had the problem, 2 if they had had the problem but not in the past two weeks, and 4 if they had had the problem in the past two weeks. The person's scores on all the separate health problems were summed to obtain his or her total health problems score.

In addition, a measure of *level of present health* is based on a self-rating of current general health as excellent, good, fair, or poor, and a report on whether he or she had been sick in the past two weeks and unable to fully carry on regular work or activities. Greater reliance is placed on the health problems index than on the level of present health measure, because respondents can be expected to provide more reliable and valid information when asked about specific conditions within a delimited time period than when asked for a general evaluation of health.

THE DIMENSIONS OF FAMILY STRUCTURE AND HEALTH/ILLNESS

The correlations between the various dimensions of family structure and the extent of health problems of men, women, children, and the combined family are shown in Table 7-1. All family structure indexes were scored so that a high score represents the energized end of the continuum. A high score on the health problems index, on the other hand, indicates a large number of health problems. Thus, a negative correlation coefficient indicates that the relationship is in the direction hypothesized—an energized family pattern associated with a low level of health problems.

Freedom and Responsiveness All four measures of the extent of the family's supportiveness of and responsiveness to its members were related significantly to the extent of health problems of family members. These measures are punishment or aversive control of children; positive support and encouragement of children's efforts to function; children's autonomy; and obstructive conflict between husbands and wives. The relationships with the level of present health index were similar.

The extent of punishment of the child by the parents is the dimension of family structure found to have the highest correlation with health problems. A high level of punishment was significantly related to a high level of health problems among men and women, as well as among children. This measure represents the extent to which parents tend to control and restrain the child by aversive means, such as physical force (slapping, hitting, spanking, confining to child's room or the house), withdrawing privileges, requiring punitive work, verbal abuse (scolding, yelling, shouting), hostile reaction, or

Table 7–1. *Relationship of the Dimensions of Family Structure to Extent of Health Problems of Men, Women, Children, and the Combined Family**

Dimensions of Family Organization	Extent of Health Problems of			
	Men	*Women*	*Children*	*Combined Family***
Freedom and Responsiveness				
Aversive control of child by parents	−.24	−.34	−.40	−.37
Obstructive conflict between husband and wife	−.27	−.34	−.12	−.25
Support of child by parents	−.17	−.18	−.16	−.23
Child's autonomy	−.06	−.24	−.16	−.19
Interaction				
Husband-wife interaction	−.15	−.09	−.01	−.05
Father-child interaction	.08	.00	.00	.07
Mother-child interaction	.02	−.09	.08	−.03
Combined family interaction	.01	−.12	−.03	−.07
Man's emphasis on father role (vs. job role)	−.01	−.06	−.13	−.10
Role Structure				
Conjugal division of task of child health care	−.12	.03	−.04	−.05
Conjugal power	−.04	−.07	.08	.01
Coping Effort				
Health training efforts by parents	.02	−.14	−.05	−.08
Links to Community				
Combined family extramural interaction	.03	−.12	−.03	−.06

* Correlation coefficients of .10 are significant at the .05 level. A negative correlation indicates that the relationship was in the direction hypothesized: an energized family pattern associated with a low level of heath problems.
** The combined family health problems index is a composite of the three family members' health problems scores.

ridicule. These techniques tend to block the child's conduct without providing positive redirection toward alternative courses of action.

A high level of autonomy for the child was associated significantly with a low level of health problems of women, children, and the combined family, but the relationship to men's health problems was not statistically significant. This measure represents the level of responsibility given to the child, opportunity to develop his or her uniqueness, and freedom to explore and to function independently, as opposed to detailed regulation of activity, intrusive parental domination, and required conformity to pre-established standards.

A high level of obstructive conflict between husband and wife was also related significantly to extensive health problems among all family members, children as well as husbands, wives, and the combined family. This measure represents the extent to which the husband and wife tended to block each other's efforts to function or to block the family's functioning by physical force (for example, by hitting), physical separation, and noncooperation or nonperformance in such matters as finances, preparing meals, and sexual relations.

Extent and Variety of Interaction Among Family Members   There was a tendency for a high level of interaction among family members to be associated with fewer health problems, but the relationship was not very consistent or strong.

Active Coping Behavior   Extensive efforts by the parents to train their children in health matters was related significantly to a low level of health problems among women, but not to the health problems of men or children. This cannot be viewed as a major influence on health.

Conjugal Role Structure   A flexible division of labor concerning the care of children's health was significantly related to a low level of health problems among men, but not among women or children. Conjugal power was not related significantly to the health problems of men, women, or children.

Family Links to the Community   Participation of family members in community organizations and activities was not found to have a strong, consistent influence on the health of all family members. But there was one significant exception: When the overall level of community participation by the whole family was high, women's health was significantly better than when the family group had a generally low level of outside participation. Notably, it was insufficient for women themselves to have a high level of participation. It may be that when a woman is the only member of the family to participate in the community, her activities tend to cut her off from other members; but when she is joined by her family in community involvement, the bonds of common interest among all the members are strengthened.

RELATIVE IMPORTANCE OF VARIOUS FAMILY STRUCTURE DIMENSIONS

The results of stepwise regression analysis presented in Table 7–2 confirm that punishment, obstructive conflict, autonomy, support for the child, and, to a lesser degree, interaction among members, were clearly the most influential aspects of family structure for the health of family members. After the influence of these measures had been taken into account, conjugal role structure and community participation had no additional influence. The pattern varied only slightly for men, women and children.

COMBINED INFLUENCE OF THE FAMILY STRUCTURAL DIMENSIONS

Table 7–2 reveals the *combined* influence of the several dimensions of family organization on the health practices of men, women, children, and the composite family group. The cumulative figure in the R^2 column shows that the combination of family structure measures accounts for about 16 percent of the total variance in men's health problems, 25 percent of women's, 23 percent of children's, and 27 percent of the total variance in the family group's combined health problems.

The findings suggest that it is not simply a number of separate factors that affect health, but that it is the family's overall pattern of arrangements

Table 7–2. *Stepwise Regression Analysis of the Relationship of Family Structure to Extent of Health Problems*

Independent Variable	Multiple R	R^2	Changes in R^2	Standardized Regression Coefficients	F Ratios	p	Simple r with Dependent Variable
Men							
Obstructive conflict between husband and wife	.27	.07	.07	−.24	21.9	.001	−.27
Aversive control of child by parents	.35	.12	.05	−.22	13.8	.001	−.24
Child's independence	.38	.15	.03	−.16	8.4	.001	−.14
Husband-wife interaction	.39	.16	.01	−.10	3.1	.05	−.15
Women							
Aversive control of child by parents	.34	.12	.12	−.27	36.0	.001	−.34
Obstructive conflict between husband and wife	.45	.20	.08	−.25	27.6	.001	−.34
Child's autonomy	.49	.24	.04	−.19	12.7	.001	−.24
Support of child by parents	.49	.25	.01	−.11	4.1	.01	−.18

Table 7-2. *Continued*

Independent Variable	Children						
	Multiple R	*R²*	*Changes in R²*	*Standardized Regression Coefficients*	*F Ratios*	*p*	*Simple r with Dependent Variable*
Aversive control of child by parents	.40	.16	.16	−.38	52.1	.001	−.40
Child's autonomy	.43	.19	.03	−.16	8.6	.001	−.16
Support of child by parents	.45	.20	.02	−.11	5.2	.01	−.16
Man's emphasis on father role (vs. job role)	.47	.22	.01	−.13	5.0	.001	−.13
Obstructive conflict between husband and wife	.48	.23	.01	−.10	3.8	.01	−.12
Child's total autonomy (in health and other matters)	.48	.23	.01	−.08	2.2	.05	−.13

Independent Variable	Combined Family						
	Multiple R	*R²*	*Changes in R²*	*Standardized Regression Coefficients*	*F Ratios*	*p*	*Simple r with Dependent Variable*
Aversive control of child by parents	.36	.13	.13	−.22	41.6	.001	−.36
Obstructive conflict between husband and wife (wife's view)	.45	.17	.04	−.11	13.1	.001	−.25
Support of child by parents	.45	.20	.03	−.15	10.7	.001	−.23
Child's autonomy	.48	.23	.03	−.15	9.5	.001	−.19
Aversive control by mother	.50	.25	.02	−.19	7.3	.001	−.36
Obstructive conflict between husband and wife (husband's view)	.52	.27	.02	−.15	7.3	.001	−.22

for relating to, and working with, each other which is important. Specifically, the pattern that tends to contribute to health is one in which members are given freedom and are supported and encouraged in their efforts to cope and to function.

FAMILY HEALTH CLIMATE

The strong association found between a supportive and responsive pattern of family relationships and the health problems of the combined family group suggests the possibility that the general level of health within a family is so inextricably intertwined with the pattern of family relations that health itself becomes a vital aspect of the fabric of family life. A family with extensive health problems may provide less support and impose greater obstacles for its members' health than a family with generally sound health.

The health problems of the various members of the family were intercorrelated as follows:

Husbands and wives	.28
Mothers and children	.34
Fathers and children	.27

A stepwise regression analysis reveals that we can account for 15 percent of the total variance in children's health problems by the health problems of their mothers and fathers, 15 percent of the total variance in the health problems of women by the health problems of their husbands and children, and 12 percent of the total variance in men's health problems by the health problems of their wives and children.

Clearly, the health climate is an influential aspect of family life, for we achieve a substantial increase in explained variance by extending the concept of energized family life to include the level of health of other family members:

	Percent of Total Variance in Health Problems That Is Accounted for by	
Extent of Health Problems of	*Family Structure*	*Family Structure and Family Health Climate*
Men	16	31
Women	25	37
Children	23	32

The combination of family structure and family health climate accounts for about a third of the total variance in health problems of the members. In fact, wives' health problems are the single most important influence on husbands' health, exceeding the family structure measures. Health problems of both fathers and mothers are very important influences on children's health, exceeded in importance only by punishment.

The question now must be reversed in order to ask: Does family structure really have an influence on health problems that is independent of the influence of family health climate? One must confront the possibility that pervasive family illness is principally responsible for poor health of members, and that family structure is only accidentally involved in the reationship, because sick persons are not able to sustain a strong and capable structure. When the health problems of other family members were held constant, the original relationship persisted between family structure and health. The relationship of obstructive conflict to men's health problems was slightly diminished under control for wives' health problems, indicating that a small portion of the influence of conflict was accounted for by the wives' health problems. Even in that case, obstructive conflict continued to exert a strong independent influence on men's health problems.

We conclude, therefore, that family structure has a strong independent influence on the health of family members, and that the climate of health in the family has a significant additional influence.

Relationship of Socioeconomic Status

Studies have revealed some differences in patterns of family structure among the various socioeconomic groups, as well as substantial differences in level of health. While in our study sample there was only a slight tendency for low SES to be associated with a higher level of health problems, and that was found only for men and children, it is desirable to rule out the possibility that SES is responsible for the apparent relationship of family structure to health.

When SES was held constant, the relationships of the family structure measures to health were fully sustained. The relationship of family health climate to the health of given family members was also fully sustained under control for SES. Thus, the relationship of family structure and family health climate to the extent of health problems among family members is fully independent of SES.

ALTERNATIVE INTERPRETATIONS

A basic challenge to our hypothesis concerns the direction of causation. The relationship might represent the influence of health on family structure rather than the influence of family structure on health. Even if that challenge was refuted, there are also alternative explanations of the nature of the influence of family structure on health. Perhaps it is the degree of stress in family relationships, rather than the extent of structural provisions for freedom and support, that is the influential force represented by the family indexes.

We will test these alternative explanations of the relationships against the energized family structure explanation. The tests are makeshift, however, because the data collection instrument used in our study was not designed to permit full-fledged testing of other explanatory models.

Cause and Effect

One could reverse our hypothesis and propose that the level of health and illness influences the type of family structure that a family is able to maintain.

It is a reasonable assumption that families whose members are sick cannot sustain an energized form as readily as families whose members are in vigorous health. In fact, evidence presented in this chapter indicated that illness in the family may impair the functioning of the family and the health of other members.

Since health probably has some influence on family structure, the tests cannot logically be expected to demonstrate that all of the relationship found is due to the influence of family structure on health. Evidence that supports our hypothesis must indicate only that the *dominant direction* of influence was family structure on health.

The best basis for establishing the direction of causation is the time order: The variable that occurred prior in time must be the determinant variable. In our study, both health and family structure were measured by respondents' reports of *current* conditions and, therefore, the fact that these variables were related does not establish that the direction of causation was as hypothesized. But a question concerning *childhood* health of men and women does provide a measure of one of the variables that occurred prior in time to the other, and this makes possible some crude tests of the direction of causation based on the time sequence.

First, if men and women tended to select marriage partners on the basis of health considerations, then the similarity in husband-wife level of health would be a feature of the family environment from the inception of marriage; and the couple's level of health could then influence their evolving family structure. There is some evidence in other studies of a tendency toward mating on the basis of health (Spuhler 1968; Kraus and Lilienfeld 1959). But we found absolutely no relationship in our sample between husbands' level of childhood health and their wives' level of childhood health ($-.02$). This suggests that mate selection was not based on health or illness, although the test is flawed by the fact that the only available measure of premarital health was childhood rather than health at the time of marriage.

Second, if family structure does have a major effect on health, as hypothesized, then we would expect that among persons who had good health as children, those who developed the unfavorable (nonenergized) pattern of family structure as adults would have poorer adult health than those with the favorable (energized) pattern of adult family structure. That is, unfavorable adult family structure would tend to offset initially good health, while favorable adult family structure would serve to sustain the person's initially good health. Similarly, we would expect to find that among persons with poor childhood health, those who developed favorable family structure would have better health than those who had unfavorable family structure as adults.

This is precisely what we found when we examined the relationship between family structure and health while holding constant childhood health. The relationships of the major family structure measures (obstructive conflict and aversive control) to current health of men and women were fully sustained. Specifically, among those who started out with *good* childhood health, a significantly larger proportion of those with low aversive control in their current families were very healthy (33 percent) than of those with high aversive control (11 percent). Among those who started out with *poor* childhood health, those with low aversive control in their present families were significantly more likely to be very healthy (43 percent) than were those with high aversive control (17 percent). Thus, family structure appears to have a significant influence on adult health that is independent of prior level of health. This helps to rule out the possibility that the major direction of influence is health on family structure, and thereby bolsters the proposal that the dominant direction of influence is family structure on health.

Third, the direction of influence between family structure and *children's* health can also be tested on the basis of the time sequence. We can do this since parents' health is prior in time to children's health because of the difference in their ages. One can examine the possibility that children's health is affected by their parents' health (for example, through genetic transmission, infection, or social transmission) rather than by family structure; and that family structure only appears to be related to children's health because parents' health influences both the type of family structure they can maintain and their children's health. This is a reasonable possibility because parents' own level of health could affect their punitiveness toward the child, sick parents showing less tolerance and more irritability, and a greater tendency to adopt rigid formulas and simplistic procedures.

The test is to examine the relationship of aversive control to children's level of health while holding constant the parents' level of health. Under control for mothers' and fathers' level of health, the relationship of punishment to children's level of health was found to be fully sustained. This rules out the possibility that it was parents' health which was the dominant influence on children's health, as well as the possibility that family structure affects children's health only insofar as parents' health influences their family structure.

None of the tests permitted a conclusive demonstration of the direction of influence between family structure and health, but all the evidence tended to support the hypothesis of our study that family structure exerts an influence on health.

How the Family Affects Health

The literature is full of discussions of the importance of stressful life situations as a cause of disease. The question arises concerning our hypothesis as to whether the measures used to represent family structure, such as aversive control, obstructive conflict, and support, may simply represent the extent of stressfulness of family life rather than a distinctive form of family structure.

This can be tested by examining the original relationship between the family structure measures and extent of health problems, while holding constant the level of general stressfulness of family life. A measure of general

Table 7–3. *Relationship of Obstructive Conflict to Women's Health Problems Under Control for Extent of Women's Worry*

Extent of Obstructive Conflict	Low Level of Worry *Extent of Health Problems*				High Level of Worry *Extent of Health Problems*			
	Low	*Medium*	*High*	*Total*	*Low*	*Medium*	*High*	*Total*
High	0	0	100	100%	3	27	70	100%
Medium	25	67	8	100%	18	36	46	100%
Low	47	37	16	100%	26	53	21	100%
				(76)				(105)

stressfulness available in our study is an index of the extent to which the person worried about nine areas of personal and family life.

We found that the original relationships of the family structure indexes to health were fully sustained under control for worry. Table 7–3 shows that among women with a high level of worry, those living in families with a high level of obstructive conflict had significantly more health problems (70 percent) than those living in families with little obstructive conflict (21 percent). The same pattern prevailed for women with few family worries.

Thus, the family structure measures represent a social influence that is independent of general stressfulness of family life, as measured here. While this does not demonstrate in a positive sense that it is family structure that the family indexes represent, it does strengthen the rationale that it is family structure which is influencing health since the study rules out a competing interpretation.

CONCLUSIONS

The dimensions of family structure that were found to have the strongest relationship to good health were a low level of aversive control and obstructive conflict, and a high level of autonomy, support and encouragement, and interaction among members. A high level of health in the family as a whole was also related significantly to good health of men, women, and children. A combined pattern of supportive family relationships and a supportive family health climate accounted for about a third of the total variance in the extent of health problems among family members.

We conclude that the level of health is greater in families that tend to support their members' personal needs and interests, assist the members' efforts to cope and function, and tolerate and encourage members' moves toward self-actualization and personal development. Clearly, freedom is favorable to health.

The aspects of the energized family model that were found to be most important for personal health practices and use of professional medical services were also found to influence health. There were differences in emphasis, however. Since both personal health practices and use of professional medical services are forms of task performance requiring competent and dedicated coping activity, those aspects of family structure that tend to facilitate effective coping behavior were the critical ones for those two forms of health behavior, but were less crucial for health. On the other hand, family freedom and support, which aid and enable persons to develop and use their full physical faculties, turned out to be the crucial aspects of family structure for health, but were of less central significance for health care behavior.

EIGHT

Problems in the Structure
of American Families

How TYPICAL OF CONTEMPORARY American society is the energized family form or its various structural components? If this type of family structure is infrequently found, that could account, in part, for the poor performance of essential health functions by large numbers of families. It would indicate that there is an incongruence between the functions the contemporary family must perform for its members and the structural resources that are available to the family for carrying out those functions.

FULLY ENERGIZED FAMILIES

Few families can be characterized as fully energized, for only 10 percent of the families in our study sample had the composite of attributes of the model. Another 20 to 30 percent were semi-energized, that is, they had some of the features of the model. On the other hand, equally few families were fully nonenergized, as only 8 percent fell at the opposite extreme.

It is not surprising to find that so few families fit the model. Because of the diversity of American life, no model could be expected to depict the majority of families. But the fact that fully energized families are uncommon raises the question of whether this form is characteristic only of an eccentric segment of the population, such as the wealthy or highly educated, or whether it has gained a foothold in the general population. While the energized form was found to be somewhat more characteristic of the higher than of the lower socioeconomic group, it is definitely not an upper-middle-class family model. Energized families were found in all socioeconomic strata, and this suggests that this family form has a broad societal base.

The uncommonness of energized families also raises the question of whether any of the energized features are commonly found, and whether any of these structural dimensions are in the process of becoming more common. We will examine each of these features.

LINKS WITH THE BROADER COMMUNITY

In spite of our democratic ideal of voluntary citizen participation in the political process, a majority of citizens have not participated extensively in public affairs. In fact, as urban patterns of life rapidly displaced the rural ideal in the nineteenth century, nonparticipation in the corrupt society came to be an accepted pattern. The home and family became idealized as a retreat from everything that was distressing in the broader community—slums, immigrants, gambling, saloons (Jeffrey 1972). In the twentieth century, as more specialized institutions undertook activities that the family formerly carried on at home, families had to come into the public arena to obtain essential services. But there has been little diminution of the fear and loathing of urban society. Some of the old symbols of evil have been reinforced by new ones, such as crime in the streets, the porno parlor, the singles bar, pollution, political corruption, and racial tension. The ideal form of escape is physical retreat to a suburban sanctuary set off in privacy from the world by grass and shrubs.

It would be incorrect to state that nonparticipation is the normatively approved position today, for Americans exhibit considerable ambivalence on this matter. A study reports that one-half of the respondents believed the ordinary person need not be active in her or his local community (Almond and Verba 1963). A majority actually do not participate actively in voluntary associations (Hausknecht 1962; Almond and Verba 1963; Smith and Freedman 1972). In our urban sample, almost six in ten men and women and more than six in ten children belonged to no organization or association. Fourteen percent of a sample of Detroit residents were members of families in which no person had ever belonged to an organization (Detroit Area Study 1952).

Of persons who do belong to some organization, only about half belong to more than one, and about half participate actively in the goals or activities of the organization. This means that only about one in five adults could be considered to be extensively or intensively engaged in associational activities. Even fewer adults are engaged to the extent that they have attempted to exert influence over events in the community. Among a group who felt competent to influence their local government, only a third had actually attempted to do so, and among those who did not feel competent to influence local government only 10 percent had ever tried to do so (Almond and Verba 1963).

One type of link to the community that was especially important for health care functioning of the family was participation in cultural activities. Yet even in a sample taken in a middle- to upper-middle-class suburban county close to New York City, fewer than a fourth of the adults belonged to any organization for the arts (Pratt 1969). In our urban sample, over six in ten families never took their children on trips to art exhibits or museums, and eight in ten did not take the children to live theater performances or concerts.

In spite of the available transportation network that potentially links the family to a variety of places and facilities, most people tend to establish a small number of narrow beats, with standardized origin and destination points which circumscribe most of their forays into the world. This bustling to and fro gives the appearance of deeply penetrating the resources, facilities, and places of their world. In actual fact, a third of the women and a fourth of the men in our study sample used only one town other than their home community in the course of a month, and this prevailed in an area of closely linked towns with easy access to New York City. A Pennsylvania study found that almost three in ten persons never shopped out of town during the course of a year (Herrmann and Beik 1968). About 5.5 million persons out of a population of over 200 million travel outside the United States during the course of a year (Bureau of Census 1972).

The trend appears to be toward an increasing proportion of citizens participating in voluntary associations. One study reported a small but notable increase between the mid-1950s and early 1960s, and the increase occurred among the poor as well as the wealthy (Hyman and Wright 1971). Nonetheless, the limited exposure to and experience with formal organizations and resources that is currently characteristic of a majority of families leaves them poorly equipped to carry out their formidable array of health care responsibilities, particularly when it comes to negotiating with the formal medical service system.

ACTIVE COPING EFFORT

To what extent do families actively seek out new ideas and information, continue to improve their skills, creatively develop solutions to suit their changing needs, analyze the implications of alternative courses of action, plan with long-term consequences taken into consideration, and strive for increased mastery over themselves and their life situation? Mythology suggests a national trait of energetic coping effort, for Americans are thought to show ingenuity in finding practical solutions to problems, to use initiative in getting things done, and to be achievement- and future-oriented.

In any one year, fewer than one in five adults engages in any formal course work or lessons to develop new ideas and skills. Most families consistently have no adult members taking formal course work or lessons. This type of activity is highly concentrated among those who already have college degrees (Morgan et al. 1966).

Efforts to develop skills in areas of family functioning usually consist of informal, individual use of various information media. A study found that nine out of ten mothers and almost as many fathers seek child-rearing information from books, pamphlets, and magazines, and over half obtain information from newspapers and television (Stolz 1967). Other data reveal that much smaller proportions regularly use these media. Three out of ten people in a national sample reported that they read no magazines, and almost half reported that they spend less than an hour a week reading books. Magazine and book reading is highly concentrated among those who are well-educated and those who belong to community organizations (Hausknecht 1962).

A majority of families makes some effort to learn about health matters and to convey information to their children, but both the learning and the conveying of information are done casually in most families. While a majority of the fathers and mothers in our study sample reported that they had attempted to train their children (aged nine to thirteen) about a number of basic health matters, very few went about this training systematically or rigorously, such as by getting a health pamphlet, using a model to demonstrate, or taking the child to a health lecture or film.

But the direction of change over time has been toward more systematic coping activity. A comparison of three generations of families showed that the latest generation of married couples were more likely than their parents' or grandparents' generation to use various methods of obtaining information and evaluating solutions before taking important actions, such as changing the family residence, making home improvements, or acquiring durable goods. The youngest generation is more likely than older generations to obtain and use information from outside the family rather than rely only on the advice of the immediate family, and to critically evaluate the wisdom of the previous decisions made and actions taken in order to plan more effectively for future actions (Hill et al. 1970).

REGULAR AND VARIED INTERACTION AMONG MEMBERS

To what extent are American families characterized by regular and varied forms of interaction? To what extent is there joint participation in tasks and leisure, structured and unstructured events, and physical activity and verbal communication?

HUSBAND-WIFE INTERACTION

A high rate of husband-wife interaction is widely held to be a central structural feature of the contemporary American family, as well as a highly valued aspect of marriage. In a study of Detroit wives, 47 percent ranked companionship in doing things together with the husband as more valuable than any other part of marriage (Blood and Wolfe 1960). Another study found that both men and women ranked affection and companionship highest in a list of nine goals for marriage (Levinger 1964).

The actual interactions of husbands and wives differ somewhat from the ideal picture of marital companionship. A majority of the couples in our study engaged in a moderate amount of joint activity, and few had a large amount. The measure used was based on the frequency with which a couple engaged together in eleven different leisure activities. The median score was just above the midpoint of the score range, although there were some couples scattered along the entire continuum, including one couple who had absolutely no joint interaction in the eleven activities, and one couple who frequently participated in all eleven. The frequency of joint participation in the eleven activities is shown below for the 273 couples.

	Often	*Occasionally*	*Never*	*Total*
Sit around and talk	65	32	3	100
Joke together	55	40	5	100
Go for a pleasure drive in a car	45	43	12	100
Visit relatives	41	54	5	100
Visit friends	37	56	7	100
Attend church	40	34	26	100

	Often	Occasionally	Never	Total
Attend some type of performance, e.g., theater, movie, etc.	14	53	33	100
Go to parties	9	67	24	100
Attend meetings	8	31	61	100
Play cards	7	32	61	100
Attend sports events	5	29	66	100

Based on these and other data, the bulk of husband-wife leisure interaction is made up of casual conversation around the house and casual drives in the car. Couples less frequently have broader social involvement, but when they do, it consists mainly of visits with relatives or friends. While joint participation in the diversified system of formal organizations and entertainment activities could potentially serve as a major source of marital integration, this has not turned out to be the fact. A majority of couples never attend a meeting or sports event together.

The joint activities of husbands and wives result in some sort of meaningful exchange for a majority of couples, because almost two-thirds of the husbands and three-fourths of the wives reported that they enjoyed very much going places or doing things with their spouses, and only 2 percent of the husbands and 4 percent of the wives did not enjoy it at all.

Most available evidence suggests that the long-term direction of change has been toward greater companionship and communication. A three-generation comparison of couples revealed greater communication between the younger spouses than the older generations (Hill et al. 1970). Another researcher concluded that "Perhaps for the first time in history, the marriage bond has become important in its own right, even after children arrive" (Blood 1964). Other evidence suggests that men are becoming increasingly companionable, both with their wives and their children (Mogey 1957), although this trend is not yet clearly established; and a minority of sociologists even dispute that men have increased their family involvement and participation (Martindale 1960).

Parent-Child Interaction

A study reveals that United States parents and their children are less companionate than Germans, and this includes less instrumental companionship —teaching and helping—as well as less friendship companionship (Devereux et al. 1962). Similarly,

> "Simple companionship between parents and children appear(s) more pronounced in Soviet society than in our own. Although ... Soviet parents may spend less time at home, more of that time appears to be spent in conversation, play, and companionship with children than in American families" (Bronfenbrenner 1970, p. 99).

Bronfenbrenner (1970, p. 98) concludes that there has been "a progressive decrease, especially in recent decades, in the amount of contact between American parents and their children." American children now spend about twice as much time with peers as with their parents (Condry et al. 1968).

In our sample, about half of the parents never spent time with their nine- to thirteen-year-old children doing such things as reading or telling stories, playing games, taking them to the movies, or taking them to a park or beach. Substantially more parents engaged in instrumental interaction with their children, that is, discussing schoolwork or problems. Even among the parents who did interact with their children in entertainment activities, well under half enjoyed it very much. Substantially more enjoyed interacting with children concerning their schoolwork and problems.

Parents are generally not doing as many things with their children as the children would like. Eight out of ten children in our study sample enjoyed doing things with both their parents very much, but only a minority of parents reciprocated the pleasure. This was especially true of the fathers; not only did they do fewer things with their children than did the mothers, but they enjoyed it less than the mothers, even though the children generally enjoyed the mother's and the father's companionship equally. There was also a discrepancy between parents and children in what they wanted to do together. The child wanted the parent to be more of a playmate-pal, while the parent wanted to be more of a teacher-social worker.

FREEDOM AND RESPONSIVENESS
TO THE INDIVIDUAL

To what extent do families encourage autonomy, foster self-actualization, and respond to the unique needs of the individual members? To what extent do families block the efforts of members to cope, function, and work toward personal objectives and fulfillment, particularly through the practice of aversive controls? It is readily apparent that this is a complex area of family behavior, about which it is difficult to draw simple conclusions.

AUTONOMY VERSUS CONTROL OF CHILDREN

A study of parents' values concerning qualities desired in their children found that both mothers and fathers valued *independence* more highly than any other quality. This included both self-reliance and individual freedom, and parents believed it was best attained by giving the child "freedom to make choices, freedom to be away from parents, encouragement to find his own answers, or, in general, freedom through lenient parental control" (Stolz 1967, p. 100). But this same group of parents valued *obedience* almost as highly as independence. This quality included respect for elders and other authority figures. Clearly, then, parents' desire for independence in their children is limited by their concern for obedience.

In addition to their concern with obedience, all parents simply do not believe unconditionally in allowing children independence and full participation within the household. Parental control is positively valued. One survey of magazine readers found that 58 percent of the parents said teenagers should not have a strong voice in setting the rules under which they live (*Better Homes and Gardens* 1972), and another study found the sample about evenly split between agreeing and disagreeing with the statement "A teenager should be allowed to decide most things for himself" (Levinson and Huffman 1955). In practice, full participation by children in family decision making is far from universal. A national study of tenth-grade boys reported that 54 percent felt they had considerable influence in family decisions that affected them, and 46 percent reported moderate, some, or no influence. Fewer than half of the boys said that their parents often or always listened to their side of the argument, or talked over important decisions with them (Bachman 1970).

Other evidence concerning children's independence is found in their degree of freedom to act independently of parental control. More than seven out of ten eleven-year-olds reported that they did not spend any time away from home when the parent did not know definitely where they were, and only 2 percent ever spent as much as two hours away from home in that manner (HEW 1971). Over three out of four women believed children should be over age twelve before being allowed to decide their own bedtime, and over a fourth felt a child should be at least twelve years old before being allowed to decide what to eat (Tavris and Jayaratne 1972). Another survey reported that very few men and women thought that parents should relinquish effective control over their children before age nineteen (*Better Homes and Gardens* 1972).

Other factors that impinge on parents' granting of freedom to children are their concern with protecting them and getting the right behavior from them, together with the joint beliefs that parents know what is best for children and that close control is the best means of getting children to conform to parents' concepts of good behavior. For example, a majority of parents in a study sample agreed with the statement "The saying that 'mother knows best' still has more than a grain of truth" (Levinson and Huffman 1955). Thus, not only is control over children valued as an end in itself, but it is also viewed as an essential instrument for molding children's behavior.

The direction of change appears to be toward more democracy in parent-child relations and more autonomy for children. As early as 1948, a study reported that "a larger percentage of the children in this sample are growing up in equalitarian-democratic and near-equalitarian families than was probably true of their parents" (Ingersoll 1948, p. 297). Content analysis of popular literature from 1950 to 1970 shows a shift toward encouraging parents to rear children to become self-actualizing persons rather than to conform to a prescribed life-style (Bigner 1972).

Use of Aversive Control

A basic characteristic of the relationships between parents and children, husbands and wives, and siblings in a majority of American families is the use of force and the threat of force to exercise control. Various studies show that from 84 to 97 percent of parents use physical punishment at some point in the child's life (Straus et al. 1973; Steinmetz and Straus 1974), and even among adolescents in their last year of high school, one-half had been threatened or actually hit by their parents (Straus 1971). When parents in our sample were asked what they usually did when the child misbehaved or failed to do something he or she was supposed to do, two-thirds of the mothers and almost as many fathers said they slapped or hit the child, and two-thirds said they would also be likely to confine the child to his or her room or to the house. In a national sample of tenth-grade boys, three in ten said their parents slapped them, and 45 percent were threatened with slapping sometimes, often, or always (Bachman 1970). Another study examined the customary behavior of mothers in feeding small children. When faced with a feeding problem, one-half of the mothers hit the child for not eating, or both hit and forcibly opened the child's mouth to put in the food (Brim 1954).

These punitive parental practices are supported by general American values. As previously discussed, there is a widespread belief that parents have a moral obligation to control their children and to demand obedience, and many parents view physical punishment as the necessary and desirable means of achieving it. Control through physical punishment receives broad societal support through its use in the school system. Only two states (New Jersey and Massachusetts) have outlawed corporal punishment in the schools, while thirteen states give positive authorization for its practice. A 1969 survey by the National Education Association found that two-thirds of the elementary school teachers and over half of the high school teachers favored judicious use of violent bodily punishment (Maeroff 1972).

Use of physical force between husbands and wives is not as common, but it is not a rare phenomenon. In our study sample, one-fourth of the husbands and wives reported that they had hit each other. Another estimate, based on extensive study, is that physical force was used in over half of all marriages (Straus et al. 1973). If threats of violence were included, as well as actual execution of violence, the estimate would be even larger. But the law no longer justifies the use of force by the husband to control his wife, and a majority do not openly support marital violence. Only one in four men and about one in six women approve of slapping a wife or husband under any circumstances (Stark and McEvoy 1970).

Husbands and wives employ a variety of other forceful techniques to block and control each other. The typical pattern of handling disagreements in over a fourth of a sample of couples was for either one or both of the spouses to try to force the other to give in (Locke and Williamson 1958); that is, control rather than voluntary compromise was the mode of operating. The techniques used include refusal to perform services or supply goods, such as the wife's refusal to cook and the husband's withholding of money. The wife's refusal to engage in sexual intercourse has been a traditional control device. Physical withdrawal is another device, for example, locking oneself in a room. An even more forceful method is walking out of the house; this may range from a few hours absence to an extended marital separation. Thirteen percent of the married couples in our study sample had at some time physically separated.

FLEXIBLE AND EGALITARIAN STRUCTURING OF RELATIONSHIPS

To what extent is there an egalitarian pattern of decision making and a flexible division of tasks and activities in American marriages? To what extent is there authoritarian decision making and rigid, traditional assignment of tasks and activities?

DECISION-MAKING POWER

While there is a widespread tendency for husbands to exercise more power in the family than their wives, there is considerable diversity among contemporary American families in the pattern of conjugal power, ranging from high equality to high inequality. The couples in our study were distributed all along a six-point index, which measured the extent to which family decisions were concentrated in the husband or wife or were jointly made. There is a significant segment of American families who hold out for greater authority for men than for women.

Men have tended to retain their traditional authority as overall head of the household in decisions regarding their own employment and to a lesser extent their wives' employment, in financial matters, and in sexual activity. Decision making has become more egalitarian in the areas of vacation and leisure time activities, household purchases, home selection, and care of children. The distribution of power has become more egalitarian in part because of the gain in influence by women, especially employed women, in men's traditional sphere of activities, and in part by the loss of power by employed women in their traditional spheres of influence, the household and children.

The direction of change has definitely been away from patriarchal power and toward more egalitarian arrangements. There was a clear trend toward egalitarian decision making over three generations of families in such matters as what housing to take, how much life insurance to buy, whether the wife will work, whether the husband will change his job, whether to call a doctor, and where to spend vacations (Hill et al. 1970). A majority of a sample of male and female college students felt that family decisions should be joint to a greater extent than was practiced in their families of orientation, suggesting that their own marriages would be more egalitarian (Lovejoy 1961). Other researchers concluded that the egalitarian pattern of family decision making was becoming institutionalized, because a majority of husbands and wives reported that both their actual and desired patterns in several areas of family decision making were to have approximately equal participation of the husband and wife (Dyer and Urban 1958). Egalitarian tendencies have advanced extensively through practically all strata of the American population, for there are no remaining subcultures that harbor the fully patriarchal form (Blood and Wolfe 1960).

But there is little likelihood that American marriages will soon become completely egalitarian, because the economic and political circumstances that produced and maintained male dominance will not be quickly eliminated. As long as men continue to hold the more influential and rewarding positions in the broader society, particularly in employment and politics, they will bring to marriage relatively greater resources and personal power than their wives, assuring them at least a slight edge in marital power.

DIVISION OF TASKS AND ACTIVITIES

There are widely differing patterns of task assignment in American marriages, ranging from sharp traditional role segregation to liberal role crossing and flexibility in task assignment, but few couples practice no traditional sex-typing of activity (Blood 1963; Blood and Wolfe 1960; Gavron 1966; Kenkel 1966; Orden and Bradburn 1969; Udry and Hall 1965).

There has been a trend away from rigid sex-typing of activities and toward sharing and flexibility in the family's division of labor (Hill 1964; Kirkpatrick 1963; Miller and Swanson 1958). The early signs of this change were seen in the period between the two studies of Middletown, 1925 to 1935 (Lynd and Lynd 1937). Analysis of three generations of families shows that while all generations followed a pattern of medium to high role specialization, the youngest generation exhibited the most role flexibility and the least conventional role allocations (Hill et al. 1970).

Traditional sex-typing has tended to break down most in recreational, political, civic, and cultural activities, while the traditional sex division of labor has shown greater persistence in household tasks. Women still had the principal responsibility for health care tasks in a slight majority of households in our sample, but in four out of ten households the husband and wife were equally responsible for such tasks as staying up with the sick child, taking the child to the doctor or dentist, knowing what to do when the child was ill or injured, and buying medicines. When wives were ill in bed, the vast majority of husbands took over or assisted with the household tasks, and practically all husbands negotiated medical care arrangements for sick wives.

Another facet of the change is the tendency for more couples to share and to carry on certain activities jointly rather than separately. There is an increasing permissiveness in leaving it to the discretion of individual couples to work out their own division of labor based on the particular capabilities and desires of the husband and wife.

CONCLUSIONS

The evidence suggests that a majority of contemporary American families are inappropriately organized for performing essential health care functions effectively. The fully energized type of family, which was found to be more effective than other types in obtaining medical services, fostering personal health practices, and sustaining the health of family members, is rare. None of the separate features of the energized model is a dominant American pattern. Families generally have rather limited links with the organizations and resources of the broader community. This leaves them poorly equipped to develop their members' capabilities for caring for personal health needs and for dealing effectively with the formal and technical system of professional medicine. The general failure of families to engage in systematic and energetic efforts to cope also hampers the development of their members' competence to take care of personal health needs and to use professional services effectively. Another factor that impedes the development of sound personal health practices is the tendency for interaction among family members to be limited and stereotyped, particularly the husband-father's involvement within the family. The tendency of families to control and block their members' efforts at self-direction and full functioning, rather than to encourage such efforts, is detrimental to health.

Some evidence does indicate that family structure is undergoing modification in the direction of more energized types of families—greater participation in the broader community, greater freedom through emphasis on self-actualization rather than conformity to a prescribed life-style, more egalitarian distribution of power, and more flexible role arrangements. But there are certainly no massive trends in the direction of a more energized family form in the United States.

The structural limitations of families are underscored when contrasted with the structural capabilities of the formal health care system, the system with which the consumer-family must negotiate for medical service, information, and guidance. Professional medicine has achieved a high degree of autonomy in establishing working arrangements to suit its own objectives rather than those of clients, organized much of its activity within powerful bureaucratic organizations, structured its relationships with clients on highly authoritarian lines, developed formal mechanisms for asserting its interests forcefully in the political arena, and collaborated with other elements of the establishment to preserve its own advantages. Not only is the consumer-family at a distinct disadvantage in negotiating for service with such a system, but consumers are also restrained from developing the knowledge, skills, judgment, confidence, and responsibility needed for caring for health on their own. Under these circumstances, energized families have a reasonable chance of success in taking care of their members, but nonenergized families do not.

If families are to perform health care activities more effectively than they currently do, adaptations are needed in the organization of either the family or the health care system, or both. The final two chapters will discuss what the family requires to function successfully within the context of societal conflict and coercion. Chapter Nine takes a social action approach, and proposes some specific strategies that could aid families in dealing more effectively with the health care system and in caring for their members' health needs. Chapter Ten takes a theoretical approach, generalizing about the requirements for an effectively functioning family system, and the nature of the family's relationships with other social systems.

PART THREE

Implications for
Social Action and Theory

The final section will discuss some practical applications of the evidence presented in the course of the book. The research findings have basic implications for designing action strategies that will prove effective in getting families to care adequately for their members' health; and they also have implications for social theory, particularly our assumptions about what type of structure a social system needs in order to function effectively.

Our investigation led to these conclusions: A major share of the responsibility for health care in the United States has been absorbed by the family, yet families are generally performing their health-related activities rather inadequately. This discrepancy between need and performance is due, in part, to the limited structural capabilities of the family itself and, in part, to the imbalance between the structural resources of the family and those of the health care system. The internal structure of families is based more on disciplining members to conform to prescribed societal patterns than on fostering self-actualization and individuality. Families' relationships with the medical care system are relatively passive and nonassertive. Family units have not generally delineated their distinctive interests and the areas of incompatibility between their interests and those of the medical care groups they deal with, and they have not developed tactics for advancing their own interests in encounters with medical care groups. Nor have families formally organized for concerted action in order to influence health policy or to control the health services. On the other hand, the medical care system is organized formally and autocratically, and has well-developed mechanisms for asserting its members' own distinctive interests in relationships with other social systems, including the family. Thus, there is an incongruence between the health functions the contemporary family must perform and structural resources available to the family for carrying out those functions in an effective manner.

Evidence from our field research indicates that those families whose structure is based on a high degree of autonomy in relationships among members, encouragement of individual development, aggressive coping effort, dynamic relationships among members, flexible and nontraditional role patterns, egalitarian power, and energetic participation in external social systems do carry out their health activities quite effectively. These families are more likely than other types of families to sustain the level of health of their members, to achieve a high level of personal health practices in their members, and to use medical services appropriately.

The empirical evidence led us to devise the label *energized family* to express the type of structure that enables the family to perform personal care effectively. The energized family is generally well adapted to perform the principal functions required of the family today. Given the regimentation, impersonality, and coerciveness of other societal institutions, the family must provide, first and foremost, a bond in which the individual is esteemed, and in which the individual is given freedom to be himself or herself and is supported in his or her efforts to fulfill personal goals. The other side of this responsibility is that families must protect and defend their members in relations with outside organizations and personnel. Health care is one aspect of this family responsibility to the individual. The family must assist persons to develop their physical capacities to the fullest and help them to protect their health in contacts with professional medicine.

Chapter Nine will propose some social action strategies, and Chapter Ten will present theoretical propositions that emerged from this evidence.

NINE
Implications for
Social Action

Marion Bernstein

THIS CHAPTER WILL reformulate the sociological question into a form designed to generate social action. The question "What type of family structure enables families to perform their health care functions most effectively?" now becomes "What modifications could be made in the family's relationships with the medical care system which would improve the family's health care performance?" The recommendations will focus on providing support to the family for relating more fruitfully and assertively to the medical care system on behalf of its members' interests.

There is reason for considerable pessimism about prospects for remodeling relationships between families and the health care system. Families are highly dependent on the medical care system, yet the services are frequently inadequate, and the professional groups are often unresponsive, rigid, impersonal, manipulative, and autocratic in dealing with clients. Consequently, it is becoming an increasingly important responsibility of families to deal assertively with the professionals in order to protect the families' interests. Even though this type of response may be called for, families do not typically advance their claims systematically and forcefully, either in the form of concerted political action or assertive interpersonal relations with professionals. Only among the aristocracy has there been a tradition of broad-scale promotion of family interests. The structural shortcomings of a majority of families preclude their taking assertive action on their own; besides, the structural strength of the health care system enables it to resist external pressures for change.

But there are elements within both systems that hold potential for generating constructive change. First, there are the energized families, which can bring pressure for change and make use of any new developments in health care arrangements. Second, there are individuals and groups in the medical care system who are responsive to the need to make the system more adaptive to client needs. This responsive element within the health care system was not discussed in the earlier analysis of the system, because it does not represent the mainstream to which most families are exposed. But it is the combined efforts of this minority element within medicine and this minority of energized families which hold promise for restructuring relationships between the family and medicine.

Some of the actions recommended depend entirely on family initiative, while others require professional initiative plus family pressure. One objective is to develop the family's power to influence the health care system and to deal with it effectively. The proposed strategies for achieving this depend on family initiative, and range from consumer control of the health services to techniques for dealing assertively with the professionals in interpersonal relations. Another objective is to involve the family more fully with the professionals in the therapeutic process. The recommendations include involving the family in hospital care and providing a full range of health services at home. This calls for joint professional and family effort.

The particular recommendations made here are not, of course, the only possible conclusions that could be drawn from our research. Other analysts might propose additional applications of the findings or disagree with the usefulness or the objectives of the ones presented. On the other hand, the proposals for action do not stand or fall only on the basis of their grounding in our research findings; for particular proposals may have merit because of their benefits to health, regardless of their possible contribution to family capabilities.

The chapter continues to pursue the goal of characterizing the family by the nature of the actions it performs. To know what the family of the future will be, one must know what its characteristic actions will be. If the proposals are implemented, families will be involved in an increased amount of health care action, and they will be engaged in more systematic and forceful management of their external relationships, which may come to include their relationships with educational, leisure, government, and other societal agencies, as well as with the health care system.

AUGMENTING FAMILY POWER

We will propose some strategies that are aimed at increasing the power of families to influence the medical care system and to deal with it effectively. Because the current level of family activism is so low and because families differ so widely in their needs and inclinations, any realistic scheme for aiding families to increase their influence over the health care system must provide them a number of alternative modes of action. Our proposals range from formal political participation to interpersonal influence, and from militant to defensive action. We will first propose some modes of concerted political action, then some strategies for increasing the family's effectiveness in direct negotiations with the health care system.

Consumer Control of Health Services

Many health planners outside the medical profession now operate on the assumption that health care is too important to be left solely to the professionals, and that as we move toward a greater commitment of public funds for making comprehensive health care available to everyone, it is obligatory that consumers participate in the governance of every aspect of the system (Aspen Institute 1971). This is not new, for union-sponsored health plans of the United Mine Workers and United Automobile Workers are well established, and there is an organization called the Group Health Association of America that represents the various consumer-sponsored plans (Wolfe 1971). But consumer control of or even participation in the governing boards of health services is still very uncommon, and the largest plan, the Kaiser program, has very limited consumer representation.

Major impetus for consumer participation has come from federal laws requiring consumer involvement. The 1966 Partnership for Health Law established comprehensive community health planning and called for State Health

Planning Councils, requiring that a majority of the membership consist of persons representing consumers of health services (Palmer et al. 1972). The Neighborhood Health Centers started in 1968 under the Office of Economic Opportunity also called for maximum feasible participation of poor people in designing and directing these health centers (Cahn and Passett 1969).

Consumer participation is expected to increase, but concerted pressure from consumer groups will be needed to bring about each new concession. A group called the People's Committee for Accountability succeeded in getting consumer councils set up in the Health Insurance Plan of Greater New York. These councils are definitely not permitted to control the centers (Lichtenstein 1972). In 1972, the first community board established in a New York municipal hospital was installed in Sydenham Hospital, but the physicians attempted to disband the board so it could be reorganized with increased physician representation (Hicks 1972; Fraser 1972).

Even when consumers do gain representation on health agencies, traditional pressures to let the professionals run things persist. Although consumers constitute a majority of the members of State Health Planning Councils, the government agencies charged with setting up health programs do not give as much credence to the advice and opinions of the lay or consumer council members as they do to the advice from health professionals. The citizens who are selected to serve come primarily from well-established community organizations, and thus the interests of many segments of the consuming public may not be represented at all (American Rehabilitation Foundation 1969). Even when a neglected minority segment of the community does get representatives on a board or agency, the representatives are often co-opted by the medical establishment; the representatives' inclinations to change the system are neutralized by offering them jobs in the organization, or by allowing them to participate with the leadership elite (Kane 1971). Some health organizations assume an ideological stance of citizen participation in relations with the public, and use this facade to buy out the complaints of clients and to neutralize community opposition, without permitting any real sharing of power (Krause 1969).

Yet consumer representation on planning bodies and health delivery systems is essential to achieve needed improvements in services. Consumers played a major role in establishing neighborhood health centers by writing some of the first proposals and by getting the health care providers and consumers to work together (Chenault et al. 1971). Consumer-family representatives in consumer medical cooperatives have been able to work for changes in the delivery system that benefit families, for example, eligibility rules that include dependents in the plan, provision of family physician service to integrate care for the whole family, home care services, and complaint procedures (Schwartz 1965).

The major problem is how consumers can proceed—how they can find other concerned people to work with, and what constructive actions they can take. There is a need for mechanisms to mobilize their efforts and provide guidance. Attempts were made to provide a mechanism for consumers who are concerned about the quality of care provided by hospitals to enable them to participate in the accreditation of hospitals. This is a vital point at which consumers can exert influence, because without accreditation a hospital can receive no money under the federal Medicare program, and interns and residents who are training at such a hospital cannot get credit for their work. Yet the process has been closed to the public. The Joint Commission on Accreditation of Hospitals (JCAH) is the accrediting agency, and it sends a survey inspection team to each hospital every two years. But the Board of Commissioners of JCAH is composed entirely of hospital administrators and representatives of the medical profession, and the JCAH refuses to allow consumers to sit on the board or even to attend its meetings.

A Consumer Advisory Council was formed which puts people in touch with others in their local area who are concerned about health issues, and supplies information about the accreditation process. The Health Law Project of the University of Pennsylvania (1973) developed a guide for local groups on how to participate in hearings held by the survey team. While the ultimate objective may be to have consumers on the board of JCAH, the first step is to have consumers influence the recommendations made by the survey inspection teams about particular hospitals. Consumer involvement, even on this level, is only beginning to occur, much less to show results. The first direct participation in the JCAH accrediting process took place in 1970, when hospital interns and residents were joined by senior citizen groups in complaints against the Washington, D.C. General Hospital, resulting in a one-year provisional accreditation (Health Law Project 1973). When the accrediting agency issued its recommendations concerning the Nassau County Medical Center in New York in 1973, it incorporated some points made by a consumer interest group, including proposals for privacy in the outpatient service, more doctors to handle the outpatient load, and interpreters to aid doctors and foreign-speaking patients (Gold 1973).

PARTICIPATION IN VOLUNTARY ASSOCIATIONS

The formal work organizations—business, government, school, and health service units—have been called the workhorses of society, while it is the voluntary associations that bring about reforms and innovations. Voluntary associations arise so that a group of people can achieve a common objective, and they often disappear when the objective is accomplished. They provide a vehicle which families can use to bring about modifications in the health care system.

The General Federation of Women's Clubs is credited with being a major force behind the enactment of the Pure Food, Drug and Cosmetic Act in 1906. The Women's Clubs were aroused by the impure milk they fed their children (Hasebroock 1965). It was through the efforts of voluntary reform groups that birth control was legalized. The reformers framed the issue as one of family well-being, emphasizing the value of birth control in strengthening the family in a secular society and in helping families to achieve upward mobility in a competitive economy (Conway 1971). More recently, women's groups have been credited with getting a bill through the New York state legislature that legalized abortion (Kovach 1970). A major theme was the right of the individual couple and, particularly, the woman to make decisions about childbearing without interference from outside agencies.

The American Parents Committee (1971) direct their efforts toward getting federal legislation of benefit to children, such as a family assistance plan, school lunch programs, family planning services, and community mental health centers. The National Council on the Aging (1972) works for a variety of health care programs beneficial to elderly persons, including measures to provide home care services and coverage of home care costs by Medicare and Medicaid.

Some of the associations that focus on a particular disease or disability work for legislation that benefits the diseased person's family. For example, the American Foundation for the Blind (1972) tried to get disability insurance benefits extended to the widow or widower of the disabled person, and federal assistance for parents of blind children to meet the costs of special facilities and medical care.

Some newer associations seek more radical solutions to family health problems. The Peoples' Coalition Against Lead Poisoning in St. Louis has taken the position that the lead-poisoning problem can only be dealt with when tenants organize and take control of the landlord's property, so they retain rent money and use it to repair the housing (*Source* 1972). The boldest efforts are those aimed at establishing alternative medical structures. The Medical Committee for Human Rights, based in Chicago, is an action organization of health workers and patients, which proposes to create a federal nonprofit corporation to produce drugs and medical supplies (*Source* 1972). Other associations have established free medical clinics in poor neighborhoods of some major cities. Staffed by local residents, these clinics try to reach the neighborhood poor by setting up in storefronts or in mobile units (O. M. Collective 1971).

The self-help group is a type of voluntary association that may turn out to be well suited for achieving radical solutions to a variety of family health problems. These groups are organized by "individuals who share a condition stigmatized by the larger community" (Traunstein and Steinman 1973). Two self-help groups that emerged in the 1930s are the National Association for Retarded Children and Alcoholics Anonymous. Today there are about 300 self-help groups in the country. Self-help groups work on the basis that people who share the same problem can provide each other with help that is not available from, or not adequately provided by, professionals and bureaucratic service organizations. While other people stigmatize those afflicted as deviant, weak, or inferior, the group members define themselves and their condition as acceptable. Self-help groups often seek, therefore, to undermine or reform the approach and methods used by the professionals and the traditional health organizations, which enforced the stigma.

COLLABORATION WITH THE CONSUMER MOVEMENT

The modern consumer movement is mobilizing many diverse groups and concerns around the central issue of reordering national priorities, so as to give greater support to individual consumers relative to corporate and professional groups. It is highly likely that families interested in using the political process to advance their interests will be able to achieve their objectives by working with some of the organizations that make up the consumer movement. On the whole, the interests of families are directly served by the general consumer movement, yet the needs of families sometimes differ from the needs of other citizen groups. To realize their own needs, families must have special representation within the general consumer activist movement.

Two nonprofit testing organizations provided the backbone for the general consumer movement. Consumers Union, founded in 1936, publishes *Consumer Reports,* and Consumers' Research, founded in 1928, publishes *Consumer Bulletin.* In 1968 Consumers Union sued the Veterans Administration for withholding information it had learned about hearing aids bought for disabled veterans. The Veterans Administration was forced to release the information. This court decision set an important precedent for other government agencies to release product information compiled with public funds (Burson-Marsteller 1970).

In 1964 the consumer movement gained an articulate national spokesman when Ralph Nader exposed the hidden dangers in automobile design. Nader subsequently organized the Center for Study of Responsive Law, which is staffed by young lawyers who represent the public interest before federal agencies and the courts. In 1968 "Nader's Raiders" were organized to investigate whether government agencies adequately protect and represent consumer interests.

In 1967 such independently influential consumer groups as the YWCA, National Farmers Union, National Council of Senior Citizens, labor unions, and state and local consumer organizations jointly formed the Consumer Federation of America. It maintains liaison with members of Congress and decision makers in federal agencies and departments, presents testimony on legislation affecting consumers, and collects and publishes facts on such matters as drugs, medical care, and safety.

A variety of agencies and supportive mechanisms are being set up to protect consumers and to advance their interests. There are consumer protection agencies on the federal, state, and local level of government. A few states have also established the position of ombudsman—a person who serves as a representative for people who have problems with government agencies. This invention has trickled down from government to hospitals, and a few large urban hospitals have an ombudsman to protect patients' rights.

Some of the legislative accomplishments of consumer activists are: labeling of drugs by their generic names; the Child Protection Law regulating hazardous substances and toys; a health warning label on cigarette packages; regulation of flammable fabrics in draperies, bedding, and clothing; and the truth-in-packaging bill.

There are some legal mechanisms that enable consumers to take action themselves when they have been wronged. The legalization of class actions makes it possible for a large number of consumers who have suffered the same type of wrong to join together in a single lawsuit and to recover damages. Other legal techniques are injunctions against businesses engaged in harmful practices, the provision of legal aid for poor people who wish to bring suit against a private or public agency, and expansion of the Small Claims Court, in which a person who has been cheated can bring a suit without a lawyer.

A central ideological feature of the consumer movement is that the producing and governing institutions should be open to the scrutiny of the consumer-citizen public. Some organizations have accepted this responsibility, and turned it to their advantage by opening themselves up to tours of inspection or by presenting special exhibits and demonstrations. Not so the health care industry. It is almost as tightly closed to public view as the penal system. Yet what better way for this fascinating industry to promote public understanding of its operations, problems, and accomplishments than to show off its teaching, research, and service endeavors. Since the health care system has not voluntarily accepted this responsibility, it would be appropriate for consumer action groups to encourage and assist the health industry to expose itself to view.

Family Assertiveness in Client-Professional Relationships

In the meantime, while waiting for changes to be effected in the health care system and the power structure by consumer protection agencies, voluntary associations, and consumer-dominated boards, each family has to carry on mundane transactions with the existing health care system. Improved strategies and techniques are needed to augment the power and effectiveness of family members in these transactions.

One long-range goal is to elevate the role of patient to the level of professional consumer, a role based on proficiency in obtaining good service in the professional-bureaucratic marketplace. The label of patient symbolizes and reinforces the impotence of the present role. Labels such as medical client or consumer are needed for the upgraded role in order to reflect its dynamic components—deliberate selection of service, commissioning of the provider, active participation in planning and executing the service, and evaluation of the provider and the provider's service. Some sociologists have concluded that patients can never interact with physicians on an equal basis because doctors have the advantage of skill, full-time work at their roles, and sound health. However, the current patient role came about by successfully stripping the person of all other attributes on entering the health care system, and dealing with the person only in terms of her or his weakness.

Strategies are needed for developing professional consumership. Families must socialize their members to negotiate effectively with officials and bureaucracies, mediate as units with these agencies on behalf of their members, join forces with other families or groups to enhance the family's bargaining power, and approach each encounter with the health care system ready for active engagement rather than passive submission.

There is a need for practical tactics that the consumer may use to force health personnel to perform according to the consumer's standards and needs, and to stimulate health personnel to do a good job, interact informatively, and deliver service in a convenient way. Here are some measures that are directed at common consumer problems. Unfortunately, no handbooks have been written on how to be an emancipated patient, and the tactics suggested here have not been tested in the medical marketplace for efficacy or safety.

Shop around for doctors and hospitals. Find out in advance of any medical need what services the available hospitals provide and what their practices are regarding participation of family members. Before selecting a physician, ask for recommendations from other doctors, various health professionals, and knowledgeable consumers. Find out such things about physicians as board certifications, what hospital(s) they are associated with, what physicians they get referrals from and to whom they refer their patients, and how they cover their patients when off duty.

Try to find a doctor who is accessible when needed. There is a doctors' joke that has one physician saying to another: "I make an occasional house call just to get away from the mob in the office," which the emancipated patient might turn around: "Never go to the doctor's office if a house call will do," and "Never call during the day if a night call will do" (McConnell and Schutjer 1971). More realistically, find out the physician's house call policy and tele-phoning arrangements. Select a physician who will talk to you directly by phone rather than through a receptionist. Do not discuss diagnosis or treat-ment with an intermediary for, as any child knows who has played the game *telephone,* the communication loses something in the translation. Find out the nature of the doctor's appointment system, usual waiting time, and how much time he or she is likely to spend with a patient.

Talk with the physician from the very beginning of the contact concerning diagnosis and treatment. Ask questions and direct the doctor to your needs; find out what alternative modes of treatment are being considered and what assumptions underly the choice among the alternatives. Encourage children to deal directly with health personnel; for example, to give their own medical history and discuss current complaints and therapy with physicians.

Ask for a copy of your medical record periodically, and whenever your family moves to a different town. Ask the physician what the fee is for a particular service, and request a copy of the physician's full fee schedule. If you are to be hospitalized, find out in advance when the doctor will be available to the family in the hospital. When dissatisfied, present the specific complaint directly to the physician, not through a receptionist. If you have been unjustly treated and the hospital or physician refuses to negotiate, make active efforts to resolve the problem by calling on, or by suggesting your willingness to call on, various sources of advice and influence: colleagues or friends within the health care system or in other positions of power, the county medical society and its grievance committee, the third party who insures you, a lawyer, or a consumer protection agency.

None of the tactics discussed provides the consumer with tested formulas for coping elegantly with the medical care system. But given the present state of the art of medical consumership, a certain amount of naïve blundering ahead is called for, with the expectation of being criticized occasionally for maladroitness. In the long run, consumers will need a codified body of techniques for adeptly manipulating the medical care situation to their advantage, techniques comparable to those developed to assist doctors in handling various situations. Here is an illustration of the type of guidebook instruction that is needed for patients. It is excerpted from a training manual, which instructs doctors in how to obtain consent for an autopsy from a bereaved family:

> "The best time for a request is from fifteen minutes to a half hour after death.... The request should be made to the nearest of kin, with as few other relatives present as possible.... The request should be made in a quiet room, at a little distance from the deceased. The room should be furnished in such a way as to give it an air of dignity. The room of the deceased, a hospital corridor, or a public waiting room are inappropriate places for the discussion.... A dignified and sympathetic approach by the interviewer is particularly important. He should review some of the more significant efforts made for the patient and, where appropriate, indicate how the advanced degree of illness may have prevented the success of treatment.... Some of the objections usually encountered in the interveiw—and answers to them—are as foliows:... 'He would not have wanted it.' This remark should be questioned by asking if the subject of an autopsy ever had been discussed. It might be suggested that if the deceased was a generous and unselfish person who thought of others, he no doubt would have been glad to help other persons afflicted as he was" (American Hospital Association 1970, pp. 51–53).

Consumers would be well served by comparable manuals devoted to developing guidelines and techniques for managing advantageously various medical care situations, especially those which are harrowing and have major implications for the family. One situation entails the proceedings for committing a person to an institution for mental illness, alcoholism, or drug addiction. In such proceedings, physician-psychiatrists may act as double agents, presenting themselves to patients as helpers, while using conversations with patients to collect evidence that may be used against them in court.

The court psychiatrist may spend too little time examining the patient to reach a sound diagnosis. Individuals and their families may not be informed that they may be represented by counsel (Scheff 1967). Other possible confrontations for families include proceedings to press claims for accidental injury or disability compensation, and to obtain medical services from the Veterans Administration or rehabilitation services from a health organization or government agency. Families may be called upon to negotiate with the school in delicate situations; for example, when the school classifies a child as handicapped or urges that the child be given drugs to make him or her more tractable. In such situations, the schoolchild and family members need a supportive and assertive family, a family armed with full information concerning their rights, knowledge of the requisite procedures, and adroitness in negotiation.

The discussion focused on tactics of assertiveness because, in contrast to professionals, families lack the ability to assert their interests in transactions. There are other dimensions of client-professional interaction in which clients need to develop proficiency. One is effective communication. To communicate effectively, the client must be both informative and responsive, and this requires advance preparation in the subject matter and thoughtful performance during the meeting. Another is the fulfillment of contractual obligations; for the client, this means paying bills and keeping appointments. As in other types of relationships, the professional-client transaction is enhanced if there is a rewarding human exchange between the participants. This calls for the client to be considerate, to respect the dignity of the other person, and to appreciate that person's humanness.

There is no inherent conflict between increasing the client's assertiveness in transactions with professionals, on the one hand, and effective communication, fulfillment of contractual obligation, and warm interpersonal exchange, on the other. In fact, both the client's and the professional's performance in all these important dimensions may be enhanced when the relationship is more egalitarian, and both parties openly express and negotiate in terms of their distinctive interests.

FAMILY MEMBERSHIP IN THE HEALTH CARE TEAM

Families must increase their involvement with professionals in the therapeutic process. Families cannot become highly responsible about their health care duties if the professionals exclude them from participating in medical management. Nor can families provide good care for sickness at home unless provisions are made for the delivery of health services in homes.

In the past, the patient has generally been treated as a passive subject to be ministered to by the professionals, and the family has either been excluded or regarded as an agent for carrying out the professionals' orders. It has suited the convenience and objectives of health personnel and hospitals to practice in this fashion, even though it has not generally been in the best interest of consumers and families to be denied a responsible role in patient treatment.

Technical changes taking place in medicine provide an opportunity to establish the family's role in the therapeutic team. The specialization of medical care brings the patient in contact with many different physicians at various times, none of whom coordinates and supervises his or her total care on a continuing basis, thus requiring that the patient and the patient's family assume the overall responsibility. Since there are now so many other professional members of the therapeutic team—social workers, nutritionists, nurses, and rehabilitation workers—it is no longer such a radical departure to admit family members. Employment of untrained members of the community to work with families as health aides also tends to erode the traditional distinction between the professional and the layman, and serves to link the family and professionals together in a joint effort. Added to these changes are the skyrocketing costs of professional care, which are stimulating proposals to transfer some of the health care work from the professional realm to the family.

FAMILY INVOLVEMENT IN HOSPITAL CARE

The problem of excluding the family from the therapeutic team is sharply manifested in hospitals, for here patients are physically separated from their families. Yet the movement toward involving families in care of their members in hospitals has been very slow to develop, because the strong professional tradition of focusing on the patient is fortified by the bureaucratic inclination to run a tight ship.

Some hospitals have established units that encourage parents' involvement in the care of critically ill children. At the City of Hope Medical Center in California, parents may attend their children from the hour of rising until bedtime and, in cases of critically ill children, at night as well (Knudson and Natterson 1960). In addition to providing support for children while they are hospitalized, parents learn how to take care of the children after release. By seeing other children with varying stages of the same disease and by meeting their parents, many of the parents are aided in coping with their own child's illness. The University of Kentucky Medical Center established a Care-by-Parent Unit, in which the mother is completely responsible for the child's care, just as she is at home. There is not even a supervisory person on duty during the night. The unit was set up in a special facility resembling a motel, which is adjacent to the other pediatric facilities. The savings in professional staff in this live-in unit make it more economical to operate than a conventional ward (Vernon and Wheeler 1969). A small number of hospitals have permitted fathers to share in the care of their newborn children as a method of training the father, as well as getting him involved in caring for the infant.

It is clear that pressure from outside the health care system will be needed to bring about major changes in hospitals' policies and practices regarding families. In 1959 in Great Britain, a commission recommended that provisions be made to admit mothers along with their children (*Platt Report* 1959), and the recommendations were adopted as official policy by the Ministry of Health. Yet it required well-organized efforts of a group of parents whose children had had bad hospital experiences to get the policy implemented (Shore 1965).

FAMILY HEATH PRACTICE

There have been attempts within the medical profession to reorient medical care toward the family unit rather than toward the isolated individual patient. The underlying philosophy is that the family is the cradle for health and illness, as well as the unit within which effective therapy can be accomplished (Reader and Goss, 1967).

A new medical specialty of Family Practice was created in an attempt to recapture some of the beneficial services formerly performed by the fast-disappearing general practitioner. The distinguishing feature of this specialty is the assumption of responsibility for comprehensive, continuous health care for patients within the context of their family groups (Warren 1970). The family physician's commitment to provide continuing and comprehensive care, rather than just emergency, episodic treatment, involves the physician in analyzing the interrelations among family members as they affect diagnosis and treatment. Hence the physician is virtually obligated to have family units as patient entities. The new specialty of Family Practice was approved by the AMA in 1969. There are thirty-nine medical schools that have approved programs, yielding about 152 family physicians per year. This specialty is not yet well established, however, and it has not achieved full acceptance from other specialists, such as pediatricians and internists.

There are also a number of programs for training nurses for family health care, which build on the public health tradition in nursing of relating to patients within their community and family setting. As a career field, this will open attractive opportunities for nurses to achieve greater independence than in other types of nursing careers. As envisioned, the family nurse practitioner will make independent judgments, and assume principal responsibility for primary health care of individuals and families (*Nursing Outlook* 1972).

Health planners are now proposing that services be organized for delivery to families and communities rather than to individuals. The Family Health Maintenance Demonstration at Montefiore Hospital in New York was organized to demonstrate the feasibility of maintaining good health through a family-centered approach to medical care (Silver 1963). In 1963, the Denver Department of Health and Hospitals embarked on a city-wide effort, involving twenty-eight different clinics and facilities, to provide team health care to one hundred thousand medically indigent patients. A medical team was responsible for coordinating the services needed by a particular family (Cowen and Sbarbaro 1972). But the programs have generally shown that the various health care specialties, hospital departments, clinics, and community agencies continue to go about their work independently of each other, and that given the present structure of services, it is very difficult to achieve coordinated and comprehensive care for families.

Federal planning and funding now emphasizes the family-centered approach. In 1972, the Department of Health, Education and Welfare began funding forty-one family health centers in areas where health resources are scarce. Each center provides outpatient services to at least 5,000 families, who enroll for a fixed monthly payment (HEW 1972). A much larger federal commitment has been made to finance the development of Health Maintenance Organizations, which are prepaid group practices that enroll families for a single monthly fee and provide complete health services. The aim is to involve the family in keeping its members healthy so as to avoid illness and its costly medical care.

HOME CARE SERVICES

Historically, there has been a shift away from the early pattern of caring for the sick in the home to a focus of care within hospitals. The concentration on institutional care went too far. Many persons could receive better care at home than in an institution and at the same time maintain a more normal life, if there were provisions for delivering health services to people at home. Now there are some efforts to shift the emphasis away from institutions. The American Hospital Association has indicated that home care has a valuable role to play in expediting recovery of the patient, preventing or postponing disability, preventing or shortening institutionalization, and maintaining the integrity of the family unit during illness of one of its members (American Hospital Association 1961). The Department of Health Education and Welfare has recognized that, "Home health services may well be one of the most promising approaches to help resolve the complex problems hampering the efficient delivery of health care in the United States" (HEW 1971).

With the passage of Medicare legislation, it was thought that home care services would be developed across the nation to serve the needs of the elderly ill. In fact, many home health agencies were established. But it turned out that Medicare may actually have depressed the development of home services rather than stimulated them. The terms of the Medicare insurance system encourage placement of a patient in a hospital or nursing home, for many essential services such as housekeeping, which are reimbursed when they are provided in an institution, are not reimbursed when they are provided in the home, unless the person was institutionalized first. The definition of a home health agency under Medicare requires only that the agency provide nursing care plus one other service. Yet the elderly population requires a more comprehensive and flexible array of services, including house cleaning, cooking, shopping, and bathing, if they are to be maintained at home (U.S. Senate 1972). Thus, the agencies have formed on the basis of the services they can be reimbursed for, but these service patterns do not meet the needs of the agencies' caseloads.

Rehabilitation programs have been developed to help persons with various types of physical disabilities. However, most of the work is done in centers, so that a majority of the people who are homebound by their disabilities are not receiving adequate rehabilitation service. Some efforts have been made to use the electronic teaching media to provide educational programs to the homebound. But vocational rehabilitation projects for the homebound have been limited mainly to arts and crafts (Rusalem 1971).

There are programs that are experimenting with treatment of specific forms of illness at home. In a program for hemophiliac patients, the clotting factor is injected at home instead of at a hospital emergency room. The patients and families report that they are able to treat their hemorrhages faster, stop their pain sooner, and lead more normal lives than was possible before (Brody 1970). Physicians send virtually all heart attack victims to a hospital for intensive care and close medical surveillance. But some British physicians treat heart attack patients in their homes and send them to hospital if complications occur. They find that many patients recuperate just as well, and possibly better, when treated at home instead of in a hospital (Altman 1971).

There has been an effort by some women in California to revive the custom of delivering babies at home. There are obstacles, however, for many physicians will not perform home deliveries because of time and costs and because better medical services are available in hospitals; doctors also fear malpractice suits. Nurse-midwives are not legally permitted to deliver babies in California, although efforts have been made to remove the legal barrier. Because of the importance of the family in all life-cycle crises, more families may care for their dying members at home instead of leaving them isolated in institutions.

If home care of illness is to increase, it will be necessary to coordinate existing medical services with home services. A comprehensive home care service must use institutional facilities flexibly, for example, for treatment during the day, weekends, or vacations, with the patients remaining in their homes and community the rest of the time. Full mobility of both the services and the consumer must be provided. Busing service to clinics and other health agencies must be provided so patients can obtain professional care. A full range of medical and supportive services are required within the home. This includes physician care, nutrition services, drugs and medical supplies, homemaker and home health aid services, provision of equipment, such as hospital beds, wheelchairs, and commodes, and all the other diagnostic and therapeutic services which can be safely delivered in the patient's home (American Hospital Assn. 1971).

LIMITS OF FAMILY INVOLVEMENT

Families' care of members' illnesses will certainly be enhanced by collaborating and assuming joint responsibility with professionals. But all types of family involvement will not benefit the family. Hospitals and professionals may transfer the most tedious and disagreeable aspects of medical care to the family, but may not reduce fees paid by families accordingly.

In newer approaches in medicine, it is considered essential that the physician evaluate the family, as well as the patient, in attempting to diagnose and select therapy. This orientation can greatly facilitate families' efforts to cope with their health problems responsibly, if the professionals openly accept the family as equal members of the health care team. But this approach can take some undesirable turns. The physician may regard the family as disease agents who have caused the patient's problems, and the family may, therefore, be expected to offer themselves as co-patients who must be treated in order to aid their sick member. As a result, they may be less able to provide support to their ill member than they could when they were being ignored by the physician. Or the family may be expected to act as indigenous therapists, helping the physician to carry out her or his therapeutic plan (Pollak 1967). But if the family is used by the physician in getting to the patient—in the fashion that a probation officer may urge the family to manipulate their delinquent child—a wedge may be driven between the patient and the family.

Finally, a family-centered approach is justifiable only insofar as it enhances individuals' opportunities to fulfill their potential; it is not justifiable on grounds of professional convenience, economy of service, efficiency, or family unity. Individuals should be free to obtain medical care from sources that are different from those used by their families. They should be protected from intrusion by their families into their health problems and medical care, if they choose, and physicians should continue to provide individuals with the traditional protection against violations of their right to privacy.

CONCLUSIONS

This chapter illustrates how sociological findings may be used in designing programs and strategies to facilitate the family's performance of its health care responsibilities. The investigation showed that the family was disadvantaged in negotiating with the health care system because of the imbalance in the capabilities of these two systems for asserting their respective interests. In the light of these findings, we propose that families must become politically active in order that family interests may be more fully reflected in health policy and in the operation of health institutions. Some possible modes of political engagement are representation of family-consumer interests on the boards of health agencies, participation in voluntary health associations, and collaboration with the consumer movement. Families also need to strengthen their hand in negotiations with physicians and health agencies by preparing to engage in these relationships as professional consumers rather than ineffectual patients.

A particular goal of family activism is to reformulate the relationship between the family and the health care system so that the client and family participate more fully and responsibly with professionals—as members of the health care team—rather than as passive recipients of professionals' ministrations. This should include the involvement of families in the care of their members in the hospital, the restructuring of medical practice to enable family units to obtain integrated and comprehensive care, and the funding and development of comprehensive home care services to permit families to obtain at home most of the services that are now available only in professional installations.

What is the feasibility of such proposals—given the facts that families are not presently fully responsive to their members' unique lines of development and are not representing their interests very effectively in public encounters? In spite of this, social systems do what they must. The major function that the family today must perform is to esteem the unique worth of the individual. This family function has become increasingly important as other institutions have come to relate to the individual on an impersonal and manipulative basis. The family must provide relief from the standardization and depersonalization of bureaucracies. The family must serve as a buffer between these institutions and the individual, mediating on behalf of its members. If families fail to foster their individual members' strivings for personal fulfillment or fail to represent and protect their interests successfully in the public arena, then the members will feel it decreasingly worthwhile to stay together as a group. On the other hand, if families are increasingly successful in serving these fundamental needs of their members, then the family's viability as a social system will be greatly enhanced.

TEN
Implications for Theory

THIS FINAL CHAPTER MOVES from the concrete level of empirical findings and action proposals concerning the family's involvement with health and professional medicine to a more abstract level. Generalizing beyond the findings about the particular task area and about dealings with the particular external social system, the issues will be formulated in this way: What structure does the family require to function effectively in contemporary society? What type of relationships does an effectively functioning family have with various external systems, including school, work, and government, as well as medicine? To what extent does the family concentrate its efforts on sustaining its members' capacities for personal fulfillment and goal attainment?

A theoretical model for an effectively functioning family-social system will be outlined: It is an energized model for a social system. Health and illness will be viewed as representing more broadly the individual's capacity for personal fulfillment and goal attainment.

A CONCEPTUAL MODEL: THE FAMILY AS AN ENERGIZED SOCIAL SYSTEM

A social system is a group of persons in interaction. The interaction is oriented around collective concerns and purposes, and results in the performance of distinctive functions for members and society. The interaction is distinctively patterned both internally and in relations with other social systems.

The key features of the proposed conception of the family-social system pertain to the system's structure, relations with other systems, and functions.

STRUCTURE

The structure of a social system is a pattern of relationships that sets some limits to what actions are possible. There is a degree of form and regularity in the way in which members of a system relate to each other, and in the way they represent the system in relations with outside systems. But the structure of a social system has a natural tendency to change rather than to remain static or fixed, and a tendency to be permissive and flexible rather than rigid.

Structure is constantly being modified in the interests of effective functioning. The tendency of the structure of a social system is to change, evolve, and adapt in the interests of effective functioning rather than to remain fixed or static. This view of structure, which is characteristic of systems theory, contrasts with the structural-functionalist view that assumes the normal state of a system to be order and stability. Here is a functionalist formulation:

"A social system is always characterized by an institutionalized value system. The social system's first functional imperative is to maintain the integrity of that value system and its institutionalization. This process of maintenance means stabilization against pressures to change the value system. ... The tendency to stabilize the system in the face of pressures to change the institu-

tionalized values through cultural channels may be called the 'pattern maintenance' function ..." (Parsons and Smelser 1956, pp. 16–17).

Buckley proposes that the functionalist emphasis on the tendency toward
system maintenance must be counterpointed by the tendency to change the
system:

> "Modern systems analysis suggests that a sociocultural system with high
> adaptive potential, or integration, ... requires some optimum level of both
> stability and flexibility: a relative stability of the social-psychological founda-
> tions of interpersonal relations and of the cultural meanings and value hier-
> archies that hold group members together in the same universe of discourse
> and, at the same time, a flexibility of structural relations characterized by the
> lack of strong barriers to change, along with a certain propensity for reorganiz-
> ing the current institutional structure should environmental challenges or
> emerging internal conditions suggest the need. A central feature of the com-
> plex adaptive system is its capacity to persist or develop by changing its own
> structure, sometimes in fundamental ways" (Buckley 1967, p. 206).

Structure enables a group to act in relation to its collective concerns and
purposes. Hence, in the process of carrying on group activities, the structure
becomes modified in the interest of successful functioning. Bertrand maintains that structural change is a regular and necessary process by which social
systems maintain and develop their capacities to function. Growth of a system is more than an increase in membership or the learning of new norms
by the members; it is mainly an increase in capabilities for meeting a wider
range of possible demands. Growth is evidenced in such structural modifications as alteration of the group's customs, rules, and techniques to accommodate to new information, goals, or external conditions. "All groups have a
growth potential, so long as their boundaries remain open and their members
are receptive to new ideas. It is possible to conceive of groups with such
rigidity that new ways are rarely if ever adopted, but such groups are doomed
to extinction" (Bertrand 1972, p. 123).

This conception applies with special relevance to the family. A family unit
must proceed to evolve and adapt its structure in order to cope with succes-
sively different circumstances—birth and death, illnesses of youth, marriage,
and old age.

Conflict theorists, to an even greater extent than systems theorists, reject
the notion that order or equilibrium is the natural state of society and its
component systems. Rather, society is thought to be characterized by a continuing contest between groups with differing goals and interests, and the
order that exists at a given moment in time is temporary because it was imposed by those whose power enabled them to establish the rules of the game
—for the time being. It is not enough, therefore, that a social group learn
the accepted procedures for negotiating with outside groups, for the outside
groups are trying to establish conditions for encounters in order to favor their
own interests. Hence, social systems must undertake critical evaluations of

their structure and must nurture structural innovations which will enable them to assert their interests ever more effectively.

Without accepting conflict as *the* basic social process, it is useful to enrich the conception of social structure by including the notion that dissension, struggle, and conflict are regular elements of group life that stimulate groups' tendencies toward structural renovation. As applied to the family and medical care, this means that both families and medical care units are stimulated to develop more effective structural patterns by their need to obtain the most favorable bargain from encounters with each other.

The findings of our empirical study are in accord with this proposition, for they indicated that a basic structural characteristic that made for effective family functioning was the family's general proclivity to grow, develop, modify, and adapt in response to pressure from members and from external sources. The features of the energized model that reflected this structural tendency are: responsiveness to the emerging needs of members; active exchanges among members, representing open lines of communication within the family and sensitivity to internal pressures for change; health training efforts, or receptiveness to information and ideas and readiness to modify conduct on the basis of new information; activity linkages by all members with outside systems, representing the members' efforts to draw on external resources for developing their coping capabilities.

The structure of a social system provides permissive ranges and alternative modes of behavior, and permits divergence and novelty. Structure implies that there are constraints operating so that only certain interactions are possible among the members and other interactions are not possible. But, in addition, structure implies some degree of freedom in the interactions.

Norms and roles have permissive ranges, and, in the family, some role specifications allow for an enormous range of variation in behavior. The overall societal norms for family roles are sufficiently loose to permit different families to establish their own interpretations of the roles. Also, the members in a particular family group can develop a personal style which is freewheeling and versatile, and which they modify as they go along.

Even in the strictest systems and in the most serious roles, there are opportunities for the member to unbend and to act contrary to the mode expected for the role, which Goffman (1961) refers to as role distancing behavior. Some opportunities for stepping out of role have received outright recognition; for example, pregnancy and illness are accepted as extenuating circumstances that legitimize unusual or even bizarre behavior. Some idiosyncratic and spontaneous departures from role expectations are tolerated or even rewarded. Role distancing often has beneficial consequences for the system. A mother who will occasionally relax her normally strict supervision of family health care routines (diet, for example) not only reinstates her own humanness, but also gives everyone a breather.

The system that provides opportunities for reserving something of oneself from the grasp of the system also aids the individual by enabling him or her to cope with and resist the tensions and absurdities of the social structure, according to Goffman. A permissive family helps individuals insulate themselves from the potential oppressiveness of the family itself, and also protects them from being overwhelmed by the indignities of other social systems. The permissive family—the one which does not insist on the primacy of playing prescribed roles to the hilt, and which allows members to break from the expected role pattern—enables the person to emerge more fully as a person, with an integrated, fully functioning self.

A system contains much deviant behavior. Buckley proposes that:

"A first imperative of a relatively orderly, need-satisfying and stress-free social system is the nurturing of nonpathological deviation and variety as the basic source of the continued critical examination and considered change of the institutionalized structures and value-interpretations" (Buckley 1967, p. 27).

This constitutes a needed modification of the functionalist view, which holds that:

"An established state of a social system is a process of complementary interaction of two or more individual actors in which each conforms with the expectations of the other('s) in such a way that alter's reactions to ego's actions are positive sanctions which serve to reinforce his given need-dispositions and thus to fulfill his given expectations" (Parsons 1964, pp. 204–205).

As Gouldner has pointed out, unvarying conformity to expectations does *not* achieve system stability for "The more Alter takes Ego's conformity for granted, the less appreciative Alter will feel and the less propensity he will have to reward and reciprocate Ego's conforming actions" (Gouldner 1959, p. 424). The husband who started out by cooking a good meal one time when his wife was ill, and went on to establish this as his routinely performed gesture of devotion, ends up with a reaction of "What have you done for me lately?" from his wife. The term social fatigue has been applied to this situation where there is no excitement in the interaction to maintain cohesiveness. It is especially important for the family that members not take each other for granted and codify their interaction into monotonous rituals; for, more than in most other social systems, the family bond is dependent on the members' finding stimulation and satisfaction from the interaction itself.

If a system is to remain adaptive, it must have, as Buckley has stated, "a source for the continuous introduction of 'variety' into the system, which may refine or revitalize the pool of commonly usable information and the set of common meanings and symbols" (Buckley 1967, p. 206). As Coser (1962) described it, the innovator serves a vital function by attacking vested interests in habitual patterns and by setting new standards, thereby helping to insure that the group is not stifled in the deadening routines of ritualism, unable to meet the challenges of today. Nett also has stressed that much deviant behavior functions to generate social organization:

"Since the creative strength of a society must be sought in the capacity of individuals to evaluate, extend, correct, and ultimately to alter existing definitions and understandings (a process which is, in effect, deviation), the problem of ordering a society becomes one of utilizing the vital element—deviation—in social-organizational context" (Nett 1964, p. 41).

While deviance has traditionally been regarded as destructive of social organization, that viewpoint is a narrow one suited to the purposes of those with a vested interest in retaining the established order and their own position of control. Constraining the innovators restricts the system's ability to apply "its own criticisms and correctives to the social process in a somewhat constant, i.e., controllable manner" (Nett 1964, p. 43). It is the insistent conformers who would render a system inflexible and allow it to decay.

The findings of our empirical study are in accord with the proposition that a family structure which provides its members with freedom to move around enables the family to function effectively. Tolerance and encouragement of individual variation was beneficial, whereas blocking of the individual's efforts to follow her or his own course of action was harmful to health. Responsiveness, permissiveness, and flexibility, rather than control, also facilitated the family's performance of its health care tasks at home and in the medical marketplace.

RELATIONS WITH OTHER SYSTEMS

Regular exchanges between all members of a social system and other systems are basic to the system's functioning and to its structural growth. In the terminology of systems theory, although all systems maintain their identity through some type of boundary maintenance, no system can maintain a completely closed character (Bertrand 1972). In fact, a viable system is continuously engaged in interchanges with other social systems across its boundary, and this interchange is an essential factor underlying the system's ability to function effectively and to adapt (Buckley 1967).

In the first place, in order for a social system to perform its functions, its members must carry on some of their activities outside the system in conjunction with other systems, as in the family wage-earner and medical care shopper roles. These extramural roles not only serve the family directly through exchange of product or service, but also by feedback of information that is vital to the family's adaptation to other systems. Systems are also linked by multiple-group memberships of individual members, and the more of these memberships outside the system, the greater the potential for feedback between the family and other systems. Open systems also have a general movement of information in and out of the boundaries through informal social relations, as well as formal communication networks.

As discussed earlier, social systems must continuously modify existing structure in the interests of continuing effective functioning. A principal means of stimulating these adaptive structural changes is extensive, though selective, exchanges with other systems. Flexibly structured systems allow all members to conduct exchanges rather freely with other systems, and this provides the system with the capacity to continue to make adaptive changes in structure. In rigidly structured systems with a clearcut power structure, gatekeepers are highly selective about who may conduct exchanges across the boundaries, what systems may be transacted with, and what type of exchange may be allowed to take place. In such systems there is rigid screening out and ignoring of feedback that is not in line with present goals and courses of action as defined by the system's power units.

In our empirical study, we found that extensive links with other systems and active efforts to bring information in from outside sources contributed significantly to the family's capacity to function effectively in the task area investigated.

Relations with other systems are often based on divergent interests and may involve conflict. An important contribution of the structural-functionalist conception is that it focused attention on the relationships between a given system and the broader society, as well as with other particular systems. These functional interchanges were viewed as being reciprocal. As Bell and Vogel described the functional interdependence between the family and other systems: "Some sort of balance is achieved in this interchange, between those contributions made by the family and those received by the family, even though the balance is not necessarily stable or perfect, particularly in the short run" (Bell and Vogel 1968, p. 9).

This conception of functional interdependence, balance, and reciprocity does not fully cover the nature of the interchanges between social systems within a society. As conflict theorists point out, the societal value consensus and institutionalization of norms which functionalists regard as unifying the whole society, turn out, upon closer inspection, to reflect the special interests of groups with the political power to enforce them at a given point in time (Dahrendorf 1968; Stolzman 1972). The goals and interests of various social systems are different and sometimes they conflict. The social systems tend to reflect and serve the special interests of their members, or at least their dominant members, to as great a degree as they represent and serve the interests of society. Even the so-called service institutions, such as the health care system, function on behalf of the interests of their members, especially the interests of the professionals, sometimes to the neglect of their service commitments to society.

Each social system tries to advance its own interests, to achieve control over its own activities, and to manipulate other systems to its own benefit. Thus, relationships between social systems include efforts to constrain, influence, manipulate, and control, as well as to serve, comply, adapt, and reciprocate. These are necessary responses and patterns of action if a system is to survive and achieve its own ends, and at the same time serve the unique interests of its members.

This conception of the relationships between various social systems applies to the family, as well as to more highly specialized systems. It is true that families, collectively, have not developed a strong sense of their common interests, because the members of the various specialized systems are also members of families, and each member brings to his or her family the distinctive perspective and interests of his or her professional and other specialized affiliations. But this lack of collective identity or action among families should not be allowed to hide the fact that the family functions within the societal context of differentiated interests and power assertion. The interests of the family in retaining sons may conflict with the military's interest in securing soldier manpower. The family's concern with jobs for its members may conflict with industry's interest in barring from employment persons with epilepsy or arrested cancer. The family's interest in managing its own adaptation to changing social conditions may be at variance with the church's need to maintain its traditional authority over family life in such matters as birth control and abortion. The family's interests diverge in many significant ways from those of the health care system. The family could not survive as a viable system if it did not respond with appropriate assertiveness within this societal context of organized struggle.

This conception has implications for the structure of social systems generally. In order for any system to function effectively within this societal context, it must have structural resources for dealing effectively with other systems, and it must develop the capabilities of its members (its extramural agents) for coping with the structural mechanisms of other systems. As has been indicated, the health care system has the advantage of effective structural mechanisms for dealing with the family, the government, and other systems, while families generally have inadequate structural resources for negotiating with formal systems.

FUNCTIONS

A social system functions to serve its members' interests. In functionalist theory, social systems exist to attain goals that are functional for the whole society, and an activity is viewed in terms of its contribution to, or dysfunction for, the existing social order. Social systems are regarded as integral parts of the organic whole of society, and the whole is integrated by institutionalized values. Hence, the goals and interests of any particular system are largely compatible with those of the whole society. This frame of reference has oriented attention toward the functions performed by social systems for the maintenance of the societal order as a whole, to the neglect of functions performed for the members of a particular system. In fact, concern with societal maintenance has tended to center attention on social control functions—how a social system gets members to comply with societal norms and role expectations. Because of the family's pivotal role in processing all members of society, the functions of this system, in particular, have been viewed as the exercise of social control on behalf of other systems and society as a whole through socialization of the young, regulation of sex, general enforcement of conformity, and loyalty to the overall collectivity (Christensen 1964).

Concepts of systems theory also foster this approach. The functions of social systems are called outputs, which justify the system's existence. Thus: "The system's product must be acceptable to the suprasystem or the larger social unit of which it is a part . . . . If a system can find no takers for its output, it has but two alternatives—to change its nature and as a consequence its output, or to be phased out of existence" (Bertrand 1972, p. 98). The very term used to indicate functions—output—indicates this focus of concern on the consequences for the external society, as opposed to concern with functions of the activity for members themselves.

No social system could survive which was oriented principally to societal maintenance. Neither the family nor a professional system can rely on other social systems to provide voluntarily and cooperatively the services it needs or to adapt services to the needs of the consuming system. Each system is attempting to encroach on the interests of others. It is necessary, therefore, to regard a social system as functioning to protect its own interests in surviving as a viable group and to serve its own members' needs, as well as functioning on behalf of the broader society. The family, along with all other social systems, is embroiled in asserting its members' interests. Within a conceptual framework of social differentiation and conflict, the family's member-serving functions are as sociologically significant as its functions on behalf of other systems and the societal whole.

A specific aspect of a system's member-serving functions is its individuating function. This can be viewed as an aspect of a system's socialization task—preparing the members to get along in society and in relations with particular systems. There has been a tendency to give the socialization concept a narrow interpretation—instilling social values and training for conformity to social norms—and to exclude the family's nurturing of its members' uniqueness, fostering novel behavior and ideas, training for constructive deviance and for resistance to dangerous rules imposed by other systems, and preparing members to assert their legitimate interests in adversarial confrontations. Not only is individuation an essential aspect of the family's socialization of members for getting along in a differentiated society, but, as indicated in the discussion of structure, the system itself needs fully individuated members as a source for introducing variety to assure its own continuing adaptiveness.

These are, therefore, functional requisites of the family system. In addition to serving and adapting to the larger societal system, the family serves its members' special interests and attempts to protect and assert those interests in relations with other systems. To accomplish this, the family strives for a balance in its socialization efforts—between preparing members to conform to essential social standards and readying them to deviate resourcefully to further their own and the family's legitimate interests.

Within this frame of reference, health functions of the family may be usefully regarded as actions within the family to foster the members' physical capacity for self-fulfillment and personal goal-attainment. This includes guarding members' health against the potentially health-destructive actions of other systems, and aiding members to get good service from the professional health service system. Health/illness, then, is viewed as *capacity or incapacity for self-fulfillment and personal goal-attainment.*

On the other hand, a model of society which is based on the premise that social systems function to maintain the societal order leads to a view of family health functions as actions within the family to maintain the health of personnel at a level that enables them to perform their societal roles adequately. The primary concern is society's need to have its essential tasks performed, and since sound health is requisite to the performance of those tasks, health is a normatively approved state, and illness is a deviant state. Society controls this deviancy by regulating the conditions under which a person may be permitted to assume the sick role and be exempted from her or his regular responsibilities. Both the family and the health care system are expected to act as monitors of sickness, rooting out malingering, and seeing to it that everyone takes appropriate care of her or his health to prevent unnecessary illness, and takes restorative measures to treat illness.

In part, one's preference for a frame of reference that focuses on people-maintenance or societal-maintenance functions of social systems is based on one's ideological leanings—whether one is more concerned about individual freedom or societal stability. There is a scientific basis for the choice as well, and it has to do with which framework more effectively accounts for the way a viable social system functions. Our empirical study findings indicated that some families are oriented more toward assisting their individual members to achieve their personal goals and toward fostering self-fulfillment than toward constraining members to conform with societal standards. These member-serving families are able to develop a higher level of health in their members and to perform their health care tasks more effectively than families oriented toward social control and conformity. The findings are consistent with this generalization: A viable social system is oriented toward serving members' goals and, in fact, sometimes asserts members' interests in opposition to broader societal goals and codes.

The functions of a social system constitute the nature of the system, to a great extent. A system is what it does to as great an extent as it is a way of doing things. Structure alone does not characterize and distinguish systems sufficiently. The family system is identified by the distinctive tasks and activities it performs. Examination of the content of the family's activities helps to account for the type of structure it develops, for the structure must be appropriate to the performance of the family's particular functions. It is also the content of the functional exchange between two systems, for example, between the family and the health care system, which characterizes the interrelationship between them.

The functionalist conception of social systems as functioning to preserve the societal order, and the family, in particular, as functioning to constrain members to conform to societal standards, tended to restrict concern with the family's functions to its social control functions. Other distinguishing tasks and activities performed in the system tended to be neglected, and structure became of greater concern. On the other hand, a conception of social systems as serving the interests of members in a societal context of differentiation and conflict forces consideration of what tasks and activities a system performs for its members. In this view, a system is what it does for its members, and its success or failure is based on whether it delivers what the members need.

Within a conceptual framework of social differentiation and conflict, the relationships between the various interest groups as they seek to serve their own interests is another focal concern. It is on the basis of their distinctive activities and tasks that groups must negotiate with each other. The negotiations between the family and the medical care system are based on a specific kind of task performance. The nature of this functional exchange is of equal concern with structural arrangements through which the negotiations are effected.

APPLICATION OF THE MODEL

The conceptual formulation that has been presented helps to provide a reasonable interpretation of certain critical issues involving the family and health.

The family does a large amount of health care work. The notion of conflicting interests and, particularly, the idea that there is less than complete reciprocity between the health care system and the family, accounts for why the system specializing in health care does not satisfactorily or fully provide for the health needs of the population. Medicine is concerned with its own needs, not just its service commitments. Thus, the family must take up the slack of health care tasks rejected by medicine, put forth effort to extract services from the professional system, and monitor the professionals to guard against faulty service. The view that social systems interrelate in harmonious reciprocity failed to account for, or even call attention to, the fact that the family performs a major share of society's health care work.

Family members are frequently sent to hospitals rather than being cared for at home. The high concentration of societal health resources in hospital complexes has been brought about by the successful efforts of the health care establishment to develop and control a vast system of research-teaching-care facilities. Patients are routinely sent to hospitals for care they might otherwise have received in different arrangements, especially at home, because families have no choice. This interpretation contrasts with the view that the principal force behind the development of hospitals was better service, technically superior care, and protection of the family against the disruptive effects of caring for ill members at home (Parsons and Fox 1952). If the driving force behind the development of hospitals had been the need to provide services to client-families that could not be performed as well at home, then hospitals would have been designed to involve rather than to exclude families.

The family performs many of its health care tasks inadequately. The social conflict formulation accounts for the fact that, in their own interests, the professionals keep the client-family poorly informed, restrict their participation in medical matters, and deliver service on terms that suit the professionals rather than the clients. This hampers the family in developing expertise, assuming responsibility, and obtaining the most appropriate services.

Associated with this is the question of why client-families are so submissive and ineffectual in dealing with professionals. The conflict formulation accounts for the professionals' drive to dominate the relationship with the client. The medical profession's effectiveness in establishing autonomy to determine their own working conditions explains how the asymmetrical pattern of client-professional relations became institutionalized.

In contrast, the frame of reference which assumes the legitimacy of established order and authority poses that the physician's dominance is functional for therapy and that submissiveness is the ill person's appropriate response to the professionals who have the assigned responsibility for helping him or her. But this formulation is not supported by the findings, for submissiveness and lack of competence in formal transactions produced poor health service for the patient.

Some families perform their health care activities more effectively than others. Within a societal context of differentiation and conflict, in which bureaucratization and control techniques are used by service agencies to assert their interests, the type of family that is required for effective health care functioning is one which fosters the full personal development of each member, and which asserts the members' interests in transactions with outside agencies. This conception of societal functioning accounts for why a family form that is based on control of members and enforced compliance with societal standards is at a disadvantage.

LIMITATIONS

We began our study with some hunches about how particular aspects of family structure might influence health and health behavior, not with a multifaceted conceptual model. The energized model for a family system emerged as the result of interplaying empirical data with various theoretical formulations of the family-social system. This chain of events has the advantage that the particular model did not dictate the study design or the analysis of data. But it has the disadvantage that the measures of family structure that were designed for the study did not provide as precise and thorough a test of the energized family model as could now be designed.

In particular, it would be desirable to have more detailed measures of transactions between the family and the health care system, including not only the structure but also the task content of the transactions. It would be valuable to measure directly the extent to which families serve as social control agents or the extent to which they act as agencies of individuation. How much do families press members to comply with societal health rules and requirements, for example, by rooting out malingering? How much do they encourage their members to be their own gatekeepers in health matters and support them in asserting their own health needs in transactions with employers, schools, and the health care system?

The validity of the energized model should also be tested in other family task areas, such as servicing of the members' leisure, cultural, or educational goals and interests. While our findings showed only that the energized form worked more effectively than the traditional form in serving its members' health needs, it is possible that it represents a general model for effective family functioning within contemporary society.

Appendix
The Study Method

The National Center for Health Services Research and Development provided funds from 1969 to 1972 for the field research discussed in Chapters Five to Seven. In accordance with requirements of the federal grant, we built safeguards into the study to assure that the rights of the human subjects involved in the study were fully protected.

THE SAMPLE AND FIELD WORK

The sample site was a northern New Jersey city of about 150,000 people, which has a heterogeneous composition of ethnic groups and socioeconomic levels, and presents the full range of urban social and health problems. The sample units were nuclear families with a father, mother, and at least one child aged nine to thirteen in residence. Because the research was funded in two phases, two waves of interviewing were conducted. In the first wave, conducted by Roper Associates, the mother and child were interviewed; in the second wave, conducted by International Research Associates, fathers, mothers, and children were interviewed.

We designed a two-stage probability sample—a sample of blocks and a sample of households within blocks. Since we could not know in advance whether a household would meet the sample requirements (father, mother, and child aged nine to thirteen), we had to deviate from probability requirements in the sampling of households. When an assigned family failed to meet the requirements, a substitute was selected within the same block—across the street (or hall, in an apartment building), or next door.

A minimum of three attempts were made to contact and interview a member of the assigned family, but in many instances more than three contacts were needed to complete the required interviews with the family. In order for a family to be included in the sample, it was necessary to obtain mother and child or mother, father, and child interviews from its household. Thus, even after one member of the family had been successfully interviewed, it often required additional contacts to interview the other member or members, and three attempts were mandated for each of the other members. Attempts were made at varying times during the day and evening and on different days of the week, and after the minimum three attempts had been made in person, additional attempts were made by telephone. Only after these efforts had been fully exhausted was a substitute family selected. The loss from the assigned sample was about 25 percent, higher than would have occurred in a sample of individuals. In the sample of family units, a family could be lost by the refusal or unavailability of any one of the members, and this sometimes happened even after one or two other members had been successfully interviewed. A strict substitution policy was applied to maintain the representativeness of the sample. The selection of a substitute family was made jointly by the interviewer and the field supervisor, according to a formula designed to obtain a family which lived near to and resembled closely the original one. The resulting sample resembles very closely the married population of the city in income and education distribution.

The sample consisted of 273 families in which the wife, the husband, and one child were interviewed separately, and 237 families in which the wife and a child were interviewed. We used the sample of 273 families with three interviews in the analysis. The additional families in which only the wife and child were interviewed were used to check reliability, and we found that the results obtained were essentially the same as the results from the 273 families.

The 273 families were distributed in socioeconomic characteristics as follows:

Income	Percentage	Education	Percentage	
			Husband	Wife
Under $6,000	18	Grade school	34	31
$6,000–7,999	25	Some high school	34	32
$8,000–9,999	24	High school graduate	22	33
$10,000 or more	33	Some college or graduate	10	4
	100		100	100

Three-fifths of the sample were white and two-fifths were black.

We employed experienced interviewers and trained them thoroughly in the use of the testing instruments for this study. English- and Spanish-speaking, black and white, and male and female interviewers were assigned to interview their counterparts in the sample. The husband, wife, and child were each interviewed privately. In families with more than one child aged nine to thirteen, the interviewer alternated between male and female and the various ages in order to assure representation of each sex and each age.

Field work was closely supervised. All interviews were edited immediately in the field, and an interviewer was sent back to the respondent in the case of any errors or omissions. Checks were made for interviewer honesty by telephone calls to selected respondents.

The interview instruments designed for the study were pretested and revised several times. There were closely parallel versions of the instrument for men, women, and children, differences being that some questions concerning reproduction and gynecological problems were asked only of women, more detailed questions concerning employment were asked of men than of women, and a somewhat abbreviated set of questions was used for interviews with children.

DATA PROCESSING

The completed interview forms were thoroughly edited for internal consistency (for example, all respondents who said they had never smoked would be expected to report subsequently that they had not smoked last week), and an interview form was returned to the field for any unresolvable inconsistencies. After IBM card punching, the data were also elaborately "cleaned" mechanically to assure internal consistency. The IBM card punching was verified mechanically and, in addition, a complete computer printout of all the punched cards was read back against all the original interview forms by research assistants. The final punch cards contained veritably no omissions or detectable errors. The data were then transferred to computer tape for processing and analysis.

We used a variety of statistical techniques to explore the data. The principal techniques used were correlation and stepwise regression analysis. In stepwise regression, each coefficient represents the amount of change in a dependent variable that is associated with a change in one of the independent variables with the remaining independent variables held constant. When comparing "various independent variables as to their relative abilities to produce changes in the dependent variable, . . . there will undoubtedly be differences in scale involved" (Blalock, 1960, p. 344). In order to correct for these differences in scale, we computed standardized regression coefficients, which show how much change in a dependent variable is produced by a standardized change in one of the independent variables when the others are controlled. A stepwise regression table lists the independent variables in rank order of their influence on the dependent variable. We computed F ratios to test the coefficients for statistical significance; the level of significance for each coefficient is shown in the p (probability) column.

The stepwise regression table also indicates the percent of variance in the dependent variable which is accounted for by each independent variable. In the Changes in R^2 column, the first figure indicates the proportion of variance accounted for by the strongest independent variable; each successive figure represents the contribution made by a particular independent variable above and beyond the contribution of the previously listed independent variables. The R^2 column shows cumulatively what proportion of the variance in the dependent variable is accounted for by a combination of independent variables. Thus, the last R^2 figure reveals what proportion of total variance in health practices, for example, is accounted for by the combined list of energized family variables.

CONSTRUCTION OF INDEXES

Each of the indexes used in the study is a composite measure, combining several questions from the interview. A respondent's score on a given index was obtained by applying a formula that assigned arbitrary weights to answer categories and summed the respondent's answers to the specified group of questions. The questions used in constructing the major indexes are shown below.

HUSBAND-WIFE INTERACTION

Which of the following do you do with your (husband) (wife) often, occasionally, or never?

Go to parties
Attend church
Attend meetings
Play cards
Visit relatives
Attend sports events
Attend some type of performance, e.g., theater, movie, etc.
Joke together
Visit friends
Go for a pleasure drive in a car
Sit around and talk

MOTHER-CHILD AND FATHER-CHILD INTERACTION

I am going to read some things children sometimes do with their mothers. Please tell me whether your mother does these things with you often, occasionally, or never. (Also asked of mothers). How about your father? (Also asked of fathers).

Read or tell stories to you
Play games with you
Go to movies with you
Go to park, beach, or picnic with you
Discuss your school work with you

Discuss your problems with you
Discuss your parents' problems with you

EXTENT OF COMMUNITY PARTICIPATION

Are you a member of any clubs, organizations, or community groups?
(If yes): How many? During the course of the year about how many meetings do you attend each week, on the average?

NUMBER OF TOWNS USED

Besides the town you live in, how many different towns or cities do you go to for any purpose at least once a month? (For example, how many towns have you gone to in the last month?)

EXTENT OF CULTURAL PARTICIPATION

In bringing up your children, have you ever:

Hired a teacher to give them lessons in music, painting, or dancing?
Bought "art" toys, such as painting kits, cameras, hand crafts, and so on?
Taken the child on trips to art exhibits or museums?
Taken the child to live theater performances, opera, concerts, or dance programs?

VARIETY OF CHILD'S ACTIVITIES

Please tell me which of the following you have done in the past four weeks: (child)

Visited with relatives
Visited with friends
Attended church
Gone to a party
Watched television
Attended a club meeting
Played cards
Attended some sports event
Participated in a sport
Attended a musical performance
Attended a movie or play
Gone for a pleasure drive in a car
Gone to a park or beach
Read a book

HEALTH TRAINING EFFORTS BY PARENTS

For each of the following tell me whether or not you have explained to your child about it? (Also asked of child).

The proper way to use a toothbrush
The proper kinds of foods to eat
The effects of smoking upon health
When and how much to exercise the body
How to clean yourself in order to maintain a healthy body
The importance of moving the bowels regularly
The effect of irregular or lack of sleep upon health
How reproduction takes place between the sexes

Have you ever done any of the following things to teach your child health habits (for example, brushing teeth, sleep habits, or eating habits)? (Also asked of child).

Gotten a pamphlet for your child about it
Read an article or pamphlet yourself about it and then explained it to your child
Obtained or made a model to show about it
Taken your child to a lecture or film about it

AVERSIVE CONTROL OF CHILD

Do your parents do any of the following? Which are they most likely to do? (Also asked of parents).

Slap or spank you
Confine you to your room or the house
Withdraw your privileges
Keep reminding you to do something or scold you
Yell or shout at you
Won't speak to or ignore you
Make fun of you

OBSTRUCTIVE CONFLICT BETWEEN HUSBAND AND WIFE

Have you and your (husband) (wife) ever been separated over a period of time due to some type of marital conflict? (If yes): Approximately how long were you separated? Have you and your (husband) (wife) ever hit one another? (If yes): How often—often, occasionally, infrequently, or only once?

Please indicate whether you and your (husband) (wife) have disagreements about each of the following:

Handling family finances
How to spend holidays
Religious matters
Choosing friends
Preparing meals
Punishing the children
Hugging and kissing the children
Doing things with the children
How often to have sexual relations
The size of your family
What method to use to prevent pregnancy

SUPPORTIVENESS OF CHILD BY PARENTS

Which of these things do your parents do when you behave very well? Which are they most likely to do? (Also asked of parents).

Hug or kiss you
Give you special privileges or a reward
Do special things for you
Praise you
Show a loving attitude toward you

CHILD'S AUTONOMY

I'm going to read some things to you and I'd like you to tell me for each one whether at nine years of age you (expect) (expected) (name child) to do the following?

To stand up for (his) (her) own rights with other children
To be willing to try new things on (his) (her) own without depending on (his) (her) parents for help
To get to know (his) (her) way around (his) (her) part of the city
To hang up (his) (her) own clothes and look after (his) (her) own possessions

Does (name child) if left to (himself) (herself) do each of these things on (his) (her) own? (Also asked of child).

CHILD'S AUTONOMY—HEALTH CARE

Tell me for each one whether at nine years of age you (expect) (expected) (name child) to do the following: Does (name child) if left to (himself) (herself) do each of these things on (his) (her) own? (Also asked of child).

To undress and go to bed by (himself) (herself)

To brush (his) (her) teeth regularly and properly
To eat the right kinds of foods
To get enough exercise
To wash (his) (her) hands after going to the bathroom
To get enough sleep

CONJUGAL DIVISION OF TASKS

Who in your family has the responsibility for each of the following: Is it the husband entirely, the husband somewhat more than the wife, both equally, the wife somewhat more than the husband, the wife entirely, or neither the husband nor the wife? (Asked of husband and wife).

Preparing meals
Punishing the children
Hugging and kissing the children

CONJUGAL DIVISION OF TASKS—CHILD'S HEALTH

Who in your family has the responsibility for each of the following?

Teaching the child the proper foods to eat
Toilet training the child
Teaching the child how to brush (his) (her) teeth
Buying medicines (prescriptions and nonprescriptions)
Staying up with the child when he is ill
Knowing what to do when the child is ill or injured
Taking your child to the doctor or dentist

CONJUGAL DIVISION OF TASKS—WIFE'S HEALTH

For each of the following, would you tell me whether or not your husband does any of these things when you're sick and have to go to bed? (Also asked of husband).

Helps with the household work
Takes over the household work
Calls from work to find out how you are
Stays home from work
Comes home from work early
Gets a doctor for you when needed
Tends to your needs and comfort

CONJUGAL POWER

Who in your family has the responsibility for each of the following: Is it the husband entirely, the husband somewhat more than the wife, both equally, the wife somewhat more than the husband, the wife entirely, or neither the husband nor the wife? (Asked of husband and wife).

Handling family finances
Deciding how to spend holidays
Religious matters
Choosing friends
Deciding how often to have sexual relations
Deciding upon the size of your family
Deciding what method to use to prevent pregnancy

ALIENATION

Tell me whether you agree or disagree with each of these:

Having "pull" is more important than ability in getting ahead
You should enjoy yourself while you can, because you never know what will happen tomorrow
A person has very little control over what happens to him
If you don't watch out, people will take advantage of you
A person should look out for his own interests and let others do the same
Almost every week I see someone I dislike

EXTENT OF HEALTH PROBLEMS

Now I'm going to read you a list of symptoms which most doctors ask about. I'd like you to tell me for each one whether you've ever had it or not. Has this happened in the last two weeks?

Sleeping problems, that is, trouble falling asleep, waking up in the middle of the night, or having bad dreams?
Constipation, diarrhea, or rectal pain?
Skin rash?
Eye, ear, or nose trouble, that is, watery eyes, unexplained nosebleeds, running nose, seeing double, or an earache?
A headache that lasted longer than one day?
Stiff joints for no apparent reason?
A fever above 100 degrees?
Mouth troubles, that is, a toothache or sore or bleeding gums?
Trouble with your feet, that is, athlete's foot, flat feet, blisters which make walking painful, or other trouble walking because of sore feet?
A cough, unrelated to a cold, which lasted more than a day or two, or shortness of breath after walking upstairs or bending over?
Heartburn, indigestion, or a stomachache or nausea other than during pregnancy?
After exercise or heavy work your muscles ache, your back aches, you have a headache, are dizzy, or you don't sleep well?

Unexplained bleeding, a sore in the genital area, a bruise or cut that was slow to heal, or swelling in your legs or feet?

LEVEL OF PRESENT HEALTH

Would you say your own health, in general, is excellent, good, fair, or poor?

Have you been sick in the past two weeks and unable to fully carry on your regular work or activities?

USE OF PREVENTIVE MEDICAL SERVICES

Tell me whether or not you have had each of the following medical services in the last three years:

Eye examination
Chest x-ray
Blood test
Urinalysis
X-ray of whole mouth
X-ray of a few teeth
Cleaning of teeth by dentist
Examination of teeth by dentist
General physical checkup when you were not ill

Which of these have you ever had?

Small pox vaccination
Polio vaccination
Measles vaccination

USE OF SPECIALIZED MEDICAL SERVICES

Tell me for each of the following types of doctors whether or not you've ever seen one?

Dermatologist (skin)
Orthopedist (foot or bone)
Optometrist or ophthalmologist (eye)
Internist (internal medicine)
Surgeon
Psychiatrist

PERSONAL HEALTH PRACTICES

(This index is a composite of the following seven indexes.)

Sleep Habits

How often do you go to bed or get up at least one hour earlier or later than your usual time—would you say very often, sometimes, seldom, or never?

How do you usually feel when you get up in the morning—do you feel exhausted, very tired, fairly tired, fairly rested or thoroughly rested?

Exercise Habits

Do you ever participate in any sports or physical games?

About how many hours did you spend last week on sports or physical games?

Do you do this on a regularly scheduled basis?

How about exercises—do you ever do exercises of any kind, such as setting-up exercises, calisthenics, or hiking or bicycling for exercise?

About how many hours did you spend last week on exercise?

Do you do it on a regularly scheduled basis?

Elimination Habits

How often do you have a daily bowel movement—would you say always, almost always, quite often, sometimes, seldom, or never?

How regular are you about the time of day—very regular, fairly regular, or not very regular?

Dental Hygiene

Did you brush your teeth yesterday?

Did you brush your teeth—
Before breakfast
Right after breakfast
Between breakfast and lunch
Right after lunch
Between lunch and dinner
Right after dinner
Between dinner and bedtime

Smoking Habits

Do you smoke, or have you ever smoked?

(If yes): About how many cigarettes did you smoke yesterday?

Alcohol Habits

How often do you consume an alcoholic beverage other than beer—would you say every day, five to six times a week, three or four times a week, once or twice a week, less than once a week, or never? (Asked of husband and wife).

The last day you had any alcoholic beverage other than beer, how many drinks did you have? (Asked of husband and wife).

NUTRITION

We are interested in everything you ate yesterday—at mealtimes as well as between meals. First, did you eat breakfast yesterday?

Would you name the specific foods you ate for breakfast yesterday, using this card as a guide to make sure you don't forget anything?

Did you eat lunch yesterday?

Again using this card as a guide, would you tell me what you had for lunch?

And did you have supper (dinner) yesterday?

What did you have for supper (dinner)?

Think about other things that you ate yesterday, from morning to bedtime, other than at mealtime. What else did you eat yesterday? Please look over the list again.

CONSTRUCTION OF FAMILY INDEXES

A major goal of this study was to investigate the functioning of *families* as distinct from the individual persons who compose family units. Our hypotheses proposed that the structure of the family unit would affect the health and health behavior of members, and so indexes were needed that would encompass the behavior patterns of the mother-father-child. In addition, the hypotheses proposed that health and health behavior of the whole unit would be affected by these structural patterns, and for this reason indexes were needed to represent the combined family's health status.

The problem was to design a way of taking the original index scores for each of the separate family members (for example, the index of the extent of health problems for mothers, fathers, and children), and combining the three individual members' scores into a new index that would represent the three-member group (for example, the extent of health problems in the family). After experimenting with various formats, the one selected for use here was this. Individual family members' (fathers', mothers', and children's) scores on a given index were dichotomized into high or low scores, and a high score was coded 1 and a low score 0. These codes (or new scores) were then summed for the three family members, giving a range on the new family index of 0 to 3.

Individual Family Members' Scores on the Original Index	Family Score on the Composite Index
All three members scored low	0
Two scored low, one scored high	1
One scored low, two scored high	2
All three members scored high	3

A family index was constructed for most of the major family structure and health/health behavior concepts.

Family Indexes

Family Structure	*Health/Health Behavior*
Extramural participation	Personal health practices
Interaction among members	Sleep habits
Autonomy	Exercise habits
	Elimination habits
	Dental hygiene
	Smoking habits
	Alcohol habits (mother–father)
	Nutrition
	Use of preventive medical services
	Use of specialists
	Extent of health problems
	Level of health

References

Abbott, John. 1972. "Exercise lack U.S. No. 1 health problem: Meyer." *Boston Sunday Globe* (April 23).

Adams, Bert N. 1971. *The American Family: A Sociological Interpretation.* Chicago: Markham.

Almond, Gabriel A., and Sidney Verba. 1963. *The Civic Culture.* Princeton: Princeton University Press.

Alpert, Joel J., John Kosa, and Robert T. Haggerty. 1967. "A month of illness and health care among low-income families." *Public Health Reports* 82, No. 8 (August).

Altman, Lawrence K. 1973. "Views on bowel habits are disputed." *The New York Times* (November 22).

———. 1971. "Heart treatment at home praised." *The New York Times* (September 5).

American Academy of Pediatrics. 1965. "Family epidemiology." *Pediatrics* 35 (May):856–863.

American Association of Fund-Raising Counsel. 1971. *Giving.* New York.

American Foundation for the Blind. 1972. "Statement to the Committee on Finance, United States Senate." (January 20).

American Hospital Association. 1971. *Report of a Conference on Care of Chronically Ill Adults.* Chicago.

———. 1970. *Guidelines on Responsibilities of American Hospital Association and State Associations for Cooperative Action on Federal Legislation.* Chicago.

———. 1970. *Postmortem Procedures.* Chicago.

———. 1961. *Home Care.* Chicago.

The American Parents Committee, Inc. 1971. *Washington Report on Legislation for Children and What You Can Do About It.* (February), No. 103, Washington, D.C.

American Rehabilitation Foundation. 1969. *Researching a Growing Force for Social Change: Citizen Involvement in the 70s.* Minneapolis.

Andelman, David A. 1973. "Ambulance aid found deficient." *The New York Times* (August 19).

Andersen, Ronald, and Odin W. Anderson. 1967. *A Decade of Health Services.* Chicago: University of Chicago Press.

Andersen, Ronald, Joanna Kravits, Odin W. Anderson, and Joan Daley. 1973. *Expenditures for Personal Health Services: National Trends and Variations, 1953–1970.* University of Chicago, Center for Health Administration Studies. Chicago: University of Chicago Press.

Anderson, Ella S., and Cleo Fitzsimmons. 1960. "Use of time and money by employed homemakers." *Journal of Home Economics* 52, No. 6:452–455.

Angrist, Shirley S., Simon Dinitz, and Lois H. Molholm. 1972. "The Home as a Sheltered Workshop." Paper presented at 67th Annual Meeting of American Sociological Association (August 28–31).

Aronfreed, J. 1968. *Conduct and Conscience.* New York: Academic Press.

———. 1961. "The nature, variety and social patterning of moral responses to transgression." *Journal of Abnormal and Social Psychology* 63 (September): 223–241.

Aspen Institute for Humanistic Studies. 1971. *Final Report of the Aspen Institute-American Assembly: The Health of Americans.* Aspen, Colorado.

Avnet, Helen Hershfield. 1967. *Physician Service Patterns and Illness Rates.* Chicago: Group Health Insurance, Inc.

Bachman, Jerald G. 1970. *Youth in Transition,* Vol. 2, *The Impact of Family Background and Intelligence on Tenth-Grade Boys.* University of Michigan, Institute for Social Research. Ann Arbor: University of Michigan Press.

Baily, Betty W. 1962. *Food Management Practices of Employed and Nonemployed Homemaker Families.* Georgia Agricultural Experiment Station, Bulletin N.S. 98.

Bashshur, Rashid L., Gary W. Shannon, and Charles A. Metzner. 1970. "Some Ecological Differentials in the Use of Medical Services." Paper presented at the Annual Meeting of the American Sociological Association, Washington, D.C. (August 31).

Baumrind, D. 1967. "Child care practices anteceding three patterns of preschool behavior." *Genetic Psychology Monographs* 75 (February):43–88.

Becker, W. C. 1964. "Consequences of different kinds of parental discipline." In M. Hoffman and L. Hoffman, eds. *Review of Child Development Research,* Vol. 1. New York: Russell Sage Foundation.

Bell, Norman W., and Robert A. Zucker. 1968. "Family-hospital relationships in a state hospital setting: A structural-functional analysis of the hospitalization process." *International Journal of Social Psychiatry* 15 (Winter):73–80.

Bell, Norman W., and Ezra F. Vogel, eds. 1968. *A Modern Introduction to the Family.* Glencoe: Free Press.

Bell, Robert R. 1971. *Marriage and Family Interaction.* Homewood, Ill.: Dorsey.

Berkman, Paul L. 1969. "Spouseless motherhood, psychological stress, and physical morbidity." *Journal of Health and Social Behavior* 10:323–334.

Bernard, Hugh Y. 1966. *The Law of Death and Disposal of the Dead.* Dobbs Ferry, N.Y.: Oceana.

Bertrand, Alvin L. 1972. *Social Organization: A General Systems and Role Theory Perspective.* Philadelphia: F. A. Davis Co.

Better Homes and Gardens. 1972. *A Report on the American Family.* New York.

Bigner, Jerry J. 1972. "Parent education in popular literature: 1950–1970." *Family Coordinator* (July):313–319.

Binkley, Lois, Agnes Podolinsky, and Frank von Richter. 1968. "Fewer auxiliaries and volunteers are providing more-and-more kinds of services." *Hospitals* 42 (March 16):60–64.

Bird, David. 1973. "Energy in the home being tested at Twin Rivers." *The New York Times* (May 27).

Birdwhistell, Ray L. 1966. "The American family: some perspectives." *Psychiatrist* 29:208–212.

Bishop, F. Marian, Edward W. Hassinger, Daryl J. Hobbs, and A. Sherwood Baker. 1969. "The family physician—ideal and real." *GP,* 40, No. 3:169–177.

Blackwell, Barbara. 1963. "The literature of delay in seeking medical care for chronic illnesses." Society of Public Health Educators. *Health Education Monographs* 16:3–31.

Blalock, Hubert M., Jr. 1960. *Social Statistics*. New York: McGraw-Hill.

Blood, Robert O. 1964. *Impact of Urbanization on American Family Structure and Functioning*. University of Michigan, Center for Research on Social Organization. Ann Arbor: University of Michigan Press.

———. 1963. "The husband-wife relationship." In F. I. Nye and L. Hoffman, eds. *The Employed Mother in America*. Chicago: Rand McNally.

Blood, Robert O., and Donald M. Wolfe. 1960. *Husbands & Wives: The Dynamics of Married Living*. New York: The Free Press.

Blum, Richard H., et al. 1972. *Horatio Alger's Children*. San Francisco: Jossey-Bass.

Boek, Jean K. 1956. "Dietary intake and social characteristics." *American Journal of Clinical Nutrition* 4, No. 3:239–245.

Booth, Alan, and Nicholas Babchuk. 1972. "Informal medical opinion leadership among the middle aged and elderly." *Public Opinion Quarterly* 36, No. 1:87–94.

Borsky, Paul N., and Oswald K. Sagen. 1959. "Motivations toward health examinations." *American Journal of Public Health* 49, No. 4:514–527.

Bott, E. 1957. *Family and Social Network*. London: Tavistock Publications.

Bowen, H. R., and J. R. Jeffers. 1971. *The Economics of Health Services*. New York: General Learning Press.

Bowman, H. A. 1970. *Marriage for Moderns*. New York: McGraw-Hill.

Breckinridge, Sophonisba P. 1972. *The Family and the State*. New York: Arno Press & The New York Times.

Brim, Orville G., Jr. 1954. "The acceptance of new behavior in childrearing." *Human Relations,* 7:473–491.

Brim, Orville G., Jr., Howard E. Freeman, Sol Levine, and Norman A. Scotch. 1970. *The Dying Patient*. New York: Russell Sage Foundation.

Britter, R. H., and T. Altman. 1941. "Illness and accidents among persons living under different housing conditions." *Public Health Reports* 56, No. 13:609–640.

Brodie, Donald. 1971. *Drug Utilization and Drug Utilization Review and Control*. Washington, D.C.: National Center for Health Services Research and Development (September).

Brody, Jane E. 1973. "Most pregnant women found taking excess drugs." *The New York Times* (March 18).

———. 1973. "Nutrition is now a national controversy." *The New York Times* (August 27).

———. 1973. "Study finds one in five women checks to detect breast cancer." *The New York Times* (November 9).

———. 1973. "Two updated first-aid manuals seek to reduce seriousness of accidents." *The New York Times* (November 7).

———. 1970. "Home clotting treatment eases life for blood disease." *The New York Times* (November 8).

Bronfenbrenner, Urie. 1970. *Two Worlds of Childhood*. New York: Russell Sage Foundation.

Brook, Robert H., and Robert L. Stevenson, Jr. 1970. "Effectiveness of patient care in an emergency room." *New England Journal of Medicine* 283 (October 22):904–907.

Brown, Esther Louise. 1967. "College students look at the basis of their food habits." *Journal of Home Economics* 59 (December):784–787.

Buckley, Walter. 1967. *Sociology and Modern Systems Theory.* Englewood Cliffs, N.J.: Prentice-Hall.

Bullough, Bonnie. 1972. "Poverty, ethnic identity and preventive health care." *Journal of Health and Social Behavior* 13 (December):347–359.

Bunker, John P. 1970. "Surgical manpower: A comparison of operations and surgeons in the United States and in England and Wales." *New England Journal of Medicine* 282 (January 15):135–144.

Bureau of Dental Health Education, Bureau of Economic Research and Statistics. 1966. "Survey of family toothbrushing practices." *Journal of American Dental Association* 72 (June):1489–1492.

Burgess, E. W., H. J. Locke, and M. M. Thomes. 1963. *The Family: From Institution to Companionship.* New York: American Book.

Burson-Marsteller. 1970. *Consumerism: A New and Growing Force in the Marketplace.* Washington, D.C.

Cahn, Edgar S., and Barry A. Passett, eds. 1969. *Citizen Participation.* The New Jersey Community Action Training Institute. (Summer).

Cancer Care. 1973. *The Impact, Costs and Consequences of Catastrophic Illness on Patients and Families.* New York.

Cant, Gilbert. 1973. "An x-ray analysis of doctors' bills." *Money* (August):23, 25–27.

Carothers, Hugh A. 1958. "Pets in the home: Incidence and significance." *Pediatrics* 21 (May):840–848.

Cartwright, Ann. 1967. *Patients and Their Doctors.* London: Routledge & Kegan Paul.

Cassel, John. 1970. "Physical illness in response to stress." In Sol Levine and Norman A. Scotch, eds. *Social Stress.* Chicago: Aldine.

Cathey, Charles, et al. 1962. "The relation of life stress to the concentration of serum lipids in patients with coronary artery disease." *American Journal of Medical Science* 244:421–441.

Cavan, R. S., ed. 1960. *Marriage and Family in the Modern World.* New York: Thomas Y. Crowell.

Cayler, Glen G., et al. 1969. "Mass screening of school children for heart disease." *Public Health Reports* 84, No. 6:479–482.

CBS Television News. 1973. (October 31).

Cerra, Frances. 1974. "Consumer group offers guide to Queens doctors." *The New York Times* (October 23).

Chen, Edith, and Sidney Cobb. 1960. "Family structure in relation to health and disease." *Journal of Chronic Diseases* 12 (November):544–567.

Chenault, William W., et al. 1971. *Consumer Participation in Neighborhood Comprehensive Health Care Centers,* Vol. 1 (April) *Interpretive Report.* McLean, Va.: Human Sciences Research.

Christensen, Harold T., ed. 1964. *Handbook of Marriage and the Family.* Chicago: Rand McNally.

Clausen, J. A. 1968. *Socialization and Society.* Boston: Little, Brown.

Clines, X. Francis. 1973. "State to check all Rx's in antidrug move." *The New York Times* (March 18).

Cohen, Albert K., and Harold M. Hodges. 1963. "Characteristics of the lower-blue-collar-class." *Social Problems* 10, No. 4:303–334.

Cohen, Percy S. 1968. *Modern Social Theory*. New York: Basic Books.

Comfort, Alex. 1967. *The Anxiety Makers*. London: Books & Broadcasts.

Commission on Population Growth and the American Future. 1972. *Costs of Children*. Washington, D.C.

Condry, John C., Michael L. Siman, and Urie Bronfenbrenner. 1968. "Characteristics of Peer- and Adult-oriented Children." (Unpublished) Cornell University.

Consumer Reports. 1971. "Some medicines you may want to avoid." 36 (February):14–17. Mount Vernon, New York.

Conway, Jill. 1971. "Women reformers and American culture, 1870–1930." *Journal of Social History* 5, No. 2:164–177.

Cooper, David. 1970. *The Death of the Family*. New York: Pantheon.

Cornely, Paul B., and Stanley K. Bigman. 1963. "Some considerations in changing health attitudes." *Children* 10, No. 1:23–28.

———. 1961. "Cultural considerations in changing health attitudes." *Medical Annals of the District of Columbia* 30, No. 4 (April).

Coser, Lewis. 1962. "Functions of deviant behavior." *American Journal of Sociology* 68 (September):172–181.

Cowen, David L., and John A. Sbarbaro. 1972. "Family-centered health care—a viable reality?" *Medical Care* 10, No. 2:164–172.

Cox, Peter R., and John R. Ford. 1964. "The mortality of widows shortly after widowhood." *The Lancet* 1 (January):163–164.

Crain, Alan J., Marvin B. Sussman, and William B. Weil. 1966. "Effects of a diabetic child on marital integration and related measures of family functioning." *Journal of Health and Human Behavior* 7:122–127.

Croog, Sidney H. 1970. "The family as a source of stress." In Sol Levine and Norman A. Scotch, eds. *Social Stress*. Chicago: Aldine.

Croog, Sydney H., and Donna F. Ver Steeg. 1972. "The hospital as a social system." In Howard E. Freeman, Sol Levine, and Leo G. Reeder, eds. *Handbook of Medical Sociology*. Englewood Cliffs, N.J.: Prentice-Hall.

Cseh-Szombathy, Laszlo. 1972. "Hungarian sociological studies." *Sociological Review Monograph* No. 17:207.

Dabbs, James M., Jr., and John P. Kirscht. 1971. "'Internal control' and the taking of influenza shots." *Psychological Reports* 28:959–962.

Dahrendorf, Ralf. 1968. *Essays in the Theory of Society*. Stanford: Stanford University Press.

D'Amico, Robert A. 1972. *Important Medical Bulletin*. New York: Dysautonomia Foundation, Inc.

Daspit, Lurline Cagle. 1959. "A Time and Motion Study of the Use of Small Food Preparation Equipment." Master's thesis, Texas Women's University, College of Household Arts and Sciences.

Davis, Fred. 1963. *Passage Through Crisis*. Indianapolis: Bobbs-Merrill.

Davis, Milton S. 1966. "Variations in patients' compliance with doctors' orders: Analysis of congruence between survey responses and results of empirical investigations." *Journal of Medical Education* 41, No. 11, Part 1.

Davis, Milton S., and Robert L. Eichhorn. 1963. "Compliance with medical regimens: A panel study." *Journal of Health and Human Behavior* 4 (Winter) 240–249.

Denenberg, Herbert S. 1973. *A Shopper's Guide to Dentistry: Pennsylvania.* Philadelphia: Pennsylvania Insurance Department.

Detroit Area Study of the University of Michigan. 1952. *A Social Profile of Detroit.* Ann Arbor: University of Michigan Press.

Devereux, Edward C., Urie Bronfenbrenner, and George J. Suci. 1962. "Patterns of parent behavior in America and West Germany: A cross-national comparison." *International Social Science Journal* 14, No. 3:488–506.

Dingle, John H., George F. Badger, et al. 1953. "A study of illness in a group of Cleveland families: IV. The spread of respiratory infections within the home." *American Journal of Hygiene* 58:174–178.

Dingle, John H., George F. Badger, and William S. Jordan. 1964. *Illness in the Home.* Cleveland: The Press of Western Reserve University.

Dubos, René. 1959. *Mirage of Health.* New York: Harper & Row.

Duff, Raymond S., and August B. Hollingshead. 1968. *Sickness and Society.* New York: Harper & Row.

Duffy, John C., and Edward M. Litin. 1967. *The Emotional Health of Physicians.* Springfield, Ill.: Charles C. Thomas.

Dunn, Halbert L., and Mort Gilbert. 1956. "Public health begins in the family." *Public Health Reports* 71:1002–1010.

Dunnell, Karen, and Ann Cartwright. 1972. *Medicine Takers, Prescribers and Hoarders.* London: Routledge and Kegan Paul.

Dyer, Doris M. 1962. "Students' Wives' Values as Reflected in Person and Family Activities." Master's thesis, Michigan State University.

Dyer, W. G., and D. Urban. 1958. "The institutionalization of equalitarian family norms." *Marriage and Family Living* (February):53–58.

Ehrenreich, Barbara, and John Ehrenreich. 1970. *The American Health Empire: Power, Profits, and Politics.* New York: Random House.

Elliott, Ruth. 1971. *Life and Leisure for the Physically Handicapped.* London: Elek Books.

Elsom, K. A., S. Schor, T. W. Clark, K. O. Elsom, and J. P. Hubbard. 1960. "Periodic health examination: Nature and distribution of newly discovered disease in executives." *Journal of the American Medical Association* 172 (January):55–60.

Emshwiller, John. 1972. "Heal thyself." *The Wall Street Journal* (December 7).

Eron, L. D., L. O. Walder, R. Toigo, and M. Lefkowitz. 1963. "Social class, parental punishment for aggression, and child aggression." *Child Development* 34 (December):849–867.

Eshleman, J. R. 1970. *Perspectives in Marriage and the Family.* Boston: Allyn and Bacon.

Etzwiler, Donnell D., and L. K. Sines. 1962. "Juvenile diabetes and its management: Family, social and academic implications." *Journal of American Medical Association* 181, No. 4.

Family Health. 1973. "Emergency." (August). New York.

————. 1973. "Warning: Epidemics ahead: Protect our school children." (August). New York.

Farber, Bernard. 1962. "Elements of competence in interpersonal relations." *Sociometry* 25:30–47.

Feldman, Jacob J. 1966. *The Dissemination of Health Information.* Chicago: Aldine.

Foote, Nelson N., and Leonard S. Cottrell, Jr. 1955. *Identity and Interpersonal Competence*. Chicago: University of Chicago Press.

Forst, Brian E. 1972. *Decision Analysis and Medical Malpractice*. Arlington, Va.: Center for Naval Analyses.

Fraser, C. Gerald. 1972. "Sydenham Hospital gets first community board." *The New York Times* (March 31).

Freidson, Eliot. 1970. *Profession of Medicine*. New York: Dodd, Mead.

————. 1961. *Patients' Views of Medical Practice*. New York: Russell Sage Foundation.

Futterman, Edward H., and Irwin Hoffman. 1973. "Crisis and adaptation in the families of fatally ill children." Mimeographed.

Gardell, Bertil. 1971. "Alienation and mental health in the modern industrial environment." In Lennart Levi, ed. *Society, Stress and Disease*. London: Oxford University Press.

Gavron, H. 1966. *The Captive Wife*. London: Routledge and Kegan Paul.

Giedion, Siegfried. 1948. *Mechanization Takes Command*. New York: Oxford University Press.

Glogow, Eli. 1970. "Effects of health education methods on appointment breaking." *Public Health Reports* 85, No. 5:441–450.

Gochman, D. S. 1971. "Some correlates of children's health beliefs and potential health behavior." *Journal of Health and Social Behavior* 12 (June):148–154.

Goffman, Erving. 1971. *Relations in Public*. New York: Basic Books.

————. 1961. *Encounters*. Indianapolis: Bobbs-Merrill.

Gold, Gerald. 1973. "The public gets voice in accreditation of hospitals." *The New York Times* (December 20).

Gottlieb, Stanley, and Herbert Kramer. 1962. "Compliance with recommendations following executive health examinations." *Journal of Occupational Medicine* 4, No. 12.

Gouldner, Alvin. 1959. "Organizational analysis." In Robert K. Merton, Leonard Broom, and Leonard S. Cottrell, Jr., eds. *Sociology Today*. New York: Harper & Row.

Graham, Ellen. 1973. "Say Ahhh: Many doctors assail tonsillectomy, say it is useless or dangerous." *Wall Street Journal* (May 21).

Gray, R. M., J. P. Kesler, and W. R. E. Newman. 1964. "Social factors influencing the decision of severely disabled older persons to participate in a rehabilitation program." *Rehabilitation Literature* 25:162–167.

Green, Lawrence W. 1970. *Status Identity and Preventive Health Behavior*. Pacific Health Education Reports 1. Berkeley and Honolulu.

Greenberg, Selig. 1971. *The Quality of Mercy*. New York: Atheneum.

Haefner, Don P., et al. 1967. "Preventive actions in dental disease, tuberculosis, and cancer." *Public Health Reports* 82, No. 5:451–459.

Hall, Florence Turnbull, and Marguerite Paulsen Schroeder. 1970. "Time spent on household tasks." *Journal of Home Economics* 62, No. 1:23–29.

Harmer, Ruth M. 1963. *The High Cost of Dying*. New York: Macmillan.

Harris, Richard. 1966. *A Sacred Trust*. New York: The New American Library.

Hasebroock, Mrs. William H. 1965. "Home remedies in household management." *Annals of the New York Academy of Sciences* 120, Article 2 (July 14):996–1001.

Hassinger, E. W., and T. M. Anderson. 1964. *Information and Beliefs About Heart Disease Held by the Public in Five Areas of Missouri.* Columbia: University of Missouri, College of Agriculture, Research Bulletin 874.

Hassinger, E. W., and D. J. Hobbs. 1972. *Health Service Patterns in Rural and Urban Areas.* Columbia: University of Missouri, College of Agriculture, Experiment Station.

Hassinger, E. W., and R. L. McNamara. 1960. *The Families, Their Physicians, Their Health Behavior in a Northwest Missouri County.* Columbia: University of Missouri, College of Agriculture, Research Bulletin 754.

Hausknecht, Murray. 1962. *The Joiners.* New York: The Bedminster Press.

Health Law Project, University of Pennsylvania School of Law. 1973. *The Accreditation of Hospitals: A Guide for Health Consumers and Workers.* Philadelphia.

Hellersberg, Elisabeth F. 1946. "Food habits of adolescents in relation to family, training, and present adjustment." *American Journal of Orthopsychiatry* 16:45–61.

Hentoff, Nat. 1974. "The child-catchers." N.Y.: *The Village Voice* (Jan. 10).

Herrmann, Robert O., and Leland Beik. 1968. "Shoppers' movements outside their local retail area." *Journal of Marketing* 32 (October):45–51.

Hershey, Nathan. 1969. "Compulsory personal health measure legislation." *Public Health Reports* 84, No. 4:341–352.

HEW. *See* U.S. Department of Health, Education and Welfare.

Hicks, Nancy. 1974. "Physicians in state to lose malpractice group policy." *The New York Times* (January 8).

———. 1973. "A second opinion reduces surgery." *The New York Times* (June 19).

———. 1972. "Freed mental patients found needing services." *The New York Times* (July 30).

———. 1972. "Laymen's growing role in health planning disturbs some physicians here." *The New York Times* (April 9).

Hill, Reuben. 1964. "The American family of the future." *Journal of Marriage and the Family* 26 (February):20–28.

Hill, Reuben, et al. 1970. *Family Development in Three Generations.* Cambridge, Mass.: Schenkman Publishing Co.

Hills, Hilda Cherry. 1973. *Living Dangerously.* Bungay, Suffolk: Tom Stacey.

Hinkle, Lawrence E., Jr., and Harold G. Wolff. 1957. "Health and the social environment: Experimental investigations." In Alexander H. Leighton, John A. Clausen, and Robert N. Wilson, eds. *Explorations in Social Psychiatry.* New York: Basic Books.

Hinton, J. M. 1963. "The physical and mental distress of dying." *Quarterly Journal of Medicine* 32:1–21.

Hobart, Charles W. 1963. "Commitment, value conflict and the future of the American family." *Marriage and Family Living* (November):405–414.

Hoberman, H., E. F. Cicenia, and G. R. Stephenson. 1951. "Useful measurement tools and physical rehabilitation programs of pre-school orthopedically handicapped children." *Archives of Physical Medicine and Rehabilitation* 32 (July): 456–461.

Hoeflin, Ruth. 1954. "Child rearing practices and child care resources used by

Ohio farm families with pre-school children." *Journal of Genetic Psychology* 84:271–297.

Hoffman, M. L., and H. D. Saltzstein. 1967. "Parent discipline and the child's moral development." *Journal of Personality and Social Psychology* 5 (January): 45–57.

Holles, Everett R. 1972. "Freed pilots begin tests and are visited by families." *The New York Times* (September 20).

Holley, Robert T. *Current Medical Malpractice Law: An Outline for the Physician.* Minneapolis: Health Services Research Center, Institute for Interdisciplinary Studies. Undated manuscript.

Houston, C. S., and W. E. Pasanen. 1972. "Patients' perceptions of hospital care." *Hospitals* 46 (April 16):70–74.

Husband, Peter, and Pat E. Hinton. 1972. "Families of children with repeated accidents." *Archives of Diseases in Childhood* 47:396.

Hyman, Herbert H., and Charles R. Wright. 1971. "Trends in voluntary association memberships of American adults: Replication based on secondary analysis of national sample surveys." *American Sociological Review* 36, No. 2:191–206.

Ingersoll, Hazel L. 1948. "A study of the transmission of authority patterns in the family." *Genetic Psychology Monographs* 38:225–302.

Inkeles, Alex. 1966. "Social structure and the socialization of competence." *Harvard Educational Review* 36:265–283.

Irelan, Lola M. 1965. "Health practices of the poor." *Welfare in Review* (October):1–9.

Jackson, Charles L. 1969. "State laws on compulsory immunization in the United States." *Public Health Reports* 84, No. 9:787–795.

Jackson, Percival E. 1950. *The Law of Cadavers.* New York: Prentice-Hall.

Jacobs, M., and A. Spiken. 1970. "Life stress and respiratory illness." *Psychosomatic Medicine* 32:240.

James, Vernon L., and Warren E. Wheeler. 1969. "The care-by-parent unit." *Pediatrics* 43, No. 4, Part 1:488–494.

Jeffrey, Kirk. 1972. "The family as utopian retreat from the city." In Sallie TeSelle, ed. *The Family, Communes, and Utopian Societies.* New York: Harper & Row.

Kahn, Robert L. 1973. "Conflict, ambiguity, and overload: Three elements in job stress." *Occupational Mental Health* 3, No. 1:2–9.

Kalish, R. A. 1969. "Experiences of persons reprieved from death." In A. H. Kutscher, ed. *Death and Bereavement.* Springfield, Ill.: Charles C. Thomas.

Kane, Daniel A. 1971. "Community participation in the health system." *Hospital Administration* 16:36–43.

Kasl, S. V., and S. Cobb. 1966. "Health behavior, illness behavior, and sick role behavior." *Archives Environmental Health* 12 (April):531–541.

Kellner, Robert. 1963. *Family Ill-Health.* Springfield, Ill.: Charles C. Thomas.

Kelly, William D., and Stanley R. Friesen. 1950. "Do cancer patients want to be told?" *Surgery* 27, No. 6:822–826.

Kenkel, W. F. 1968. "Influence differentiation in family decision-making." In J. Heiss, ed. *Family Roles and Interaction: An Anthology.* Chicago: Rand McNally.

Kieren, Dianne, and Irving Tallman. 1972. "Spousal adaptability: An assessment of marital competence." *Journal of Marriage and Family* 34, No. 2:247–256.

Kihss, Peter. 1972. "Study says 550 were born addicted to drug-users." *The New York Times* (November 2).

King, Stanley H. 1962. *Perceptions of Illness and Medical Practice*. New York: Russell Sage Foundation.

Kira, Alexander. 1966. *The Bathroom*. New York: Bantam.

Kirkpatrick, C. 1963. *The Family—As Process and Institution*. 2d ed. New York: Ronald Press.

Kirscht, John P., Don P. Haefner, S. Stephen Kegeles, and Irwin M. Rosenstock. 1966. "A national study of health beliefs." *Journal of Health and Human Behavior* 7 (Winter):248–254.

Knapp, David A., and Deanne E. Knapp. 1972. "Decision making and self-medication." *American Journal of Hospital Pharmacy* 29 (December):1004–1012.

Knight, James A. 1967. "Psychodynamics of the allergic eczemas." *Annals of Allergy* 25 (July):392–396.

Knudson, Alfred, Jr., and Joseph M. Natterson. 1960. "Participation of parents in the hospital care of fatally ill children." *Pediatrics* 26, No. 3, Part 1:482–490.

Komarovsky, Mirra. 1964. *Blue-Collar Marriage*. New York: Random House.

Koos, E. L. 1954. *The Health of Regionville*. New York: Columbia University Press.

Kovach, Bill. 1970. "Rockefeller, signing abortion bill, credits women's groups." *The New York Times* (April 12).

Kraus, Arthur S., and Abraham M. Lilienfield. 1959. "Some epidemiologic aspects of the high mortality rate in the young widowed group." *Journal of Chronic Diseases* 10:207–217.

Krause, Elliott A. 1969. "Functions of a bureaucratic ideology: 'Citizen participation'." *Social Problems* 16:129–143.

Kuchler, Frances W. H. 1957. *The Law of Support*. Dobbs Ferry, N.Y.: Oceana.

Lader, S. 1965. "A survey of the incidence of self-medication." *The Practitioner* 194 (January):132–136.

LaHorgue, Zeva. 1960. "Morbidity and marital status." *Journal of Chronic Diseases* 12 (March):476–498.

Landis, P. H. 1970. *Making the Most of Marriage*. New York: Appleton-Century Crofts.

Langer, Elinor. 1970. "The shame of American medicine." In Jerome H. Skolnick and Elliott Curie, eds. *Crisis in American Institutions*. Boston: Little, Brown.

Langone, John. 1972. *A View of the End of Life*. Boston: Little, Brown.

Lantz, H. R., and E. C. Snyder. 1962. *Marriage*. New York: John Wiley.

Lazerson, Jack. 1971. "The prophylactic approach to Hemophilia A." *Hospital Practice* (February).

Leary, Jean A., Dolores M. Vessella, and Evelyn M. Yeaw. 1971. "Self-administered medications." *American Journal of Nursing* 71, No. 6:1193–1194.

Leslie, G. R. 1967. *The Family in Social Context*. New York: Oxford University Press.

Levinger, George. 1964. "Task and social behavior in marriage." *Sociometry* 27:433–448.

Levinson, D., and P. Huffman. 1955. "Traditional family ideology and its relation to personality." *Journal of Personality* 23:251–273.

Lewis, Howard, and Martha Lewis. 1970. *The Medical Offenders*. New York: Simon and Schuster.

214   *References*

Lichtenstein, Grace. 1972. "Members ask a voice in H.I.P. Service." *The New York Times* (February 20).
Lieberman, Morton A. 1961. "Relationship of mortality rates to entrance to a home for the aged." *Geriatrics* 16 (October):515–519.
Lindemann, Erich. 1950. "Modifications in the course of ulcerative colitis in relationship to changes in life situations and reaction patterns." In Harold G. Wolff, Stewart G. Wolf, and Clarence C. Hare, eds. *Life Stress and Bodily Disease.* Baltimore: Williams & Wilkins.
Linnett, M. 1968. "Prescribing habits in general practice." *Proceedings of the Royal Society of Medicine* 61:613–615.
Litman, Theodor J. 1971. "Health care and the family: A three-generational analysis." *Medical Care* 9, No. 1 (January–February).
———. 1964. "The views of Minnesota school children on food." *Journal of American Dietetic Association* 45:438–440.
———. 1962. "The influence of self conception and life orientation factors in the rehabilitation of the orthopedically disabled." *Journal of Health and Human Behavior* 3, No. 4.
Locke, Harvey J., and Robert C. Williamson. 1958. "Marital adjustment: A factor analysis study." *American Sociological Review* 23, No. 5:562–569.
Lovejoy, B. D. 1961. "College student conceptions of the roles of husband and wife in family decision making." *Family Life Coordinator* 9 (March–June): 43–46.
Ludwig, Frederick J. 1955. *Youth and the Law.* Brooklyn: The Foundation Press.
Lund, Lois A., and Marguerite C. Burk. 1969. *A Multidisciplinary Analysis of Children's Food Consumption Behavior.* University of Minnesota, Agricultural Experiment Station, Technical Bulletin 265.
Lynd, Robert S., and Helen Merrell Lynd. 1937. *Middletown in Transition.* New York: Harcourt, Brace.
Lyons, Richard D. 1973. "Medicare held 'gold mine' for doctors in Manhattan." *The New York Times* (November 19).
———. 1973. "Physicians oppose monitoring plan." *The New York Times* (December 6).
———. 1972. "Sex called problem in half of marriages." *The New York Times* (June 19).
Mabry, John H. 1959. "Toward the concept of housing adequacy." *Sociology and Social Research* 44 (November–December):86–92.
Macqueen, Ian A. G. 1960. *A Study of Home Accidents in Aberdeen.* Edinburgh: E. and S. Livingstone.
Maeroff, Gene I. 1972. "Corporal punishment ban in schools sought." *The New York Times* (May 8).
Male, Charles Thomas. 1968. "An Attempted Correlation of Home Accident Fatalities and Housing Quality." Master's thesis, Cornell University.
Manis, M. 1958. "Personal adjustment, assumed similarity to parents, and inferred parental evaluations of the self." *Journal of Consulting Psychology* 22:481–485.
Manning, Sarah L. 1968. *Time Use in Household Tasks by Indiana Families.* Purdue University, Agricultural Experimentation Station, Research Bulletin 837 (January).

Maronde, R. F., et al. 1967. "Physician prescribing practices: A computer based study." *American Journal of Hospital Pharmacy* 26 (October):566–573.

Martin, Purvis L. 1964. "Detection of cervical cancer." *California Medicine* 101 (December):427–429.

Martindale, Don. 1960. *American Society*. Princeton: D. Van Nostrand.

McClintock, Martha K. 1971. "Menstrual synchrony and suppression." *Nature* 229, No. 5282:244.

McCollum, Audrey T. 1971. "Cystic Fibrosis: Economic impact upon the family." *American Journal of Public Health* 61 (July):1336–1340.

McConnell, James V., and Marlys Schutjer, eds. 1971. *Science, Sex, and Sacred Cows*. New York: Harcourt-Brace-Jovanovich.

McGhee, Anne, James Drever, and J. H. F. Brotherston. 1961. *The Patient's Attitude to Nursing Care*. Edinburgh: E. and S. Livingstone.

McKey, Robert M., Jr. Cystic Fibrosis: A Family Shattering Disease. (Undated).

McKinlay, John B. 1973. "Help seeking behavior of the poor." In J. Kosa, A. Antonovsky, and I. K. Zola, eds. *Poverty and Health*. Cambridge, Mass.: Harvard University Press.

McKinlay, J. B., and S. M. McKinlay. 1972. "Some social characteristics of lower working class utilizers and underutilizers of maternity care services." *Journal of Health and Social Behavior* 13 (December):369–382.

McKinley, Donald. 1964. *Social Class and Family Life*. Glencoe, Ill.: The Free Press.

Medical Economics. 1970. "Malpractice alert: The newest trends in claims." (June 8):79–93.

Meissner, W. W. 1966. "Family dynamics and psychosomatic processes." *Family Processes* 5, No. 2:142–161.

Merrill, F. E. 1959. *Courtship and Marriage*. New York: Henry Hall.

Metropolitan Life Insurance Company. 1973. *Statistical Bulletin* 54 (March):2–5.

Meyer, Roger J., and Robert J. Haggerty. 1962. "Streptococcal infections in families." *Pediatrics* 29 (April):539–549.

Meyers, David W. 1970. *The Human Body and the Law*. Chicago: Aldine-Atherton.

Miller, D. R., and G. E. Swanson. 1958. *The Changing American Parent*. New York: John Wiley.

Miller, Eddie. 1971. "Harris study stresses health education need." *Blue Cross Association Bulletin* (December 29).

Miller, Hyman, and Dorothy W. Baruch. 1950. "A study of hostility in allergic children." *American Journal of Orthopsychiatry* 20:506–519.

Mintz, Morton. 1967. *By Prescription Only*. Boston: Beacon Press.

Mishler, Elliot G., and Nancy E. Waxler. 1968. *Family Processes and Schizophrenia*. New York: Science House.

Mogey, J. M. 1957. "A century of declining parental authority." *Marriage and Family Living* 19 (August):234–239.

Moneysworth. 1971. "The third most expensive item you'll ever buy." 1, No. 20 (July 12). New York.

Moody, Philip M., and Robert M. Gray. 1972. "Social class, social integration, and the use of preventive health services." In E. Gartly Jaco, ed. *Patients, Physicians and Illness*. 2d ed. New York: The Free Press.

Morgan, James N., Ismail Sirageldin, and Nancy Baerwaldt. 1966. *Productive Americans*. University of Michigan, Institute for Social Research. Ann Arbor: University of Michigan Press.

Moser, Robert H., ed. 1964. *Diseases of Medical Progress*. 2d ed. Springfield, Ill.: Charles C. Thomas.

Muller, Charlotte. 1972. "The overmedicated society; Forces in the marketplace for medical care." *Science* 176 (May 5):488–492.

Murphy, H. B. 1961. "Social change and mental health." *Milbank Memorial Fund Quarterly* 39:385–445.

Nathanson, C. A., and M. B. Rhyne. 1970. "Social and cultural factors associated with asthmatic symptoms in children." *Social Science & Medicine* 4 (September):293–306.

National Association for Retarded Children. 1966. *Voices in Chorus*. New York.

National Council on the Aging. 1972. *Recommendations for Action in the 70s*. Washington, D.C.

National Electronic Injury Surveillance System (NEISS). 1972. *Product Safety News* (October).

National Health Council. 1972. *Discussion Guide for the 1972 National Health Forum: People Keeping Healthy: Goals and Approaches to Consumer Health Education* (March 21–22).

National Heart Institute. 1969. *Cardiac Replacement: Medical, Ethical, Psychological, and Economic Implications: A Report by Ad Hoc Task Force on Cardiac Replacement*.

National Research Council. 1968. A Report to the Committee on Tissue Transplantation from the Ad Hoc Committee on Medical-Legal Problems. Washington, D.C.

Nett, Roger. 1964. "Conformity-deviation and the social control concept." *Ethics* 64:38–45.

New Jersey Statutes. "9:6–1 Abuse, abandonment, cruelty and neglect of child; what constitutes." Trenton, N.J.

New York. 1972. *New York Handbook: Abortion Clinics: An Evaluation* 2, No. 4 (July):31–38.

The New York Times. 1974. "Labor and A.M.A. top list in '74 spending on politics." (October 29).

———. 1972. "A.M.A. urges drive to help doctors combat addictions." (November 29).

Nickell, Paulena, J. M. Dorsey, and M. Budolfson. 1942. *Management in Family Living*. 3d ed. New York: John Wiley.

Nickerson, Hiram. 1972. "Patient education." *Health Education Monographs* 31.

Nimkoff, M. F., ed. 1965. *Comparative Family Systems*. Boston: Houghton Mifflin.

Nursing Outlook. 1972. "Preparing nurses for family health care." 20, No. 1:53–59.

Nursing Research Report. 1971. "Effects of family goals on performance of tasks and use of resources during acute illness." (March):3–7.

Nye, F. Ivan. 1957. "Child adjustment in broken and in unhappy unbroken homes." *Marriage and Family Living* 19:356–361.

Occupational Mental Health. 1973. "Emotional disorders: An occupational hazard for physicians?" 3, No. 1 (Spring).

Ogburn, W. F., and C. Tibbits. 1934. "The Family and Its Functions." In *Recent Social Trends in the United States: Report of the President's Research Committee on Social Trends*. New York: McGraw-Hill.

Olim, E. G. 1968. "The self-actualizing person in the fully functioning family." *The Family Coordinator* 17 (July):141–148.

The O. M. Collective. 1971. *The Organizer's Manual*. New York: Bantam.

Orden, S. R., and N. M. Bradburn. 1969. "Working wives and marriage happiness." *American Journal of Sociology* 74:392–407.

Otto, Herbert A. 1963. "Criteria for assessing family strength." *Family Process* 2, No. 2:329–338.

Palmer, Boyd Z., et al. 1972. "The mandate for community participation." *Health Education Monographs* No. 32.

Palmore, Erdman, and Frances C. Jeffers. 1972. *Prediction of Life Span*. Lexington, Mass.: Heath Lexington Books.

Parkes, C. Murray, 1964. "Effects of bereavement on physical and mental health —a study of the medical records of widows." *British Medical Journal* 2 (August):274–279.

Parsons, Talcott. 1964. *The Social System*. New York: The Free Press.

Parsons, Talcott, and R. F. Bales. 1955. *Family Socialization and Interaction Process*. Glencoe, Ill.: The Free Press.

Parsons, Talcott, and Renée Fox. 1952. "Illness, therapy and the modern urban American family." *Journal of Social Issues* 8, No. 4:2–3, 31–44.

Parsons, Talcott, and Neil J. Smelser. 1956. *Economy and Society*. New York: The Free Press.

Peterson, Evan T. 1972. "The impact of adolescent illness on parental relationships." *Journal of Health and Social Behavior* 13 (December):429–437.

Peterson, O. L., L. P. Andrews, R. S. Spain, and B. G. Greenberg. 1956. "An analytical study of North Carolina general practice: 1953–1954." *Journal of Medical Education* 31, Part 2.

Pickens, B., et al. 1969. "Family patterns of medical care utilization." *Journal of Chronic Diseases* 22 (August):181–191.

Platt Report: The Welfare of Children in Hospital. 1959. Ministry of Health, Central Health Services Council. London.

Podell, Lawrence. 1970. *Studies in Use of Health Services by Families on Welfare: Utilization by Publicly Assisted Families, PB 190 390*. Washington, D.C.: National Center for Health Services Research and Development.

Pollak, Otto. 1967. "The outlook for the American family." *Journal of Marriage and the Family* 29 (February):193–205.

Pollak, Otto, and Alfred S. Friedman, eds. 1969. *Family Dynamics and Female Sexual Delinquency*. Palo Alto, Calif.: Science and Behavior Books.

Pomeroy, Richard. 1970. *Studies in the Use of Health Services by Families on Welfare*. Washington, D.C.: National Center for Health Services Research and Development.

Pratt, Lois. 1973. "Child rearing methods and children's health behavior." *Journal of Health and Social Behavior* 14 (March):61–69.

———. 1973. "The significance of the family in medication." *Journal of Comparative Family Studies* 4, No. 1:13–35.

———. 1972. "Conjugal organization and health." *Journal of Marriage and the Family* 34, No. 1:85–94.

———. 1971. "The relationship of socioeconomic status to health." *American Journal of Public Health* 61, No. 2:281–291.

———. 1967. *A Report on a Program to Upgrade the Knowledge Among Health Workers Concerning Social and Environmental Influences on Health.* Madison, N.J.: Fairleigh Dickinson University.

———. 1956. "How do patients learn about disease?" *Social Problems* 4, No. 1:29–40.

Pratt, Lois, Arthur Seligmann, and George Reader. 1957. "Physicians' views on the level of medical information among patients." *American Journal of Public Health* 47 (October):1277–1283.

Pratt, Samuel. 1969. "The public and the arts." *Meadowlands: Cultural, Artistic, Esthetic Potential Report.* Trenton: New Jersey State Council on the Arts.

Preston, J. A., Corporation. 1972. *Preston Equipment for Physical Medicine and Rehabilitation, Catalog 1080.* New York.

Price, James L. 1968. *Organizational Effectiveness.* Homewood, Ill.: Irwin.

Putnam, William J., Robert M. O'Shea, and Lois K. Cohen. 1967. "Communication and patient motivation in preventive periodontics." *Public Health Reports* 82, No. 9:779–780.

Queen, S. A., and R. W. Habenstein. 1967. *The Family in Various Cultures.* New York: J. B. Lippincott.

Radomski, J. L., et al. 1966. "Pesticide concentrations in the liver, brain, and adipose tissue of terminal hospital patients." *Food and Cosmetics Toxicology* 6, No. 21:209–220.

Rainwater, Lee. 1968. The lower class: Health, illness, and medical institutions. In I. Deutscher and E. J. Thompson, eds. *Among the People.* New York: Basic Books.

———. 1965. *Family Design.* Chicago: Aldine.

Rainwater, Lee, Richard P. Coleman, and Gerald Handel. 1959. *Workingman's Wife.* New York: Macfadden.

Ranney, Elizabeth M., Helen E. McCullough, and W. H. Scheick. 1950. *Handbook of Kitchen Design: A Report of an Investigation in Space Use.* University of Illinois, Small Homes Council. Urbana: University of Illinois Press.

Reader, George G. and May E. Goss. 1967. Comprehensive Medical Care and Teaching. Ithaca: Cornell University Press.

Rees, L. 1964. "The importance of psychological, allergic and infective factors in childhood asthma." *Journal of Psychosomatic Research* 7:253–262.

Remmers, H. H. 1965. *Report of Poll 74: The Purdue Opinion Panel.* Purdue University, Purdue Research Foundation.

Rice, Dorothy P. 1969. "Measurement and application of illness costs." *Public Health Reports* 84, No. 2 (February):95–101.

Rice, Dorothy P., and Barbara S. Cooper. 1972. "National health expenditures, 1929–71." *Social Security Bulletin* 35, No. 1 (January):3–18.

Richards, N. David, and Lois K. Cohen, eds. 1971. *Social Sciences and Dentistry: A Critical Bibliography.* U.S. Public Health Service, Division of Dental Health.

Richardson, W. C. 1970. "Measuring the urban poor's use of physicians' services in response to illness episodes." *Medical Care* 8 (March/April):132–142.

Riley, Conrad M. 1956. *Living with a Child with Familial Dysautonomia.* New York: The Dysautonomia Association.

Ritvo, M. M. 1963. "Who are 'good' and 'bad' patients"? *The Modern Hospital* 100, No. 6:79–81.

Robinson, David. 1971. *The Process of Becoming Ill.* London: Routledge and Kegan Paul.

Roney, J. G., and M. L. Nall. 1966. *Medication Practices in a Community: An Exploratory Study.* Menlo Park, Calif.: Stanford Research Institute.

Rossi, Peter H. 1955. *Why Families Move.* Glencoe, Ill.: The Free Press.

Roth, Julius A. 1972. "Staff and client control strategies in urban hospital emergency services." *Urban Life and Culture* 1, No. 1:39–60.

Rusalem, Herbert. 1971. "A capsule research review." *Rehabilitation Literature* 22, No. 7:194–207.

Samora, Julian, et al. 1961. "Medical vocabulary knowledge among hospital patients." *Journal of Health and Human Behavior* 2, No. 2.

Scheff, Thomas J. 1967. "Social conditions for rationality: How urban and rural courts deal with the mentally ill." In Thomas J. Scheff, ed. *Mental Illness and Social Processes.* New York: Harper & Row.

Schmale, A. H., and H. Iker. 1971. "Hopelessness as a predictor of cervical cancer." *Social Science & Medicine* 5:95–100.

Schmeck, Harold M., Jr. 1973. "A.M.A. criticized on drugs policy." *The New York Times* (February 7).

———. 1973. "Women smokers warned of fetal and infant risks." *The New York Times* (January 18).

Schor, S., T. W. Clark, H. L. Parkhurst, J. P. Baker, and K. A. Elsom. 1964. "An evaluation of periodic health examinations: The findings in 350 examinees who died." *Annals of Internal Medicine* 61:999–1005.

Schwartz, Doris R. 1958. "Uncooperative patients." *American Journal of Nursing* 58:75–77.

Schwartz, Doris, et al. 1962. "Medication errors made by elderly, chronically ill patients." *American Journal of Public Health* 51, No. 12:2018–2029.

Schwartz, Jerome L. 1965. "Participation of consumers in prepaid health plans." *Journal of Health and Human Behavior* 6:74–79.

Scotch, N. A., and H. J. Geiger. 1962. "The epidemiology of rheumatoid arthritis: A review with special atention to social factors." *Journal of Chronic Diseases* 15:1037–1067.

Sears, R. R. 1961. "Relation of early socialization experiences to aggression in middle childhood." *Journal of Abnormal and Social Psychology* 63 (November):466–492.

Sears, R. R., J. Whiting, V. Nowlis, and P. Sears. 1953. "Some child rearing antecedents of aggression and dependency in young children." *Genetic Psychology Monographs* 47 (May):135–236.

Sedgwick, Peter. 1974. "Medical individualism." *Hastings Center Studies* 2, No. 3:69–80.

Seeman, Melvin, and John W. Evans. 1962. "Alienation and learning in a hospital setting." *American Sociological Review* 27 (December):772–782.

———. 1961. "Stratification and hospital care: I: The performance of the medical interne." *American Sociological Review* 26, No. 1:67–80.

———. 1961. "Stratification and hospital care: II: The objective criteria of performance." *American Sociological Review* 26, No. 2:193–204.

Shenker, Israel. 1972. "Government bookstore is full of advice for your health, education, and welfare." *The New York Times* (September 3).

Shore, M. F., ed. 1965. *Red Is the Color of Hurting: Planning for Children in the Hospital: Proceedings of a Workshop on Mental Health Planning for Pediatric Hospitals, New York.* Washington, D.C.: U.S. Department of Health, Education and Welfare.

Silver, George A. 1963. *Family Medical Care.* Cambridge, Mass.: Harvard University Press.

Skipper, James A., Jr., and Robert C. Leonard. 1968. "Children, stress, and hospitalization." *Journal of Health and Social Behavior* 9, No. 4:275–287.

Slater, Philip E. 1962. "Parental behavior and the personality of the child." *Journal of Genetic Psychology* 101:53–68.

————. 1961. "Parental role differentiation." *American Journal of Sociology* 67 (November):296–311.

Smart, Reginald G., and Dianne Fejer. 1972. "Drug use among adolescents and their parents: Closing the generation gap in mood modification." *Journal of Abnormal Psychology* 79, No. 2:153–160.

Smith, Constance, and Anne Freedman. 1972. *Voluntary Associations.* Cambridge, Mass.: Harvard University Press.

Smith, Lawrence, Jr., and Robert Kane. 1970. "Health knowledge and symptom perception: A study of a rural Kentucky county." *Social Science and Medicine* 4 (December):557–567.

Smith, Lee. 1972. "Get me to the ward on time." *New York* (Dec. 18):59–62.

Smith, W., E. K. Powell, and S. Ross. 1956. "Manifest anxiety and food aversion." *Journal of Abnormal and Social Psychology* 50:101–104.

Sofranko, Andrew J., and Michael F. Nolan. 1972. "Early life experiences and adult sports participation." *Journal of Leisure Research* (Winter):6–24.

Soriano, A. 1966. "Comparison of two scheduling systems." *Operations Research* 14 (May–June):388–397.

Source Catalog: Communities/Housing. 1972. Chicago: Swallow Press.

Spuhler, J. N. 1968. "Assortative mating with respect to physical characteristics." *Eugenics Quarterly* (June):128–140.

Stark, Rodney, and James McEvoy. 1970. "Middle class violence." *Psychology Today* 4 (November):52–65.

State of Florida, Department of Health and Rehabilitation Services. 1971. *Community Care for the Elderly.*

Steinmetz, Suzanne K., and Murray A. Straus, eds. 1974. *Violence in the Family.* New York: Dodd, Mead.

Stockwell, Felicity. 1972. *The Unpopular Patient.* London: Royal College of Nursing.

Stolley, Paul D., and Louis Lasagna. 1969. "Prescribing patterns of physicians." *Journal of Chronic Diseases* 22:395–405.

Stolley, Paul D., et al. 1972. "Drug prescribing and use in an American community." *Annals of Internal Medicine* 76, No. 4:537–540.

Stolz, Lois Meek. 1967. *Influences on Parent Behavior.* Stanford, Calif.: Stanford University Press.

Stolzman, James D. 1972. "Edward Shils on Consensus: An Appreciation and Critique." Paper presented at Eastern Sociological Society, Boston.

Stott, Leland H. 1951. "The problem of evaluating family success." *Marriage and Family Living* 13, No. 4:149–153.

Stouffer, Samuel A. 1955. *Communism, Conformity and Civil Liberties*. New York: Doubleday.

Straus, Murray A. 1971. "Some social antecedents of physical punishment." *Journal of Marriage and the Family* 33 (November):658–663.

———. 1964. "Power and support structure of the family in relation to socialization." *Journal of Marriage and the Family* (August):318–326.

Straus, Murray A., Richard J. Gelles, and Suzanne K. Steinmetz. 1973. "Theories, Methods, and Controversies in the Study of Violence Between Family Members." Paper presented at American Sociological Association Annual Meeting, August 27–30, 1973, New York.

Stroup, A. L. 1966. *Marriage and Family: A Developmental Approach*. New York: Appleton-Century-Crofts.

Suchman, Edward A. 1965. "Social patterns of illness and medical care." *Journal of Health and Human Behavior* 6 (Spring):2–16.

———. 1965. "Stages of illness and medical care." *Journal of Health and Human Behavior* 6, No. 3:114–128.

———. 1964. "Sociomedical variations among ethnic groups." *American Journal of Sociology* 70, No. 3:319–331.

Sunshine, Irving. 1965. "Use and misuse of self-medication." *Annals of the New York Academy of Sciences* 120 (July 14):931–941.

Sussman, Marvin B. 1972. "Family, kinship, and bureaucracy." In A. Campbell and P. E. Converse, eds. *The Human Meaning of Social Change*. New York: Russell Sage Foundation.

Tagliacozzo, Daisy L., and Hans O. Mauksch. 1972. "The patient's view of the patient's role." In E. Gartly Jaco, ed. *Patients, Physicians and Illness*. New York: The Free Press.

Tavris, Carol, and Toby Jayaratne. 1972. *How Do You Feel About Being a Woman? The Results of a Redbook Questionnaire*. New York: McCall.

Taylor, Carol. 1970. *In Horizontal Orbit: Hospitals and the Cult of Efficiency*. New York: Holt, Rinehart and Winston.

Taylor, P. J. 1968. "Personal factors associated with sickness absence." *British Journal of Industrial Medicine* 25:105–118.

Time. 1972. December 18:72.

Titmuss, Richard M. 1971. *The Gift Relationship*. New York: Pantheon.

Traunstein, Donald M., and Richard Steinman. 1973. "Voluntary self-help organizations: An exploratory study." *Journal of Voluntary Action* 2, No. 4:230–239.

Tunley, Paul. 1966. *The American Health Scandal*. New York: Harper & Row.

Turner, Ralph H. 1970. *Family Interaction*. New York: John Wiley.

Twaddle, Andrew C. 1969. "Health decisions and sick role variations." *Journal of Health and Human Behavior* 10, No. 2:105–115.

Udry, J. R., and M. Hall. 1965. "Marital role segregation and social networks in middleclass middleaged couples." *Journal of Marriage and the Family* (August): 392–395.

Ulrich's International Periodicals Directory 1971–1972, Vol. 1, 14th ed. New York: R. R. Bowker Co.

U.S. Bureau of the Census. 1972. *Statistical Abstract of the United States, 1972*.

———. 1972. *We, the Americans—Our Homes.* Social and Economic Statistics Administration.

———. 1970. *Current Housing Reports, Series H–111, Nos. 55 and 63.*

U.S. Department of Agriculture, Agricultural Research Service. 1972. *Toward the New: A Report on Better Foods and Nutrition from Agricultural Research.* Agriculture Information Bulletin No. 341 (February).

U.S. Department of Health, Education and Welfare. 1973. *Report of the Secretary's Commission on Medical Malpractice.*

———. 1972. *Acute Conditions, Incidence and Associated Disability, United States, July 1968–June 1969. Series 10, No. 69.* Public Health Service.

———. 1972. *Family Health Centers.* Press Release (August 18).

———. 1972. *Periodontal Disease and Oral Hygiene among Children, United States, June. Series 11, No. 117.* Public Health Service.

———. 1972. *Physician Visits, United States, 1969. Series 10, No. 75.* Public Health Service.

———. 1972. *A Study of Health Practices and Opinions* (June). Food and Drug Administration.

———. 1972. *Time Lost from Work Among the Currently Employed Population, United States, 1968. Series 10, No. 71.* Public Health Service.

———. 1972. *U.S. Kidney Transplant Fact Book.* Public Health Service.

———. 1971. *Catastrophic Illnesses and Costs.* Office of the Assistant Secretary for Planning and Evaluation.

———. 1971. *A Guide for Promoting Home Health Services. No. HSM–71–6404.* Public Health Service.

———. 1971. *Parent Ratings of Behavioral Patterns of Children, United States.* Public Health Service.

———. 1971. *Persons Hospitalized by Number of Hospital Episodes and Days in a Year, United States, 1968. Series 10, No. 65.* Public Health Service.

———. 1971. *Report on Licensure and Related Health Personnel Credentialing* (June).

———. 1971. *The Size and Shape of the Medical Care Dollar.* Social Security Administration.

———. 1971. *Teenage Smoking: National Patterns of Cigarette Smoking, Ages 12 through 18, in 1968 and 1970.* Public Health Service.

———. 1970. *Mortality from Selected Causes by Marital Status, United States. Series 20, No. 8A and 8B.* Public Health Service.

———. 1970. *Persons Injured and Disability Days Due to Injury, United States, July 1965–June 1967. Series 10, No. 58.* Public Health Service.

———. 1969. *Chart Book on Smoking, Tobacco, and Health. Public Health Service Publication No. 1937 (June).* Public Health Service.

———. 1969. *Chronic Conditions Causing Activity Limitation, United States, July 1965–June 1967. Series 10, No. 58.* Public Health Service.

———. 1969. *Family Use of Health Services, United States, July 1960–June 1964. Series 10, No. 55 (July).* Public Health Service.

———. 1966. *Obesity and Health.* Public Health Service.

———. 1966. *Oral Hygiene in Adults, United States, 1960–1962 (June).* Public Health Service.

———. 1965. *Health Interview Responses Compared with Medical Records, United States. Series 2, No. 7.* Public Health Service.

————. 1963. *Length of Convalescence After Surgery, United States, July 1960–June 1961. Series 10, No. 3.* Public Health Service.

U.S. Senate, Special Committee on Aging. 1972. *Home Health Services in the United States (April)*.

U.S. Water Resources Council. 1968. *The Nation's Water Resources.* Washington, D.C.

Vayda, Eugene. 1973. "A comparison of surgical rates in Canada and in England and Wales." *New England Journal of Medicine* 289 (March 8):1224–1229.

Vernon, Glenn M. 1970. *Sociology of Death.* New York: Ronald.

Vincent, Clark. 1973. *Sexual and Marital Health: The Physician as a Consultant.* New York: McGraw-Hill.

————. 1967. "Mental health and the family." *Journal of Marriage and the Family* 29, No. 1:18–39.

————. 1966. "Familia Spongia: The adaptive function." *Journal of Marriage and the Family* (February):29–36.

Walker, Kathryn E., and William H. Gauger. 1973. *The Dollar Value of Household Work.* Cornell University, New York State College of Human Ecology.

Wang, V. L., L. W. Green, and P. H. Ephross. 1972. *Not Forgotten but Still Poor.* College Park, Maryland: University of Maryland Press, Cooperative Extension Service.

Warren, Perry S. 1970. *Family Medicine: Working Papers in Comprehensive Health Planning, No. 13.* Ithaca: Cornell University Press, Center for Urban Development Research.

Warren, Virginia Lee. 1973. "Backaches multiply, but country takes threat lying down." *The New York Times* (August 22).

————. 1972. "Sugar—the question is, do we need it at all?" *The New York Times* (July 4).

Watkins, Julia D., et al. 1967. "Observation of medication errors made by diabetic patients in the home." *Journal of the American Diabetes Association* 16, No. 12:882–885.

Wessen, Albert F. 1972. "Hospital ideology and communication between ward personnel." In E. Gartly Jaco, ed. *Patients, Physicians and Illness.* New York: The Free Press.

Westley, William A., and Nathan B. Epstein. 1970. *The Silent Majority: Families of Emotionally Healthy College Students.* San Francisco: Jossey-Bass.

White, Kerr, L., et al. 1961. "International comparisons of medical-care utilization." *New England Journal of Medicine* 277 (September 7):516–522.

Wilensky, Harold L. 1964. "The professionalization of everyone?" *American Journal of Sociology* 70 (September):137–158.

Williamson, R. C. 1966. *Marriage and Family Relations.* New York: John Wiley.

Wilner, Daniel M., et al. 1962. The Housing Environment and Family Life. Baltimore: Johns Hopkins Press.

Wilson, Robert N. 1970. *The Sociology of Health: An Introduction.* New York: Random House.

Winch, R. F. 1971. *The Modern Family.* New York: Holt, Rinehart and Winston.

Witkin, H. A. 1969. "Social influences in the development of cognitive style." In D. A. Goslin, ed. *Handbook of Socialization Theory and Research.* Chicago: Rand-McNally.

Wolf, Stewart. 1971. "Patterns of social adjustment and disease." In Lennart Levi, ed. *Society, Stress and Disease.* London: Oxford University Press.

Wolfe, Samuel. 1971. "Consumerism and health care." *Public Administration Review* 31 (October):528–536.

Womble, D. L. 1966. *Foundations for Marriage and Family Relations.* New York: Macmillan.

Young, Michael, Bernard Benjamin, and Chris Wallis. 1963. "The mortality of widowers." *The Lancet* 2 (August):454–456.

Index

225